How ISLAM PLANS to CHANGE the WORLD

updated edition

How ISLAM PLANS to CHANGE the WORLD

william **wagner**

Kregel
Publications

How Islam Plans to Change the World, Updated Edition

© 2012 by William Wagner

Published by Kregel Publications, a division of Kregel, Inc., P.O. Box 2607, Grand Rapids, MI 49501.

Library of Congress Cataloging-in-Publication Data
Wagner, William.
   How Islam plans to change the world / by William Wagner.
     p. cm.
Includes bibliographical references and index.
   1. Islam—Controversial literature.   2. Islam—Relations—Christianity.   3. Christianity and other religions—Islam.
I. Title.
BT1170.W34   2004
297.7—dc22   2004009618

ISBN 978-0-8254-3929-2

Printed in the United States of America

16 / 5 4 3 2

To my wonderful wife, Sally,
and our two precious children,
Mark and Candice.
All have helped greatly during our thirty
years on the mission field.

Contents

Foreword

A dramatic gap in our understanding of world religions was recently exposed. Since September 11, 2001, Islam—the world's second largest religion after Christianity—has come under the spotlight of social, political, and religious scrutiny. For Western nations, gaining an understanding of this Middle Eastern religion has been an elusive pursuit. Vast worldview differences have, by and large, prevented political and religious dialogue from taking place. Instead, colonial categories were applied to interpret the clash of our cultures.

At last the obvious can be ignored no longer: *Islam is in search of world dominance* . . . a fact consistent with Islamic theology and worldview. The West, cast in the mold of its Judeo-Christian worldview, is left to conclude that it is viewed as competition for world dominance.

In this book, Dr. William Wagner gives us helpful insights into Islam, drawing from the Qur'an and referencing Islamic spokesmen who have taken good advantage of the new media prominence to promote their faith in the West. All are "in search of a friendly face" for Islam as it meets the West on the platform of human history. Dr. Wagner's many years of overseas experience in Europe as well as in the Middle East, along with his role as a distinguished professor, qualify him as a witness and a scholar in pursuit of understanding what is behind the clash of Muslim and Judeo-Christian based cultures and worldviews.

This book, more than any I know, speaks forthrightly to the issues that precipitated the horrors of the World Trade Center attacks, and that continue to affect world events. Exposing Islamic missionary strategies, defining *jihad* (or holy war) initiatives, addressing issues of democratic failure, speaking to global expansion realities—all are part of the discussion. For some, the phrase "the truth hurts" will take on new meaning as you read this. But ignoring the facts that have led to this historical clash and contemporary challenge would be even more painful. In this matter, too, it is correct to say, as Jesus did, "you will know the truth, and the truth will set you free" (John 8:32).

Open marketplace discussion, with a plea for peace and love to prevail, is a worthy goal to pursue. To that end, I commend this book to you for your understanding.

2004   —Dr. J. Ray Tallman
                                          Director and Professor
                    David and Faith Kim School of Intercultural Studies
                         Golden Gate Baptist Theological Seminary

Preface to the Updated Edition

One of the greatest preachers of the last one hundred years, Dr. Billy Graham, recited an interesting story. He related:

"Recently I was reminded of Albert Einstein, the great physicist, who has been honored by *Time* magazine as the Man of the Century. Einstein was once traveling from Princeton on a train when the conductor came down the aisle, punching the tickets of every passenger. When he came to Einstein, Einstein reached in his vest pocket. He couldn't find his ticket, so he reached in his trouser pockets. It wasn't there, so he looked in his briefcase but couldn't find it. Then he looked in the seat beside him. He still couldn't find it.

"The conductor said, 'Dr. Einstein, I know who you are. We all know who you are. I'm sure you bought a ticket. Don't worry about it.' Einstein nodded appreciatively. The conductor continued down the aisle punching tickets. As he was ready to move to the next car, he turned around and saw the great physicist down on his hands and knees looking under his seat for his ticket.

"The conductor rushed back and said, 'Dr. Einstein, Dr.

Einstein, don't worry. I know who you are . . . no problem . . .
you don't need a ticket. I'm sure you bought one.'
"Einstein looked at him and said, 'Young man, I too
know who I am; what I don't know is where I am going.'"

From time to time, it is necessary to stop and look at where we
are going. The world seems to be moving at a faster pace every day.
The increase of knowledge is such that most people are experiencing
future shock—the inability to absorb the rapid changes now taking
place in society. It is difficult enough to try to live in the present
without having to look at the future. Under the impact of this distorted world, it is necessary at least to evaluate the present and prepare for what will come.

Marin County near San Francisco, one of the wealthiest counties in the United States, had a world-renowned theologian speak
at a breakfast dealing with social issues. The speaker, Os Guinness,
opened his remarks by saying that "those living in the West have to
deal with three major issues today." He listed them as:

1. The future of China in the world of tomorrow
2. The battle between secularists in the West and those supporting Judeo-Christian principles
3. The rise of Islam

In many regards, the answers to these three issues could determine the future of civilization as we know it. First, in looking at
China, it is apparent that this vast country is even at present a major
political, economic, military, and social power. With every passing
day we see its growth. A little known fact is that one of the greatest
revivals in the history of the Christian church is now taking place in
that country. By 1945, after more than 250 years of missionary work,
the Christian church, including both Roman Catholics and Protestants, had only approximately two and a half million members. Then
the Bamboo Curtain closed and all missionaries were expelled. After
about forty years, when the Curtain was partially raised, the number

of Christians had grown to somewhere between sixty and eighty million. The church continues to grow exponentially.

The second issue is one that most in the West deal with every day. Decisions made by politicians affect this debate, and both sides experience gains and losses. All signs point to continuing disagreement on these issues in the West. A good example of this battle is the growing emphasis on homosexuality as an acceptable lifestyle. More and more the Western world approves this "alternative" lifestyle with great consequences in the social fabric of society. The battle continues and is rapidly changing America's moral values.

Islam, however, is possibly the most critical issue of this generation. In the first edition of this book, I show how certain leaders in Islam have created a very effective strategy to convert the world by the year 2080. In 2004, when the book was first published, it was determined that those developing the strategy had three major prongs to implement their plans:

1. *Da'wah,* or missions
2. *Jihad,* or Holy War
3. The building of mosques

Not long ago, a fourth prong became apparent. It actually started to be an important part of the strategy in the 1980s and 1990s, but more and more its success has became noticeable.

4. Immigration

One major reason for writing a new edition of this book was to include this fourth element in a new chapter—"Changing Demographics."

No other studies on Islam's strategies have stated that these four points exist. I have identified them by putting together all the facts on the growth of Islam, and by studying Islamic strategy for more than ten years. It became apparent that in order to really understand what certain leaders in Islam are doing, their varied tasks and activities needed to be named in a way that could be understood. At the very least, these four prongs give the reader a beginning point in comprehending a complex program of world domination.

I understand that by simply limiting Islam's worldwide macro strategy to only four points, I offer the student of Islam only a limited view of the subject's complexity. This book offers a starting point to more intensive studies of Islam.

Whenever I present this topic via television, radio, or personal appearances, the number one question I am asked is, "OK, we understand the Muslim plan, but what can we do about it?" In planning for this second edition, it became apparent that a chapter needed to be added to provide an answer; thus chapter 12, "What Can We Do About It?" came into being.

Another topic of interest today is the Muslim Brotherhood. There is much new information concerning this organization—some of it contradictory—so I felt it necessary to include an appendix on this very active movement. The so-called "Arab Spring" contains many elements from the Brotherhood, and so to correctly understand this phenomenon, we need to study both the beginnings and the goals of this organization.

Statistics on Islam remain fuzzy. Different sources give widely varying statistics concerning both the size of Islam and its growth. For instance, the estimated number of Muslims in the world today varies from just over 700 million to over 1.4 billion. Reasons given for this wide difference vary from the simple fact that many countries do not keep good records to bold accusations of exaggerated numbers. Thus, the figures from the first edition have been carried into the second edition.

One thing is certain: no one can tell the future. In light of the imminent second coming of Christ, however, it behooves us to understand what is happening today. The question remains whether those in the West are still convinced of the validity of their religion and value system; if so, then we need to understand all the forces now in play that are trying to change the Western world order. The purpose of my writing is not to cause fear but rather to issue a call for action and a return to the root of Western culture and society—God's holy Word.

Preface to the First Edition

The "Clash of Civilizations" was an expression popularized in Samuel P. Huntington's article in the summer of 1993 in the journal *Foreign Affairs*. Since then, many have spoken about the possible coming conflict between the Christian-oriented West—led by the United States—and the Islamic world with its center of influence permeating from the Middle East. Interaction between these two culturally different societies could present the world with continuing conflict, which would include terrorism, suicide bombings, and even the possibility of nuclear weapons.

The attacks on September 11, 2001, seemed to testify to the fact that the official beginning of the "clash" has already occurred. Despite numerous warning signs over the past several decades, many were caught off guard and still are not sure what will come of the new world situations.

I am assuming that there is a real danger of the clash becoming more and more of a reality in the future. Coming events could radically change the relationship between these two global world blocs. My purpose is not to try to explain the problems of such an impending conflict, nor is it to explain the religion of Islam to the Western reader. Rather, the premise is simple: *Islam is a world religion with a well-defined culture and a developed strategy for taking control of the world.* This is not meant to be a condemnation of Islam; most Christian missionaries have a similar rallying cry: "We will win the world to Christ." It is not wrong to desire a world unified under one set of beliefs. However, it is necessary to understand that the expansion of Islam has a planned growth strategy and one that is well orchestrated.

I am simply presenting what is now happening in the Christian–Islamic encounter, and combining the contemporary events with writings from both the secular press and Islamic writers. In doing this, it becomes clear that Islam's growth is not accidental but, rather, is a part of a loose strategy that is based upon the Qur'an and has its center in Mecca.

I use the phrase "loose strategy" because many Muslims who are actively involved in the proclamation of Islam are not aware of how they fit into the overall plan. Because Islam is growing so rapidly, there is a spontaneity to its growth that defies explanation, but when closely studied it becomes apparent that there is a strategy. The average person will not be able to find a master document that forms the basis of this strategy. Rather, there are numerous capable Islamic strategists who are articulating their faith's strategies and working toward a desired end.

Islamic leaders are well aware of Christian missiological methods and strategies, and they have borrowed what they feel will help them to achieve their ultimate aim. The best article I have read on the subject of contextualization—putting the desired message into the cultural context of the hearer—came from the *Muslim World League Journal,* published in Mecca. This article (as well as others) shows that Muslims are strategically mature in their understanding of what it takes for a religious group to grow.

In analyzing the Muslim strategy, I have come to the conclusion that they have a three-pronged plan, which is as follows: *jihad* (holy war), *Da'wah* (missions), and mosques (presence). In the writings of the many Muslim scholars and strategists, I could not find mention of their dividing up their strategy into these three methods. This trinitarian definition of methodology is mine. However, I did find that several Islamic writers explain the concept of three levels of work. Generally speaking, they could be classified as *micro* (work with individuals and local groups), *intermediate* (work with large groups and institutions), and *macro* (work that attempts to change a whole society and its thinking). Each of these is covered in more detail throughout the book.

My intent in this book is not to condemn Muhammad, or Islam as a religion, but to show how this religion plans to take over the world. Both successes and failures are listed.

It is not always easy to write a book on Islam. The difficulty is not in the writing itself but, rather, in the results that might come from the finished work. Take for example a recent book that appeared in Germany under the title *War in Our Cities*. It was written by Udo Ulfkotte, an investigative reporter for one of Germany's most respected newspapers. In the book, he identifies and explains how extreme Muslims are working in Germany to try to undermine the government. Germans bought the book in such great quantities that it went on the top-ten best-sellers list in that country. The author had to contend with numerous lawsuits and received many threats, and certain Muslim organizations tried to get the book banned in Germany. Other authors who have written about the political side of Islam have experienced similar pseudo-persecution.

When I began this book, I was well aware of the likely consequences. In the past, because of my work with Muslims in both Europe and the Middle East, unknown critics have sent me threatening letters. One, postmarked from Saudi Arabia, mentioned that the names and schools of my children were known, and if I did not cease my work with their people, all in my family would be in danger. It is important that those of us in the Western world take this clash of civilizations seriously. The Muslims certainly do.

In the June 30, 2002, issue of *Time* magazine, an article titled "Under Cover" reported about Christians who were working to proclaim Christianity in the Muslim world. At the start of the article the following statement was made: "Throughout this article, for the safety of missionaries working in potentially hostile environments or returning to them, pseudonyms are used. They will be indicated on first usage by quotation marks. Many locations will also be omitted."

The necessity of protecting people working in the Muslim world is very real. Often in this book I have given stories of real people working in real places. Generally, I have recorded the story but have not given detailed information. From an academic standpoint, this is not correct, but the topic demands that security issues be respected. As well, I have received important information in many discussions with Islamic leaders. Such persons have been quoted without any identifying documentation. Again, this is due to the sensitive nature of the topic.

Arabic words such as *jihad* and *Da'wah* form the basis of this book. These and many other Arabic words and phrases are used. Some Arabic words have such wide usage in the West that the English dictionary defines them as if they were English. Generally speaking, words that are defined in a recognized English dictionary are not italicized or treated as foreign words. For the sake of simplicity, however, I have chosen to italicize all Arabic words. The glossary at the back of the book will help the reader to understand their meanings. Because of the richness of the Arabic language, it is not always easy to give short definitions to every word, but at least an attempt has been made to help the reader understand some of the basic concepts of each term.

The world is now in a period of unsettledness. The 2003 war in Iraq has given the world a good picture of the chaos and confusion that could possibly be ahead. Many are saying that it was a mistake for the United States to go into a country so far away from home, only to lose so many of our brightest and best. This war was not about oil but, as Thomas Friedman says, "This is a war over ideas and values and governance." He adds, "In short, America's opponents know just what's at stake in the postwar struggle for Iraq, which is why they flock there: beat America's ideas in Iraq and you beat them out of the whole region; lose to America there, lose everywhere." The war is just a microcosm of the larger problem facing the world as Islam spreads around the globe. The continuing wars and acts of terrorism are a result of the unfolding conflict between Islam and the West. Many Muslim leaders feel that it is Allah's will that the whole world accept Islam. This is the seed of the problem.

An important aspect of the discussion about the "Clash of Civilizations" is the expansion not only of radical Islam, but also of Islam as a whole. If Islam were to succeed in its bid to create one global Islamic state, would it be a radical or a moderate form of this religion? This should be a concern of all who live in the West.

At the end of the book, I have tried to show possible scenarios of the final results from the "Clash of Civilizations." In playing the role of a futurist, I find that it is very difficult to be exact. As a believing Christian, however, I am convinced that the world is moving rapidly toward a final climax. I see the situation being so acute that we could easily be living in the last days. The description of exact events preceding the end must be left to others who specialize in that area of theology.

The Bible does state, "False Christs and false prophets will appear and perform great signs and miracles to deceive even the elect—if that were possible" (Matthew 24:24). On the positive side, Jesus also said, "this gospel of the kingdom will be preached in the whole world as a testimony to all nations, and then the end will come" (Matthew 24:14).

Some might read this book and feel alarmed, but the real antidote for the problems before us is clear-cut: We should become much more active in living out our Christian faith and in proclaiming the truth as found in Jesus Christ. Together, let's dedicate our lives anew to those all-important tasks.

2004

Acknowledgments

The preparation and writing of a book such as this entails many years of work. It could not have been written without the help and encouragement of many of my associates as well as those in my family. I want to thank Sally, my wife, and my two children, Candice and Mark, who lived with me during the eighteen years that I was associated with Muslims in Europe and the Middle East. Their support has been invaluable.

After my retirement from the mission field, I was given the wonderful opportunity of being the professor of missions at Golden Gate Baptist Theological Seminary. Many of my students helped with the research for this book while taking my courses on Islam. I am grateful for their help and prayers. Also, the faculty at the seminary helped to provide a working environment that allowed me to research and write this manuscript. Others have read the manuscript and given many valuable suggestions. Three people I would like to mention are Dr. Ray Tallman, my esteemed colleague; Dr. Ray Register, a former missionary to Muslims in the Middle East; and Dr. John Landers, a well-respected leader in Christian publishing. All three have been a great help.

Stephen Barclift and Jim Weaver from Kregel Publications have given me valuable advice and encouragement during the final phases of publishing this book. And I thank Dawn Anderson for her excellent help on the second edition. Additional help was also provided by Renée and David Sanford, Sanford Communications, Inc., Portland, Oregon.

Much of the typing and work on the format was accomplished by my longtime coworker Alice Webb. Also helping in this area was my teaching assistant Jeff Summers. Many others have made smaller contributions, but each one has added valuable content to the finished product.

chapter **one**

Don't Panic

Islam's Plans for World Dominance

It was a normal summer day in Central Asia. Several of my colleagues and I were scheduled to take a flight from Alma Ata in Kazakhstan to Moscow. The airport was crowded, the smell was stifling, and confusion seemed to be the rule of the day.

Our flight was supposed to take off at 8:00 AM, but, as usual, we were informed that it would be late. After waiting for eight hours and still not knowing when or if we would leave, we boarded the plane. It was packed not only with people but also with various packages and suitcases of many sizes and shapes. Most were piled in the aisles.

As our plane rolled to the runway, we all felt that we had finally crossed the last hurdle. The Boeing 727 of Trans-Aero Airlines began its takeoff, but just before we rose into the air, there was a loud explosion under the wing. A tire blowout. The pilot tried to get the plane airborne, but ten seconds later there was a second explosion as the second tire on that same side also gave way.

As the plane was shaking terribly and swerving to and fro on the runway, one person was heard to cry out, "Don't panic! Don't panic!" Those instructions seemed strange at a time like that. Only in frightening situations do people ever cry out, "Don't panic!"

Thankfully, the pilot was able to get the aircraft under control and bring it to a stop. We disembarked, only to have to wait for two more days in Alma Ata.

After the horrific attacks of September 11, 2001, many were heard to say, "Don't panic! Don't panic!" Many were asking themselves how these warlike events could be happening in a peaceful, advanced society like the United States. As leaders tried to understand the chemistry of what had taken place, it seemed that some unknown forces were at play that made life different from the way it was the day before.

What were these forces that made the world sit up and take notice? Certain names and concepts now were on the lips of thinking people. Suddenly, average Americans were talking about Osama bin Laden, *jihad*, Muslim extremism, the Taliban, and so forth. New words and new ideas were now forming the basis of coffee table discussions.

A new day had dawned. Muslim extremism was now recognized as a more powerful force than most had imagined. It seemed like only yesterday that Christians and Muslims stood shoulder to shoulder when the Berlin Wall came down. Both saw Marx's brand of atheism as an enemy of monotheism, and both saw a brighter day ahead. Faith had won out over disbelief. Christians felt that their ideas of individualism, liberalism, constitutionalism, human rights, equality, liberty, the rule of law, democracy, free markets, and the separation of church and state were now the norm, but suddenly another force had raised its head—one that was in total opposition to their basic belief patterns.

September 11 could best be described as "the twenty-first century shot heard around the world." What happened in just one short day was the start of a new relationship between Islam and the West. "Don't panic" seemed to be the cry, not only because of the terrible events of 9/11 but also because of the realization that a clash of civilizations was now much more visible than ever before.

Many awoke to the fact that the attacks on that date were not an isolated occurence but part of a well-planned and highly financed movement that has a desire to dominate the world. In the year 2000, bin Laden announced the formation of the World Islamic Front for the *jihad* against Jews and Crusaders (bin Laden's term for Christians)—an umbrella group of radical movements across the Muslim world. He issued a *fatwa* stating that it is the duty of all Muslims to kill U.S. citizens and their allies.

Also, it has been publicized that Islam is the second largest and fastest growing religion in the world, at best estimates, numbering between 1.0 and 1.3 billion—about one-fifth of the population of the world. Many areas of the world have regional conflicts, such as Jews versus Palestinians, Hindus versus Muslims in Kashmir, and Russians versus Muslims in Chechnya. Are all of these related, or should they be seen only as separate occurrences in world history? After taking a closer look, it is apparent that there is a worldwide objective for world dominance by Islam.

Understanding both the history and the dynamics of the plan might help us. A simple explanation for the problem is not possible since there are political, cultural, economical, sociological, and religious implications. One writer, John Esposito, has stated that, in light of 9/11, we in the West must ask three questions:

1. Is there a clash of civilizations between Islam and the West?
2. Why do they hate us?
3. Is there a direct connection between Islam, anti-Americanism, and global terror?[1]

These questions, taken with the many facts before us, are reasons for concern. Attempts will be made to address all three in this book.

The growth of the Muslim population in the West and particularly in America has been both silent and alarming. Between 1989 and 1999, the Muslim population grew by more than 100 percent in Europe, to fourteen million (2 percent of the population), and in America by 25 percent. There are fifteen hundred mosques in Germany, and five million Muslims in France. The number of the followers of Muhammad in the rest of the European Union is between twelve and fifteen million.[2]

Many believe that Islam will be the second largest religion in America by 2015. The number of participants in American mosques has increased by more than 75 percent during the past five years and there are now more than twelve hundred mosques in the United States.[3] Islam is definitely on the rise.

From a worldwide perspective, it is also interesting to note that, according to a United Nations demographic report, Muslims will represent at least half of the global birthrate after the year 2055.[4] Islam's rapid growth gives us new impetus to ask, What strategy is Islam employing to facilitate such growth?

ISLAM'S BASIC STRATEGY

While living in Germany, I had a long discussion with a Muslim leader from that country who stated, "Islam's race to win the world was detoured for about four hundred years, but now it is back on track to achieve our ultimate goal—the setting up of a worldwide *ummah* [Islamic community]."[5]

One school of thought, founded in 1953 by Sheik Taqiuddin an-Nabhani, states, "Muslims nowadays live in *Dar-al-Kufr* [the world of infidels]."[6] To them this is intolerable, and "the only solution to the problem is for Muslims to reestablish the *Khalifah*, or Islamic State."[7] According to this school of thought, the Islamic state does not yet exist in the world since *Khalifah* implies one large Islamic state, ruled by a single leader (called a *caliph*), without national boundaries. Just as the founders of Communism felt that world conquest by Marxism was inevitable, so many Islamic scholars and politicians feel that the depravity of the West, coupled with the dynamism of Islam, sets the stage for a future worldwide Islamic state.

One well-known strategist was Ayatollah Khomeini of Iran. During his years of exile (supposedly supported by the French government), he developed the strategy that was so successful in bringing about revolution in his homeland. Literally hundreds of thousands of his taped sermons advocating an Islamic revolution flooded the country. His overthrow of the well-established Shah has been studied by many as an example of how a religious revolution against a contemporary secular government can be accomplished. It was common knowledge in Iran that Khomeini had as his goal a five-stage plan. It was as follows:

Step 1:   The overthrow of the Shah and the establishment of an Islamic Republic in Iran.

Step 2:   Encouraging the creation of Islamic Republics in the surrounding Muslim countries either by revolution, war, or negotiations (thus the war against Iraq).

Step 3:   The defeat of Israel.

Step 4:   The Islamic takeover of Europe.

Step 5:   The fall of the Great Satan (United States of America) as the last step in the creation of a worldwide Islamic *ummah*.

Khomeini was one of the more important influences in the Islamic strategy. Some have said that only the *Wahabi Sunnis* have taken a hard-line position, but Khomeini, a *Shiite,* was probably the ultimate revolutionary leader. President Jimmy Carter's ambassador to Tehran reported that Ayatollah Khomeini was a "twentieth century saint." It is said that Carter himself, being a religious man, felt that it would be possible to deal with him. History has clearly shown that this was a wrong assumption. As we look at Khomeini's plans for world dominance, it is interesting to see what he thought of the West:

> Those who know nothing of Islam pretend that Islam counsels against war. Those who say this are witless. Islam says, "Kill all the Unbelievers" just as they would kill you. Islam says, "Kill them, put them to the sword and scatter their armies." Islam says, "Kill in the service of Allah." Whatever good there exists is thanks to the sword, and the shadow of the sword. People cannot be made obedient except by the sword. The sword is the key of Paradise, which can only be opened for Holy Warriors.[8]

In reading Khomeini's *Islamic Government,* one has a tendency to compare it to Adolf Hitler's *Mein Kampf.* Both state clearly their grand ideas of world conquest, but people today do not take such writings seriously. The key difference between the two is that Hitler was an atheist while Khomeini claimed to be a man of God.

Another so-called twentieth-century saint, the Mullah Mahammad Taqi Sabzevari, who also worked in Iran, was quoted as saying:

> Allah has promised that the day will come when the whole of mankind will live united under the banner of Islam, when the sign of the Crescent, the symbol of Muhammad, will be supreme everywhere. But the day must be hastened through our *jihad,* through our readiness to offer our lives and to shed the unclean blood of those who do not see the light brought from the heavens by Muhammad. . . . The Satanic rulers must be brought down and put to death.[9]

It is no wonder that large numbers of Muslims claim to be international revolutionaries. They form an important part of the Muslim global strategy.

In the past few years, various strategies have been proposed by either Muslim clerics or organizations. Some go so far as even listing which of America's fifty states will be the first to become Islamic. On one list Michigan was given this honor. It is not so foolish as one might think, since one well-known Christian demographer, Jim Slack, the director of research for the International Mission Board of the Southern Baptist Convention, stated that in the year 2000 more than 50 percent of the population of Detroit proper was Islamic or of Islamic background. He also mentioned that Washington, D.C., and London, England, were not far behind.[10] A news report from Voice of America stated, "Dearborn, Michigan, is said to have the largest population of Muslims of any American community. Other cities with large Muslim populations are New York, Los Angeles, and Chicago."[11]

When we look at the military scene, we are appalled. Among the nine largest purchases of arms in the world since 1983, four were by

Arab states: Iraq, Saudi Arabia, Libya, and Egypt.[12] Most of the Arab states have twice as many of their people in military service as Western countries have in theirs. On television, Benjamin Netanyahu, the former prime minister of Israel, has stated that the day would come when the West must fight against the Arab world. If it is now, it will be easier, but if we wait, it will be much more difficult since they are gaining military strength every day. Weapons of mass destruction are not far away for several Muslim states.

Some have said that 15 percent of all Muslims are sympathizers of extreme Islam. How many Muslims in America would fit into this category? What would happen if hundreds of thousands of soldiers from a foreign power invaded the United States? A great alarm would be sounded. Americans would be called upon to fight and defend the flag, our country, and our way of life. Yet, many Muslims in America *are* now politically sympathetic with the goals of the *al Qaeda* movement—yet we do almost nothing.

When did the Islamic revolution begin? What are its plans for the future? There has been contact and conflict between the Christian and Islamic worlds since the founding of Islam in A.D. 621. The Golden Age of Islam was said to be between the seventh and the fourteenth centuries. At the end of that period, they began to suffer a number of defeats at the hands of Western empires. The era of colonization was then introduced, and the growth of Islam was halted. Some say Islam entered into its own "Dark Ages," similar to the Middle Ages. Their period of enlightenment then began in the twentieth century.

THE NEW DAWN FOR ISLAM (1945–1969)

A little-known fact is that the Muslim Brotherhood grew up in Egypt in the 1920s as an imitation of European fascism, which itself was a revolt against modernity. In Italy and Germany they were known by their black or brown shirts. In Egypt they had green shirts, which symbolized the Muslim Brotherhood. Fascism failed in Europe but survived in Egypt and spread to other parts of the

Islamic world.[13] The influence of this radical movement is still very powerful in Egypt. It became fiercely anti-Western in the 1940s and 1950s under the direction of Sayyid Qutb, an Egyptian fundamentalist. This movement was credited with many assassinations, including that of Anwar Sadat.

It was always easy to identify those who belonged to the Brotherhood in the Middle East. In 1983, when I attended a meeting of Baptists in Egypt, I and two of my younger colleagues were told that we all had to shave our beards. When we asked for a reason, we were told that in Egypt the only ones who wore beards were members of the Brotherhood. (For more on the Islamic Brotherhood, see appendix C.)

This movement planted the seeds that were to grow during what Ralph Winters identifies as "the twenty-five unbelievable years" in his book by the same title.[14] No matter how you look at it, the twentieth century was amazing, but no period had more change and more influence on today's problem than did the twenty-five years described by Winters. This period could be termed "the official end of political imperialism," or better, "the retreat of the West." In his book, Winters shows that before 1945, 99.5 percent of the non-Western world was under Western domination. By 1969, 99.5 percent of the same area was independent.[15] Political colonialism was ended. Economic, national, and cultural imperialism, however, remained.

Among those countries that experienced this new freedom were the Arab nations that form the cradle of Islam. Those who talk about the Arab world are talking about the citizens of the states that are members of the Arab League created in 1945. It started with seven states (Egypt, Iraq, Saudi Arabia, Syria, Lebanon, Jordan, and Yemen) and expanded its membership to twenty-two states, including relative latecomers such as Djibouti, Comoros, and Palestine. Also included are Algeria, Bahrain, Kuwait, Libya, Mauritania, Morocco, Oman, Qatar, Somalia, Sudan, Tunisia, and United Arab Emirates.[16] Non-Arab countries such as India, Indonesia, Malaysia, and other countries with large Muslim populations also escaped out from under the thumb of Western colonialism.

The extension of Islam into the West had many sources. Europe still had a remnant of Muslims after the Moors were expelled from Spain and the Turks were defeated in the southeastern part of their continent. There continued to be some limited contact in America when Muslims were first brought over as early as 1717 during the African slave trade period. Years later, Muslims migrated voluntarily to America in five separate waves from 1875 to 1967. Most of those coming were unskilled Arabs who found work in the larger urban areas of the Northeast and the Great Lakes regions.

During the period of time prior to Winter's closing date of *The Twenty-Five Unbelievable Years,* Muslims seemed to have little or no effect on the society. They either became a part of the "melting pot" or they hid themselves in small groups, so as not to be too conspicuous. The only exception to this was the Nation of Islam among African-Americans, but their form of Islam was so radically different that more orthodox Muslims shunned them.

After 1969, the more orthodox Muslims seemed to fall into one of two groups as described by Larry Poston. He said they were either "offensive-activist Muslims" or "defensive-pacifist Muslims." The offensive-activists usually come from a traditional Islamic country like Saudi Arabia and seek to "propagate their faith and persuade Americans to abandon their current religious beliefs or secular life-style and convert to Islam."[17]

Their goals do not always include political conquest, but they refuse to assimilate into American society. The defensive-pacifist Muslims have come to America in search of greater economic and political freedom. They have assimilated into American culture and have played a huge role in the establishment of mosques and Islamic institutions for the purpose of helping Muslims preserve their Islamicity in the midst of "Christian" America.

Jane Smith, in a book she wrote prior to 9/11, describes it differently; "Many Muslims living in the United States . . . want to assimilate as much as possible into American culture and try not to emphasize elements of their identity that would differentiate them from others."[18] She goes on to add, "Many others, however, are tired of what they see as the biased and unfair representations of Islam and Muslims in the American media and take opportunity to correct those images by providing in their own lives public examples of what 'real Islam' looks like when practiced by conscientious and faithful adherents."[19] The end of colonization and the new world order now gave Muslims a new identity and a readiness to reawaken their original dream of world domination.

Muslim countries were now also free to determine their own religious future but still had to work under the constraints of cultural and economic imperialism. Radical Islam grew under these ripe conditions. The West was blamed for the lack of a better life as radicals took the moral high ground. The fact that most of the new developing countries established dictatorships actually helped fundamentalists, even when those leaders drew in the reins out of fear of a revolutionary takeover.

In Islamic thinking, the failures of the past or present can be blamed on economic oppression by the West, and Christianity in general. Fatema Mernissi, a Muslim, stated, "Today few Arab heads of state would dream of a . . . [large scale] solution to the problems of unemployment and instability; their solution would more likely be to send an army into the streets or to imprison the rioters."[20] I would add "or to declare a *jihad* against the West to divert the criticism." If the new nations did not flourish economically with their newly gained freedoms, Islam as a religion did.

As early as the 1950s, the situation in America began to change. There was an influx of a new type of Muslim. The new immigrants were better educated, and they came to live in the "land of freedom" because of the higher standard of living. Many had studied in America and grew to genuinely love their new homeland. One article says of the 1950s:

> This was the period which saw the formation of the early Muslim communities and mosques in such places as Detroit, Ann Arbor, Gary (Indiana), Cedar Rapids (Iowa), Sacramento and the like. Visiting scholars and missionary

groups from the Middle East and the Indo-Pakistan subcontinent also began to arrive. And Islam began, in a very slow manner, to gain adherents among white Americans.[21]

This was also a time when the Muslim population of America began to look for their roots. They began to have conferences, find places to worship, and create organizations that could help them live as a people in a Western world. New national Islamic groups such as the Muslim Students Association of the United States and Canada began to spring up. Even in the small town of Abique, New Mexico, there was the creation of a large training center for Islam. Many Muslims began to find their way back into the faith they had previously seen as dormant. Now a new dynamic was introduced into the community. For the first time Americans had to face the fact that the existence of Islam in their country was a reality.

Meanwhile in the home area of Islam, the newly founded countries of the Middle East began to see a growth of a more fundamental Islam—following the lead of the Egyptian Muslim Brotherhood. Other groups formed. The mixture of weak economies, oppressive governments, and frustration drove many back to their faith, one that allowed them to use might to find fulfillment, if necessary. The radical groups set up terror networks that distilled a host of economic, cultural, and political problems into a concentrated toxin of hatred aimed at Western cultures and their perceived flagship, America.

Many in the West saw this movement toward fundamentalism as only a small sect of Islam. However, in an article in *Newsweek* dated October 15, 2001, a Muslim leader, Fareed Zakaria, said, "To say that *al Qaeda* is a fringe group may be reassuring, but it is false. The problem is not that Osama bin Laden believed that this is a religious war against America. It's that millions of people across the Islamic world seem to agree."[22]

Around the globe new movements gave hope for Muslims living in poor conditions. From Indonesia to Nigeria, a new enthusiasm emerged out of the former colonial, secular societies. The awakening appeared not only in the historic Islamic homelands but in all countries where the followers of Muhammad lived. The groundwork for September 11 had been laid.

The Death of the West

While this new vibrancy in Muhammad's religion was growing, the Christian foundation of the West was taking a beating. Patrick Buchanan, in his controversial book, *The Death of the West,* outlined how America and the West were losing the cultural wars. Buchanan wrote:

> The West is dying. Its nations have ceased to reproduce, and their populations have stopped growing and begun to shrink. Not since the Black Death carried off a third of Europe in the fourteenth century has there been a graver threat to the survival of Western civilization.[23]

Among the threats to our present-day society are (1) secularism, (2) immigration, (3) ethnic population decline, and—last but not least—(4) Islam. Buchanan gives a convincing argument for the secularism of the West. It is a secularism that tends to disapprove of the Christian heritage of the West, with the separation of church and state—once a strong Baptist issue—now being used to rid the society of all remnants of its Christian heritage. Through the courts of the land and the media, a concerted attack is being made against the very soul of the West. It was an unprecedented attack against a faith that had stood for two thousand years.

It would appear that this decline of Christianity in the West has paralleled the rise of Islam in the West. In Europe, the death of the church is much more advanced, as is the rise of Islam. In America the process is more inhibited by a lingering faith. Buchanan and others have asked the question, "Where is the sense of outrage?" As the battle unfurls, the church seems to be silent. Buchanan quotes Jim Nelson Black as writing:

But one of the greatest reasons for the decline of American society over the past century has been the tendency of Christians who have practical solutions to abandon the forum at the first sign of resistance. Evangelicals in particular have been quick to run and slow to stand by their beliefs. In reality, most Christians have already vacated "the public square" of moral and political debate by their own free will, long before civil libertarians and others came forth to drive us back to our churches.[24]

What is the major problem facing the West? James Kurth, in "The Real Clash," contends: "The real clash of civilizations will not be between the West and one or more of the Rest. It will be between the West and the post-West, within the West itself. This clash has already taken place within the brain of Western civilization, the American intellectual class. It is now spreading from that brain to American body politic."[25]

While some see the major clash as being between Islam and the Christian West, I see that in reality there are three entities, each fighting against the other. The first two are already recognized as Islam and the Christian West. I dare to add a third—secularism. Christianity views this humanistic form of thought as a· problem. Islam sees the resulting atheism as a residue of Western nonbelief that erodes Islamic influence with both Western Muslims as well as those in the predominately Islamic countries. Television, the Internet, radio, and international travel all seem to present a threat to their faith. The faith-based entities see humanistic secularism as a non-option in their plans to win the world for their faith. The reason is obvious. Secularism preaches the oneness of man and the idea of pluralism but detests any group that claims to hold the true faith including Islam and Christianity. As the two largest religions of the world seek to further their own goals, they must keep a close eye on the third.

The second threat to the West is the mass migration of peoples, which has gained in intensity over the past twenty years. The world is going through a demographic change of a magnitude never before seen. People of many nations and tribes seeking a better way of life are invading the more affluent countries of North America and Europe. Uncontrolled immigration threatens to change the West at its very core. Muslims do not always desire to become a part of the new chosen land. For a variety of reasons (which we will look at later), many prefer to remain distant and distinct. I find it ironic that those from the Islamic cultures want to come to the West because of the failure of their own system, yet at the same time seek to impose their failed system upon the West.

Americans are growing more concerned about the problem. Many Americans now want immigration reduced, and others want English to be America's official language. The remainder are human secularists who see a union of people as the salvation for mankind (with a liberal agenda, of course).

Europe is in a more difficult situation. It has immigrants trying to enter into it from the south, east, and west. Today, many of the socialist-led governments (such as in Belgium, the Netherlands, France, Austria, and Germany) are in danger of falling because of their unqualified support for immigration. Only recently has there been an outcry from the far right for immigration reform. These governments are now changing and instituting laws that limit the numbers that can come into the country. Immigration is changing the face of many countries, and many of the immigrants are Muslims. In France it has been said that more Muslims participate in weekly religious services than do Roman Catholics and Protestants combined.

The decline of the ethnic (European) population is also a great concern. Today, it is as difficult to find a Western nation where the native population is not declining as it is to find an Islamic nation where the native population is not exploding. Secularization and the "good life" have presented us with a new problem. A combination of an extremely high number of abortions, the desire for higher economic security, and a better standard of living often hinders the formation of large families. Muslim families are generally two, three, or four times larger than non-Muslim families in the West.

The growth of Islam and the changing immigration patterns were seen as a positive aspect of a free global society simply trying to find itself. Many uttered soothing words about the positive aspects of political and religious pluralism. On September 11, many began to wake up and notice the dangers within pluralism. All acknowledged that the West was not at war with Islam, but it seemed clear that Islam was at war with the West.

THE CLASH OF CIVILIZATIONS

In the summer of 1993, *Foreign Affairs* published an article, written by the highly respected Samuel Huntington, which created a worldwide debate. It warned that a clash between Western culture and Islam would dominate global politics. Huntington followed up on the article by writing a book titled *The Clash of Civilizations and the Remaking of World Order.* He does not see much possibility of a cordial cohabitation of Islam and the West. He writes that people are trying to define themselves and find their cause to serve. He states, "In the modern world, religion is a central, perhaps *the* central, force that motivates and mobilizes people."[26]

Huntington is aware that the fault line between Islam and the West is not the world's only major problem. He identifies eight distinctive civilizations: Islamic, Sinic (centered on the "core state" of China), Western (with the United States as its core), Orthodox (with Russia as its core), Japanese, Hindu, Latin American, and (somewhat tentatively) African. He says that divisions between each of these civilizations could be problematic. The major players in the forthcoming struggle are Islam and the Christian West. In a review of the Huntington book, A. J. Bacevich writes:

> Huntington does not attribute the West's recent difficulties with Islam to the influence of a handful of fanatics. "The underlying problem for the West is not Islamic fundamentalism. It is Islam, a different civilization whose people are convinced of the superiority of their culture and obsessed with the inferiority of their power."[27]

Have politicians and analysts defined the current crisis accurately? Some describe the struggle as between democratic and non-democratic forms of government. In theory, Islam is an inherently political religion. As well as being the bearer of divine revelation, the prophet Muhammad founded a political state. Those who followed him were primarily political leaders and heads of governments and empires rather than pious religious leaders. It is interesting to note that few of the Muslim states in the world are truly democratic. All of the Arab states seem to have a leader for life. When Hosni Mubarak of Egypt was asked if he was ready to allow free elections in his country, he answered that he had spent his entire life preparing to serve his people and he would be letting them down by not leading.

For Huntington, the concept of religion is extremely important since it signifies "who we are" and "who we are not." Many see the fault lines of the next conflict as geographical, but neither Islam nor Christianity fits into this category. The problem today is not a clash of governments or cultures but rather of civilizations—which include governments and cultures. Increasingly, it is a clash of religions. Both Islam and Christianity now have adherents in all the countries of the world and are actively seeking to increase their numbers. Huntington refers to the global aspects of both religions as "an inter-civilizational phenomenon." Both faiths continue to be vibrant and alive. The coming conflict will be between these two world religions and their related cultures.

THE AMERICAN JIHAD

At the beginning of this new century, most Americans felt that they were secure. Communism had been defeated, the economy was strong, and there was, after all, only one real world power—the United States of America. But when New York's twin towers fell, this security began to unravel. For the first time, many began to see Islam as a threat. Most, however, had little or no idea of what Islam was and what Muslims believed.

After that fateful day in September, many Americans from foreign countries began to bear the brunt of persecution or were looked upon with suspicion when they boarded a plane. Among them were Hindus and Sikhs. Because they wore different types of clothing or hats, they were viewed as Muslims, but they also had their own problems with Muslims. Many assumed that the new situation would be a distraction for Islam in its goal of converting America, but the opposite was true. When isolated instances of persecution occurred, many rushed to the side of those being threatened and harmed. This was to be expected since it is the American (and, I might add, the Christian) way. What was not apparent was that the Muslims capitalized on the situation and made great gains in making their faith known to the American people. Americans were asking, What is Islam?

Mosques in America were put on the alert, and many of them immediately began to have open houses and public meetings so that they could explain what Islam teaches. Letters were sent to mosques telling their people how to take advantage of the events. I went to one of these meetings and was amazed to hear that Islam was a religion of love, peace, and forgiveness. The speaker distanced himself and his mosque from the evil events of destruction while promoting the positive aspects of his belief. It worked. Many mosques reported large numbers of Americans converted to Islam after 9/11.

Democratic America has been an excellent breeding ground for not only Islam as a religion but also for radical Islam. As the FBI and the CIA began to search for terrorist cells, they found numerous Muslim organizations with varying ties to radicals. In his book *American Jihad*, Steven Emerson gives a fascinating description of the various Muslim organizations now operating in America and their ties with various terrorist organizations. The political freedom afforded in this country gives a convenient cover to those who seek the establishment of a global Islamic state.

The key to understanding the link between Islam as a religion and the terrorist movement now dominating the news is to understand the *Wahabi* movement. Emerson quotes Sheik Muhammad Hisham

Kabbani who spoke to an open forum at the U.S. State Department on January 7, 1999. Kabbani stated:

> The man who brought it to the tribes was a Muslim scholar by the name of Muhammad ibn Abd al-Wahhab. This was in the Eastern part of what we call Saudi Arabia during the seventeenth and eighteenth century. These ideas were going forth and back. Sometimes they were put down and other times they were supported. There was a struggle with the Muslims trying to keep them down with the support of the Ottoman Empire. They were successful until the Ottoman Empire dissolved and finished in the middle of 1920 and the new regime came—it was the secular regime of Mustafa Kemal [Ataturk]. They then found an opportunity in the tribes, which no longer had the support of the Ottoman Empire in that area. They had freedom to go and change the ideas and brainwash the minds of the Muslims in this area. Slowly, slowly in the many years from 1920 until today they were very successful in establishing a new ideology in Islam that is very extremist in its point of view. It was not so militant [at first], however; it didn't take the form of militancy, but it took the form of revival or renewal of Islamic tradition.[28]

Wahabism (or *Wahhabism*) was the religion of the al-Saud family when they unified the tribes of the Arabian Peninsula in the 1930s and seized power, establishing the kingdom of Saudi Arabia. They are very orthodox and puritanical in their theology and tend toward a form of Islamic militancy that advocates reform through the use of the sword. Some have even stated that the religion of all of Saudi Arabia is *Wahabism*. It is no wonder that Osama bin Laden considered himself an adherent of this movement. Perhaps the most disconcerting part of this is that Saudi Arabia is taking the lead in the worldwide missionary work of Islam. Together with its seemingly unlimited economic strength and its religious fervor, this is where the main threat to the West lies.

Stephen Schwartz, author of *The Two Faces of Islam,* says we should not be alarmed by the growth of Islam in the United States but by who controls it. "I would say billions of dollars have been spent in the United States to advance Wahhabism," Schwartz said. "The Wahhabi sect, backed by Saudi Arabia, controls 70 to 80 percent of the mosques in the United States. That means they control the teaching, the preaching, the literature that's distributed, and they control the training of the Imams."[29]

Dale Hurd of CBN News gives another example of this situation. He says, "American Muslim leaders have said they are not under the control of Saudi Arabia because they don't take money from the Saudi government, but only from private Saudi citizens. However, one spokesman admitted to the Associated Press that the 'money does not come free. It always comes with strings attached.'"[30]

Da'wah consists mainly of motivating Muslims to do mission work, and many Muslim missionaries are heavily financed by Saudi sources. The main missions organization is the Muslim World League, which is a worldwide Islamic organization.[31] Since the Saudis finance them, it is natural that they embrace the stricter form of *Wahabism* that is a part of the Saudi society. In his interview with the State Department in 1997, the moderate Sheik Kabbani made two controversial assertions: "80 percent of all mosques and Muslim charitable organizations in the United States had been taken over by 'extremists' who did not represent the mainstream community; and Osama bin Laden represented an imminent threat to America."[32]

From many different sources I have heard that 80 percent of all *imams* in the mosques in America are *Wahabis.* My own experience in speaking with many *imams* has confirmed this assertion. Often I will take a class of students to pay a friendly visit to a mosque. In our dialogue concerning what Islam believes, I often hear words of peace, love, and forgiveness, but when I enter the political realm, I find a completely different atmosphere. Bitterness and hate take the forefront; words that claim a future world conquest for Islam are spoken. At the end of the conversation, there is a reverting back to peace, forgiveness, and love. *Wahabism* has made its mark not only on individual faith communities within Islam but on all of America.

In the fall of 2001, there was a strong debate in the halls of Washington, D.C. The question was simply, "Can we trust the Saudis?" In a briefing from the Rand Corporation to a Pentagon advisory board, the briefer charged that "the Saudis are active at every level of the terror chain from planners to financiers, from cadre to foot soldiers, from ideologist to cheerleader."[33] There was an equally strong rebuttal from the Saudi ambassador. He denied that they were to be blamed for all that they were accused of doing. In a sense, both were telling the truth. Those in Washington have been taught to separate religion and politics in their thinking. In the Arab mind these two are one. Those from the Rand commission could look at the heavy financial aid given to groups in America that support terrorism as proof that they are seeking to aid terrorists and overthrow democracy. The Saudis see it as a legitimate function of the state to support all Muslim work, no matter what form it takes.

CONCLUSION

The question must still be answered: Is Islam a threat? My experience of working with Muslims both in the Middle East and in the West has shown that the answer is a strong yes. Years before the fall of New York's twin towers, I was saying there were storm clouds ahead. The rain has now begun to fall. I could give many hundreds of examples to support my answer. People have suffered greatly under Islam; some have lost loved ones, others have been beaten or had their homes burned down, and still others have been ambushed while worshiping peacefully in their church. Almost every day in some part of the world, there are news reports of brutalities against non-Muslims by Muslims. Those suffering often tell of the loud cries of *"Allahu Akbar"* ("God is the greatest") shouted by those who perform the evil deeds.

chapter **two**

The Quiet Revolution

Islam's Mission Strategy (Da'wah)

The story of the camel and the Arab is often recited in the Middle East. An Arab was making a long trip across the desert. During the day the heat can be scorching, but at night it can get bitter cold. On one especially cold night, the Arab was in his nice warm tent where some embers kept the environment warm. As the man began to go to sleep, he noticed a large camel nose sticking in under the tent.

"Camel," he said, "why is your nose in my tent?"

"O Master," he replied, "it's so cold out here, and if only my nose were warm, then I could have a good night's sleep."

The Arab thought it over and allowed him to keep his nose in. A little later the man awoke and saw that the camel now had his whole head in the tent.

"What are you doing, Camel? You said you only wanted your nose in the tent."

"O Master, you just do not know how cold it is out here, and if my head is in the tent, then I will be satisfied."

After thinking it over, the Arab agreed and he went back to sleep. Once again he was awakened, this time to find that the camel had his head, neck, and two feet in the tent.

"Camel, this is too much. You must stop."

"O Master, now I am really comfortable. I can sleep the whole night."

"OK," said the Arab, "but just this and no more."

Later in the night, the Arab awakened to discover that the tent was now full with the whole body of the camel inside the tent, and the Arab had little room.

"Camel!" he shouted. "What are you doing?"

"Get out of my tent, you stupid man," was the camel's reply.

Most Americans see Islam as a threat to the West mainly through *jihad* or holy war. They are not aware that there are actually four easily definable elements in the Muslim world strategy. The four are:

1. *Da'wah*—the Islamic equivalent to Christian missions
2. *Jihad*—holy war
3. The Mosque—their physical presence
4. Immigration

This and the next three chapters will study, in depth, each of these four elements. The first, *Da'wah*, is the same slow but effective method that the camel used to gain possession of the tent.

UNDERSTANDING *Da'wah*

A friend of mine who is the leader of a mosque in Europe says, "You in the West do not use the correct translations of Arabic words." This critique is generally aimed at Westerners who use the word *jihad* and call it "holy war." There are two main reasons why Westerners have a difficult time understanding the complexities of Arabic. First, translating from a more complicated language into a simpler one poses significant problems. Several years ago a group of linguists concluded that the most difficult languages for a foreigner to learn are Navajo, Arabic, and Mandarin. Second, because Muslims believe Arabic is the heavenly language, for many years it was prohibited to translate the Qur'an into any other language. This prohibition is now gone, but many of the more orthodox schools still have problems with the issue.

Da'wah (or *da'wa* or *daawah*) is one of those words that has several valid meanings.

Jane I. Smith, professor of Islamic Studies at Hartford Seminary in Connecticut, in her book *Islam in America,* gives three perspectives on *Da'wah* for various practitioners:

> For some, *da'wa* means the active business of the propagation of Islam with the end of making conversions. . . . For others, *da'wa* involves the effort to bring those who have fallen away from Islam back to active involvement in the faith. . . . And for still others, *da'wa* means the responsibility to simply live quiet lives of Muslim piety and charity, with the hope that by example they can encourage wayward coreligionists as well as others that Islam is the right and appropriate path to God.[1]

Dr. Ghassan Khalif, president of the Arab Baptist Seminary in Beirut, Lebanon, said, "The two words *ad-da'wah* mean the invitation, the calling, and/or the vocation."[2] The verb form of *Da'wah* is the often used word *Dah'u,* which means to invite or to call.[3] Others have given the meaning "come" to the word. *Da'wah* is the extending of an invitation to come into a close fellowship with Allah through Islam.

Another important word is *daa'i,* which is the nearest Islamic equivalent of the Christian missionary or mission worker. *Daa'i* could be defined as a preacher or a worker for Islam. Since every Muslim is to be a witness to Islam, each member of the faith should be a *daa'i.* This, however, has taken on another significance and is used for those who have felt a definite call to be involved in the work of spreading Islam. A *daa'i* has six different responsibilities. They are:

1. To oneself
2. To one's family
3. To one's neighbors
4. To one's fellow citizens
5. To one's countrymen
6. To one's fellow human beings[4]

The doing of *Da'wah* is an important part of the work of all who profess to be *daa'i*. There are large numbers of these Islamic missionaries working in both Islamic and non-Islamic countries. *Time* magazine reported:

> More recently the Saudis have focused on nearby Kosovo. Half of the $1 million the Saudi Joint Relief Committee spent in the two months after the 1999 war there went to sponsor 388 religious "propagators" intent on converting Kosovars to Wahhabism.[5]

These "propagators" also carry the title of being *daa'i*. Sometimes these Islamic missionaries are fully funded, and other times they do their work on a bivocational basis. There are likely more *daa'i*s preaching Islam in the West than there are missionaries preaching Christianity in Muslim countries.

COMPARISON TO CHRISTIAN MISSIONS

Both the Bible and the Qur'an give the command that their followers are to be involved in the proclamation of their faith. Here are two examples:

> Go, then, to all peoples everywhere and make them my disciples: baptize them in the name of the Father, the Son, and the Holy Spirit, and teach them to obey everything I have commanded you. And I will be with you always, to the end of the age. (Matthew 28:19–20 GNT)

> And thus we made you an *ummah*, a party equally balanced on a Presidential party so that you be Witness to the people (Shahid al an Naas) and the Prophet be a witness upon you. (*Surah* 2:143)

Both Islam and Christianity are missionary religions. They have some of the same goals and both believe that the widespread propagation of their message is God's will. These similarities can lead to conflict. David Kerr of Selly Oaks College in England has stated: "The absolute commitment of the Christian to missions and of the Muslim to *Da'wah* has undoubtedly been one of the principal contributory factors to the tension. . . . Each feels itself to have been abused by the other."[6] Since many in the West understand missions, it might be a help to make a short comparison of the two in order to gain a better understanding of *Da'wah*.

As stated earlier, *Da'wah* is defined as "an invitation" or "to come." This was the same approach made in the Old Testament by God's people, the Israelites. To know God you needed to come to his land and his people to find him. The abode of God was the Holy of Holies located in the temple at Jerusalem. Much is the same in Islam today. To find God you must come to his people and his abode, which is the *Ka'aba* located in Mecca. Of course both religions realize that God is not limited to a single definable space, but their missions concept was nuanced by their identification of the location of his presence.

Christianity broke from this concept of mission when it built its strategy for proclamation on the words of Jesus when he told his disciples to "Go into the world." The very word *missions* means "to be sent." Christianity is a "go" faith while Islam is a "come" faith. Muslims are very much aware of the different emphasis in this wordplay, and they take seriously the missionary and evangelistic visions of Christianity. One Islamic leader told me that prior to 1990 the greatest enemy to Islam was Communism, but after that date the greatest enemy became Christian missions.

Two words are on the blacklist of the Muslim psyche. They are the Arabic words *irsalyyat* (missions) and *tabshir* (evangelism). These two words are not used by Muslims to describe their work of *Da'wah*. In fact, when missionary activities are taking place among Muslims, their preachers feel responsible to warn their people of Christian missions and evangelism. The very use of these two words in Arabic sends an intensely negative message. While Christian mission and Islamic *Da'wah* run parallel, they are not the same. The following sections outline their differences and similarities.

Differences

Christian Mission	Islamic *Da'wah*
1. Christian mission has used social action as a means of showing a love that could lead to conversion.	1. Islam uses social service within their mosque as a part of the service that a believer can obtain after conversion, but most do not consider it a part of *Da'wah*.
2. Christian mission uses large numbers of full-time missionaries who are involved in a cultural incarnation ministry.	2. Islam depends mostly on semi-trained laypeople and mosque leaders in their work of expansion.
3. Christian mission emphasizes a cultural divergence that seeks to create indigenous churches within the existing social system.	3. Islam seeks to bring uniformity in law, culture, and religious practices.
4. Christian mission emphasizes going.	4. Islamic *Da'wah* emphasizes coming.
5. Christian mission invites people to become members of churches.	5. Islamic *Da'wah* invites people to become members of the *ummah* (Community of God).
6. Christian mission engages in the establishment of schools, hospitals, and other benevolent institutions through cooperative methods.	6. Islamic *Da'wah* stresses the construction of a mosque and then establishes its ministries.
7. In Christian missions, the church is to be responsible for the propagation of the faith.	7. In Islamic *Da'wah,* the *ummah* is responsible for the propagation of the faith.
8. Conversion through conquest is no longer considered a valid form of missions.	8. Conversion through armed conflict is considered helpful to *Da'wah*.

Similarities

1. Both have well-defined philosophies as well as fully thought-out methodologies.
2. Both see their faith as a worldwide faith, although their areas of strength are localized.
3. Both see the source of their communion as issuing from their holy book, which gives support to their position.
4. Both have mission organizations that have as their main purpose the furtherance of their faith.
5. Both see conversion to their belief as a positive aspect of their actions.
6. Both see the actions of the other as satanic and have some fear of the other's successes.
7. Both Christianity and Islam are "fractured religions," which have many different expressions and theologies. This plurality carries over to mission and *Da'wah.*
8. Both are aware of the paradigm shift taking place worldwide and feel there is a spiritual vacuum that they can fill.
9. Both see Eastern Europe as fertile fields for expansion.
10. Both extend a call for people to enter into a broad community of believers, Christians into the kingdom of God and Muslims into the *ummah.*

METHODS OF *DA'WAH* IN THE WEST

When people think about the expansion of Islam, most are concerned about *jihad,* yet *Da'wah* is more subtle and possibly more successful. As they look upon the world in general and the West in particular, Muslims see the circumstances as very conducive for new growth. Three reasons why Islamic scholars feel the time is right for the progress of Islam:

1. There is a great aptitude toward ungodliness. The world has not found true happiness. Because of this, the world is more

receptive than ever before. People still have an emptiness that can only be filled with Islam.

2. The world today is rational and open. Once the truth in Islam is heard, all will surely accept it.

3. In this age, many people are going back to mankind's true nature. This is at least a right direction on the path of life. People's desire to harmonize nature and mankind with God will actually bring them to Islam.[7]

Let us look at several of the ways that *Da'wah* is effectively used today.

DA'WAH IN THE ACADEMIC WORLD

American universities and colleges are prime targets of Islamic propaganda. Marsha Snulligan Haney states: "Their main goal is to promote Islamic education in both public schools (from elementary grades to the University level), as well as in the mosques and Islamic centers."[8] She goes on to add, "Strong Islamic education and knowledge is the key to both the future of Islam in this country and to attracting the interest of non-Muslims to Islam. One cannot help but notice the sense of *Da'wah* that motivates and accomplishes such practices in reality."[9] The number of Muslim students on university and college campuses is growing.

There are approximately one thousand to fifteen hundred international students from twenty-five Islamic countries in the greater Los Angeles area alone. The majority are affiliated with the Islamic Society of North America and are preparing to work for the establishment of Islamic governments. Muslim alumni who remain in this country are encouraged to establish and organize mosques wherever they live.[10]

Muslims seek to evangelize not only American students but also other international students studying at American universities. Several years ago I was invited to speak at an English class in Morocco. The room was filled with more than two hundred young, intelligent students. One of my first questions was, "Why do you want to learn English?" One student answered, "So that we can win the world to Islam." I then asked, "How many feel the same?" Every hand was raised. After class a group spoke with me and said they wanted to become *daa'is* and work in universities for Islam.

Fatema Mernissi wrote: "Some Westerners are surprised to find that today university science departments and technological and scientific institutions are the breeding ground of [Islamic] fundamentalism; it is there that a large number of fundamentalists are recruited."[11]

One method of penetrating the university communities is by using the immense economic strength of Middle Eastern Islamic countries. Financially strapped institutions receive offers to endow a chair of Islamic studies or build a nice building to house an institute of religion. One report states that "Saudi Arabia has given tens of millions of dollars to Harvard University and the University of Arkansas to fund Islamic study centers."[12] In many of the poorer countries of Africa, fundamentalist groups with the financial backing of Saudi Arabia will send a large number of professors to teach in their universities. The main aim of these projects is to promote Islam.

A short time ago, there was a national debate on the work of South Florida University Professor Sami Al-Arian. As a tenured professor, he could not be released without due cause. Much evidence was brought forth to show that he and his department were supporters of terrorist groups, including videotapes in which he called for "death to the Jews." The FBI named two of his associates with him as members and leaders of terrorist organizations. When the university attempted to fire him, cries of free speech and intellectual freedom rang out in his defense. While Professor Al-Arian later was indicted for his actions and fired from the university, he and many others have found that in the West educational institutions provide a safe and profitable base from which to operate.

Muslims also see possibilities for *Da'wah* in primary and secondary schools. Behind the veil of freedom of speech and pluralism, they are promoting Islamic instruction. In California, one of the approved textbooks had the students role-play such activities as wearing Muslim dress, taking Muslim names, and taking the pilgrimage to Mecca. When several school boards were challenged on this, their reply was that they were simply helping the students appreciate other cultures.

CBN News reported a more disconcerting example of this on February 8, 2002. A segment titled "Islam Taught in Public Schools" featured a textbook required by all California schools for seventh grade social studies. The textbook is *Across the Centuries* and is a "world history textbook published by Houghton-Mifflin. Chapters three and four outline the origins and early growth of Islam, including a detailed account of the life of Muhammad."[13] During the study of Islam there is a "10 to 15 day simulation," the purpose of which is "to be the first group to complete a pilgrimage to Mecca. Students pretend to travel in caravans, engage in trade, dress up, and even pick a Muslim name, and even stage their own jihad as part of a dice game."[14] The curriculum also states "one important phase three activity is learning Islam's five pillars of faith by imitating a requirement of each pillar." This means that, at some point in the simulation, students could be asked to imitate a Muslim profession of faith, Muslim prayer, the giving of alms, a Ramadan fast, and/or a pilgrimage to Mecca.[15]

Another book that has been published by Interaction Publishers of Carlsbad, California, is intended as a curriculum manual for use by history teachers in grades six through twelve. The book *Islam: A Simulation* consists of lesson plans and handouts for a three-week program of classroom instruction in which students "will simulate becoming Muslims" and allegedly "will learn about the history and culture of Islam."[16] One reviewer of the book, William J. Bennetta, a fellow of the California Academy of Sciences and president of the Textbook League, stated, "Page for page, this is the most malignant product that I have seen as a reviewer."[17] If the same students were required to take Christian communion or to read the Bible, numerous lawsuits would immediately follow.

Dr. Ralph Winters, former professor of missions at Fuller Seminary, related his story of attending an open house at his child's high school. The whole program was planned so that each parent could attend each of his child's classes for a ten-minute lecture. In the class on American history, the teacher listed the many customs and habits that America received from its European heritage. When she finished, she asked if there were questions. Dr. Winters stood and simply asked the teacher if she had mentioned that we had also received much from Europe in relation to the Christian faith. Immediately other parents stood and complained that if he spoke about Christianity, then he needed to speak about other religions as well. His answer was, "This is true if they were a part of our European heritage, but the fact is that they were not."

Islam has taken advantage of American openness and has made great progress in *Da'wah* in our schools that are closed to Christianity. The educational institutions of the West will be a major battleground for Islam in the future.

Soon schools may be challenged to provide history courses that deal with Islamic history instead of one examining Western civilization in detail. The fact that America has been built on Judeo-Christian principles will fall into the trash heap.

A sometimes bitter debate in Europe and recently in America is the issue of Muslim girls being allowed to wear their head scarves in school. Often it goes against the dress code of the school, and even though there is not a requirement in the Qur'an that the younger students do so, it has become a point of testing. Generally the schools allow it on the grounds of pluralism.

Understanding the youth culture of the West has not escaped the eyes of the strategists of Islam. One item carried by the Associated Press on January 3, 2003, was titled "Hip-hopping on Faith." It was a report of a new Muslim music group made up of African-Americans founded with the intent to educate Americans about Islam. The three friends who formed the group called "Native Deen," after the Arabic word for "religion" or "way of life," describe their beliefs as mainstream Islam. The article stated, "Their lyrics address topics including tensions between Islamic and secular lifestyles, pride in Islamic culture and fulfilling religious obligations. The chorus of their signature song is, 'M-U-S-L-I-M, I'm so blessed to be with them.'"[18] At present, the group's fan base is almost exclusively Muslim; although they say they would like someday to have a greater reach. Their eyes are on the $918 million in annual sales by religious performers, most of whom are Christian.

DA'WAH IN THE PRISONS

An important mission field for Islam in America, particularly but not exclusively among African-Americans, is the prison system. The life of Malcolm Little was portrayed in the film *Malcolm X*. In it Malcolm is converted in prison and then becomes a model for many young desperate blacks searching for meaning. The success of Islam in the prisons is hard to specify, but Jane Smith writes: "It is estimated that more than three hundred thousand prisoners are converts to Islam and that the rate of conversion may be more than thirty thousand each year."[19]

A recent report found that "nearly a third more African-American men are incarcerated than in higher education." The study also found that in the year 2000, 791,600 black men were in jail or prison, compared to 143,000 in 1980.[20]

The appeal is simple. Islam presents African-American inmates with the possibility of not only a changed life but also a changed culture. Prisoners who accept their new faith can do so by reciting the *shahada,* or confession of faith, before several witnesses. The prisoner then takes on a new identity, which includes a new name and new habits. Personal hygiene is improved, as is the cleanliness of the cell. The new convert is then invited into the community of Muslims, which in some prisons is rather large and influential. Muslims on the outside then take on the responsibility of caring for the families of those in prison and even help the prisoner when he is released. Prison authorities say that the rate of recidivism, the return to crime and imprisonment, is lower among Muslims than other groups. In spite of the adverse conditions that befall prisoners, they have definite felt needs, and Muslims have tried to both understand and meet these felt needs.

Recently, one area director for the Prison Fellowship Ministries informed me they now face a new strategy that has been developed by Muslims in prison. When the Christian chaplain holds a Bible study that is open to all inmates, well-trained Muslim inmates will attempt to lead the discussion in a direction that is favorable to Islam. After the meeting, anyone who appears to be seeking God will be immediately confronted and Islam will be presented. This Prison Fellowship chaplain ministers to a large number of prisons and states that the consistency of the approach shows a well-planned strategy instead of isolated incidents.[21]

There are a growing number of Muslim chaplains working alongside Christian and other chaplains. At least one significant Muslim organization, the Junior Association of Muslim Men (JAMM), was actually founded in prison. It was established in a Sing-Sing prison in 1994. It targets inmates under the age of thirty-five and helps them become integrated into the Muslim community. Thus for *Da'wah*, Muslims work on both sides of the prison wall enlisting more people to Islam. *Da'wah* is alive and well in the prisons of America.

Da'wah and the Building of Community

Whether prisoners or students, all people have a felt need for a sense of belonging. We crave a feeling of oneness with our fellow man. Islam reaches out, promising to fill that void. Sometimes it appears as if they have met this need, but a closer look shows that it is just an empty promise. The Muslim community continues to live in both fear and denial.

The center of this outreach is the mosque, the responsibility and importance of which will be covered later. Most outreach and acts of welfare issue from the mosque, the center for both religious and secular meetings. Much as Christian churches sponsor schools, the mosque will also house an Islamic school. Churches that do not have schools during the week usually have greatly underutilized buildings, while the mosque is a hub of activity during the whole week, partly due to the *"Salah"* or prayer five times a day. In the West, the average Christian will visit church only once or twice a week; a Muslim will visit a mosque as often as thirty-five times a week. The actual building is vitally important to the followers of Islam.

Muslims will first build a mosque in a city and then proceed to start other mosques in the same city. Using the mosques as a foothold, they then enter into other forms of *Da'wah*.

Other organizations that attempt to propagate their faith are connected with the mosques. Joseph Gudel states:

> The Muslim Student Association is probably the most active Islamic organization in America. Their stated objectives are " . . . producing and disseminating Islamic knowledge, establishing Islamic institutions, providing daily requirements, initiating *daawah* (the propagation of the faith), recruiting and training personnel, [and] promoting and nourishing the unity of Muslims."[22]

Reaching out is nothing new. Christianity began and flourished in an urban environment. The apostle Paul sought to plant and establish churches in the megacities of his time and then to use these as stepping-stones into the surrounding areas. However, Islam started in the backwaters of the known world. Mecca and Medina were hardly world-class cites but rather towns with a rural mind-set. Over the centuries these roles have reversed. Christianity is now more a rural-suburban faith while Islam is targeting the inner cities of the world. In America today, Islam is growing rapidly in the cities, where its appeal has three dimensions.

First, the faith is well presented and easy to comprehend. If you ask a Muslim to define his belief system, the answer will immediately contain the five pillars and the seven basic beliefs. All Muslims, no matter to which sect they belong, will know the basics. Ask a Christian the same questions and the answer will be like a shotgun blast, with all types of descriptions.

Second, Islam tries to portray dignity, self-discipline, and a sense of community to those living in an inner-city environment where disorder prevails. Those seeking simple answers to the complexity of urban living can better understand Islam.

Third, Muslims reach out to the minority populations that form the core of most inner cities. African-Americans and others are targeted with a message of equality, mixed and flavored with anti-Western rhetoric.

Strategically, Islam is right on target since 80.3 percent of all Americans live in metropolitan areas.[23] The government welfare reform of the late 1900s left the city dwellers looking for a unification of the social, political, and religious aspects of life. The system offered by Islam combines the three areas of life into one, offering simplistic solutions that are readily accepted but seldom delivered. The offerings come under the guise of community. At a meeting in New Mexico at the *Dar al Islam* center, according to one observer: "There was a sense that there is a certain urgency to beginning work on the next phase of Islamic work in America. The last decade was the mosque-building phase, and the focus was on communities and physical structures. We have now entered an *ummah* (community) building phase, and the focus is on relationships and linking those communities and the individuals within communities. We must begin to build bridges, find common ground and connect the various elements of the community."[24]

*Imam*s and mosque communities receive detailed instructions regarding the next step. First, they are told why Americans are suspicious of Islam. One year after 9/11 the Pew Forum on Religious and Public Life took a poll covering "American opinion of Islam." The poll stated that fully 45 percent of white evangelical Christians have an unfavorable opinion of Islam. Another 36 percent of highly committed white evangelicals told Pew pollsters that Islam is more likely to encourage violence than are other religions. Of secular and white mainline Americans, 34 percent have an unfavorable opinion of Islam. Between one-forth and one-third have no opinion.[25]

In addressing these concerns, Dr. Jamal Badawi sees several

problems faced by Muslims as they attempt to build community in the West. In answer to the question, "Why does the West distrust Islam?" Badawi says:

1. People are not receptive to change.
2. The bad image of Islam—many Muslims want to hide their faith.
3. Many people in the West have not been guided in the truth of Islam.
4. Many have been taught that Islam is not a religion but a culture.
5. Some people feel that Islam is a simplistic religion.
6. People understand this religion as being opposed to rational thought.
7. Some people are instructed not to inspect other religions because they can be satanic.
8. Some people are apathetic to religion in general.
9. Some people are governed by national pride. They see Islam as the religion of the Third World. Islam and Arabs are equated, even though only about 15 percent of Muslims are Arabs.[26]

These are expressed concerns for Muslims operating in the Western world.

The terrorist attacks on the World Trade Center in New York and the Pentagon in Washington have resulted in a two-edged attitude toward Islam in the West. First, they created a negative attitude toward Islam, thus making it more difficult for dedicated Muslims to carry out *Da'wah* in the Christian-oriented West. Second, and conversely, the attacks renewed interest in Islam as a world religion. The old political saying might apply here: all publicity, whether negative or positive, can get you elected.

Badawi suggests ten points for Muslims that could be used in successful outreach:

1. Be aware of our duties to Islam and to bringing the truth to all people.

2. We must motivate each other to offer *Da'wah.*
3. Islam spreads by *Da'wah.*
4. Just be a good example.
5. Organize functions where we can invite non-Muslims. Do not condemn others.
6. We must explore the use of mass media. This can be done in the West.
7. We should use literature. Put books in libraries and public schools.
8. Invite contacts with school boards so that Muslims can have access.
9. Create seminaries for *Da'wah.*
10. Emphasize the good ways that people see Islam.[27]

More and more Islamic institutions are giving better training in the use of more effective methodology for *Da'wah.* Christian missions, at the present time, still have a lead in this area, but there have been tremendous gains by Islamic strategists in the past ten years.

DA'WAH AMONG MINORITIES

Unquestionably, Islam is successful with many African-Americans. Many converts have come into the more indigenous Nation of Islam, which is highly criticized by orthodox Islam. In the last ten years, however, membership in orthodox Islam has also grown among blacks.

A good deal of attention has been given to the importance of making more converts from the worldwide Hispanic community, especially those living in the United States. In their strategy planning, Muslims recall that prior to 1492 the Muslim Moors occupied Spain. In the 1990s, the government of Spain declared a new readiness to accept different religions and several villages turned back to Islam, claiming they never left that faith. Building on this historical fact, the strategists see a real possibility for quick gains with this growing segment of the American population. The Hispanic community in the United States now outnumbers African-Americans, and they, too, have a disproportionate population in the prison system. The August 1997 issue of an Islamic mission magazine, *The Message,* was titled "Ole to Allah" and described their new emphasis. Many of the articles were devoted to work among American Latino Muslims.[28]

Several new missionary organizations have sprung up with the purpose of spreading Islam among Spanish-speaking people. One effort in New York City is PIEDAD (Propagación Islámica para la Educación y Devoción de Ala'el Divino), which focuses on Latinos who are married to Muslims. Another organization in California is the Asociación Latina de Musulmanes en las Américas (ALMA). It "seeks to spread Islam among Spanish-speaking people, educating them about the contribution of Islam to their society and culture, with the hopes of bringing them back to their ancestors' way of life."[29]

Native Americans have not been ignored, and some Muslims see significant commonalities between Native North American and Middle East worldviews. They point to the fact that both have a reverence for sacred sites, both have a deep awareness of the divine nature, both have a respect for nature and God's law regarding how to treat God's creation, and both are minorities in a predominantly white Christian environment.[30]

While the number of Muslim Native Americans at this time is small, they are a definite target. Recently when traveling through my home state of New Mexico, I passed through Gallup, which calls it-self "The Indian Capital of America." On the main road now stands a large mosque. I asked if there were many Muslims in the area. The answer was, "No, but they are growing."

Jane Smith shows how Islam sees its commonality with Native Americans:

> Seminoles in Florida claim that some of their number are descended from African slaves who before emancipation managed to escape and mingle in their ranks, even convert-ing some of the Seminoles to Islam. The Algonquian and Pima languages are said to contain words with Arabic roots.

Cherokees claim that a number of Muslims joined their ranks and say that the chief of the Cherokees in 1866 was a Muslim named Ramadhan Ibn Wati.[31]

Islam is focusing on people groups in America and the West and is creating strategies to meet the needs of these target peoples. As of now, the numbers are not large; however, as Christians have learned, people who feel displaced or alienated are more open to conversion than those who have deep roots. The minorities in America fit into this category.

MACRO, INTERMEDIATE, AND MICRO MISSIONS

There is a true sense that *Da'wah* must also be done among weaker or nonpracticing Muslims as an attempt to reinforce their sense of identity and devotion, but for our purposes we will continue to concentrate more on *Da'wah* as it relates to the non-Muslim. Khurram Murad sees three levels at work in the creation of a global Nation of Islam. They are:

1. The macro level: the level of overall *ummah* and Muslim societies and states.
2. The intermediate level: the level of very large groups, institutions, and structures.
3. The micro level: the level of the individual person and small organizations.[32]

Murad admits that, though the goal of Islam is much broader, in the present situation most persons involved in *Da'wah* must be active on the third and possibly the second state. Their plan is to have a high enough percentage of Muslims in a democratic society to use the election process to establish an Islamic Republic.

In respect to the micro-level, Murad sees *Da'wah* as a "state of mind, a worldview, an attitude of life, indeed a kind of life."[33] This definition runs parallel to the view of Islam as not just a religion, but as a full-time life mission in total surrender to the will of God. The micro-level will include existing Islamic groups and organizations that work closely with people.

The intermediate level works more with larger groups that have broader influence. Examples might be a mosque, a business, a school, or a training center. It is not enough to simply exist in community; for the sake of Islam, Muslims should enter the political scene. This can best be done by success in business. One area of great gains is in the motel and hotel business in America.

While individuals are the best suited for missions on the micro-level, finances are needed for effective intermediate and macro-missions. These funds are used to influence a society. And this level has been very successful in the materialistic West. A doctor who worked many years in Saudi Arabia was speaking about the tremendous wealth of Saudi Arabia and the Gulf States. He said all you need to do is some simple math. Saudi Arabia produces approximately eight million barrels of oil every day of the year. They receive a pure profit of twenty dollars a barrel. There is immense wealth in oil revenues alone. This does not take into consideration the large investments they have in the West. Some of this wealth is used for their people (which number less than six million), but much is used in the promotion of *Wahabi* Islam in the world. More will be said later about macro-level *Da'wah* when we look at the building of mosques and Islamic public relations.

There are only three global religious organizations that operate successfully on all three levels at once. They are Mormons, Roman Catholics, and Muslims. Obviously the most successful of the three in the past fifty years have been Muslims.

Conclusion

Let us end by stating an obvious but disturbing truth. What is being done among non-Muslims in the world today? In a quiet but effective way, Islam is gaining both respect and converts. It is not *jihad* that will be successful in the West but rather *Da'wah*. The importance of *Da'wah* has been stated well by Khurram Murad:

Da'wah among non-Muslims cannot, and should not, be
treated as an isolated phenomenon. We will not undertake
it properly unless we recognize its proper place at the center
of the Islamic life that we as Muslims must live. We will not
devote our energies to it as we ought to unless it forms an
integral part of our total endeavor and struggle. . . . *Da'wah*
among non-Muslims must not be merely an appendage attached to our Islamic existence.[34]

Islam sees *Da'wah* as an important and useful tool in their search
for world dominance. It is not right for Christians to condemn what
is done through *Da'wah,* but it will be helpful to understand the dynamics of *Da'wah* as we seek to reach Muslims with the message of
Jesus Christ.

A mosque towers over the neighboring church in Alexandria, Egypt.

chapter three

Jihad

Understanding the Muslim Concept

A close missionary friend in the Middle East once suggested that the movie *Khartoum* was one of the best portrayals of the Islamic-Christian conflict. Charlton Heston played General "Chinese" Gordon, a legendary British officer who was well known as a strong Christian. Laurence Olivier played the charismatic *Mahdi*, a leader of the Muslim forces in Sudan. Khartoum was in danger of being overtaken by rebellious forces led by the self-proclaimed *Mahdi*, who many felt was the "chosen one." Gordon, who had previously served as governor of Sudan for Great Britain, returned to Sudan to bring a solution to the crisis.

Agreement was hard to achieve despite the deep religious convictions of both. The *Mahdi* was driven by the conviction that he was ordained to unite the Arab nations, and even the world, under himself, the promised chosen one. Gordon, a Westerner, felt it was possible to reach a compromise.

In the end, both lost. As the true history unfurled, Khartoum was defeated, Gordon was killed in the battle, and the *Mahdi* died not long after that, failing to secure for himself a place in world history. Some see the "Clash of Civilizations" in the same light—a continuous conflict with no winners but with great losses for civilization.

Through the centuries, most religions have been involved in wars and conflict. But sharp contrasts exist between the teachings and practices of Jesus and Muhammad, and between the New Testament and the Qur'an when it comes to war and violence. It can be said that Islam is the only major faith that can truly be defined as political.

Generally, when a discussion on *jihad* begins, someone will immediately bring up the Crusades to show that both faiths have their violent history and nature. The best starting point, however, is not history but rather the holy books that form the foundation for belief—the Bible for Christians and the Qur'an for Muslims.

Again, I refer to my many conversations with adherents of both faiths. When we speak about religion being the basis of violence, many will point to the Old Testament and say that it forms an important basis for the Christians' belief system. In it we find examples of tremendous violence, especially in the book of Joshua, as the children of Israel were commanded to take the land. Some see this as proof that Christianity is just as violent as some make Islam out to be. However, most Christian theologians see the Old Testament as a book of progressive revelations—God slowly revealed his will for humanity in the people of God, the priests of God, and the prophets of God. This revelation was continuous until the coming of Jesus Christ, the Son of God. It is in him that mankind received the full revelation of God.

When comparisons are made between Islam and Christianity concerning the issue of war and violence, they must be made between the two founders, Muhammad and Jesus Christ, and between the Qur'an and the New Testament. It is here that we see tremendous differences.

The use of violence was never commanded or even suggested in the New Testament. When Peter took up the sword to protect Jesus, he was rebuked: "Jesus commanded Peter, 'Put your sword away! Shall I not drink the cup the Father has given me?'" (John 18:11). In the development of the early church as recorded in the book of Acts, not once were people influenced to become Christians by use of the sword. The use of war, conflict, and violence is totally foreign to the New Testament. This is not the case in Islam. Most Islamic authorities will admit that Muhammad was both a political and military leader later in life. His battles with Jews and others form an important part of the history of Islam.

To understand what Islam teaches about holy war, it is necessary to understand the meaning of the word *jihad*. While Christians see *jihad* as meaning holy war, Muslims generally want to have a much broader interpretation of the word. What does *jihad* really mean?

THE MEANING OF *JIHAD*

What significance does *jihad* play in the life of a Muslim? This is a complex question about a complex word. Most people from the non-Islamic world consider *jihad* an excuse for terrorist behavior from an extremely volatile part of the world—the Middle East.

The term *jihad* has, as its root meaning, "struggle" or "striving." *The Muslim Almanac* defines *jihad* as "striving." This is a Qur'anic concept that encompasses the idea of a just war as well as other forms of striving by which individuals or the community extends the practice of Islam and safety for Muslims.[1]

In Islamic textbooks the concept of *jihad* is often mentioned as the sixth pillar of Islam. The reason for this is that all the other pillars—prayer, giving of alms, fasting, faith, and the pilgrimage—are considered struggles in one's attempt to walk the path to God. For a Muslim, *jihad* is a system of related ideas to help in the struggle against all forms of temptations and difficulties that one must face as he attempts to live for Allah. This struggle can be both spiritual and military.

It is written that Muhammad, upon having returned from fighting a battle with some of his enemies, said, "We have returned from the lesser *jihad* to the greater *jihad*." When the people heard him, they said, "O Messenger of God, what *jihad* could be greater than struggling against unbelievers with the sword?" He replied, "Struggling against the enemy in your own breast."[2] Thus, Muslims define this greater *jihad* as a warfare against sin and all that is against Allah and his teachings. It is the struggle in one's own heart to follow the will of Allah and is an internal battle for righteousness.

The lesser *jihad* is what we know as the traditional holy war that is declared in the name of Allah and is used to spread his will. While all Muslims must undertake the greater *jihad,* not all are required to participate in the lesser *jihad,* but they must support it when it does occur.

Many Muslim teachers state that a lesser *jihad* is allowed in only two circumstances. The first is in defense. *Jihad,* according to Muslims, is never an offensive war but only a defensive war. Only after the Muslims have been attacked in some way are they permitted to fight back, or if in some way their freedom, peace, or justice has been taken away. Some of this takes place only in theory and not in actuality. Muslims claim that *jihad* is to be implemented as a last resort, only under extraordinary circumstances. Aggression from either side is not to be tolerated. Yet a study of history shows this is not the case. Muslims have engaged in many wars with aggression as the root cause, often so they can gain territory or wealth.

Today, Muslims will often state that the violence they are committing is in retaliation for what was originally done to Islam. If there is no recent reason, they will cite the need to defend Islam against the imperialistic designs of the West. Often the person issuing the call for *jihad* will list the Crusades as a reason for attacking Christians. In one *fatwa,* Osama bin Laden mentioned that the West had robbed the Arab people of its oil; thus, the West needed to pay every Muslim in the world $30,000. If this was not paid, then there was justification for *jihad.*[3]

The second reason for the lesser *jihad* is "to right a wrong." Some say that this is also a Christian argument for a just war. An example is the Gulf War of 1991, when the allies fought to repel the invasion of Iraq into Kuwait. History has shown that in many cases Christian countries could call a war just if it fit into their plans; thus the second reason given for lesser *jihad* does have an equal in Christian countries.

Rollin Armour, professor emeritus at Mercer University, gives an example of Islam's second reason for *jihad* when he writes: "The expansion of Islam in the seventh century would also be an example of righting a wrong, the idea being that it was wrong for the Middle East and North Africa not to be exposed directly to Islam and ruled by Islamic Law."[4] With this line of reasoning, lesser *jihad* could be used in all parts of the world in order to usher in a utopian society under Sharia law. Precisely this argument is used by many of the more extreme Muslims in the world.

Muslims explain that *jihad* is implemented to proclaim the religion of Islam to all the nations. It was their desire to spread Islam to all the peoples who surrounded them, to take them out of a state of "ignorance" of Allah and into a state of following his will. We cannot be sure whether people converted out of a true change of heart, fear of death, or the desire to not have to pay the tax that would be imposed on non-Muslims. It may have been a mixture of all these reasons, but we know historically that Islam has often spread by means of *jihad*.

THE RULES OF *JIHAD*

A *jihad* must observe several rules in order to be considered a true *jihad*. For most people, it is difficult to perceive that a religious war could have well-established rules. However, the sole purpose of a *jihad* derives from Allah, and therefore the "warring actions" must abide by his rules.

Although "outsiders" have considered some wars as *jihad,* they cannot technically be referred to in that manner because of specific actions taken during the event. On the other hand, if Muslims were attacked first, they would be justified in entering into war. For example, "when Rome sanctioned war against Islam, the Muslims could not be denied the full right to fight back on any battleground."[5] As mentioned before, *jihad*'s primary purpose is to spread the message of Allah. Any action that causes the message of Allah to expand is a justifiable *jihad*.

Finally, *jihad* can be used as a means to terminate or eliminate oppression. The *jihad* must not be used for selfish or economic gain. Ultimately, *jihad* must be performed with a motive that is

Allah-centered and can further the expansion of Islam and its people. There are definite benefits for those who engage in *jihad*. Those who are not killed in the battle and return home are allowed to take the spoils from their conquests. A man killed while fighting is automatically guaranteed entrance into paradise, and his family will receive an honorable name because of his great heroism. About this, *Hadith* 9:413 states:

> To the person who carries out *jihad* for His cause and nothing compelled him to go out but the *jihad* in His cause, and belief in His words, Allah guarantees that He will either admit him into Paradise or return him with the reward or the booty he has earned to his residence from where he went out.[6]

Much has been made of the fact that Islam promises paradise to those killed in *jihad*. One cleric stated to me that only when a person is killed in *jihad* is there the uncompromising guarantee of paradise. Since women were not encouraged to go to war (and in some cases forbidden), a false theory was started that said that in Islam women could not go to heaven. This is untrue, but it is clear that the path to paradise for a woman is a difficult one. It is implied in one of the *Hadiths* that many women are in hellfire because ingratitude toward their husbands is also ingratitude toward God. The *Hadith* states, "The Prophet said: 'I was shown the Hell-fire and that the majority of its dwellers were women who were ungrateful.'"[7]

When an Islamic state goes to war, Muslims observe certain rules for killing. There are different rules, however, for fighting a war against non-Muslims *(harb al-kuffar)* than fighting a war against Muslims *(harb al-bughah)*. Khaled Abou El Fadl describes some of the rules:

> If Muslims fight one another, the fugitive and wounded may not be dispatched. Muslim prisoners may not be executed or enslaved. Children and women may not be intentionally killed or imprisoned. Imprisoned male Muslims must be released once the fighting, or the danger of continued fighting,

ends. Furthermore, the property of Muslims may not be taken as spoils, and any property taken must be returned after the cessation of fighting. Even . . . means of mass destruction such as mangonels, flame-throwers, or flooding may not be used unless absolutely necessary.[8]

Since Fadl is a contemporary writer, it is of interest to read between the lines and see that "infidels" will be treated differently than fellow Muslims.

THE TWO FACES OF JIHAD

Westerners are often confused when they hear two entirely different explanations of *jihad*. Americans are faced with two differing views, one saying Islam is a religion of peace, love, and forgiveness, while the other says that Islam promotes and rewards war. Which of these two options is correct? The answer is simple. There is a dichotomy in the faith that allows for both views to be held at the same time. Again it is necessary to return to the Qur'an to understand how two vastly differing opinions could be accepted without major problems by the worldwide fellowship of Muslims.

The Qur'an was written in two cities and at different times in the life of Muhammad. Of the total, ninety-two Surahs were written at the beginning of his ministry, and the last twenty-four were written in Medina during the later years of his life. Muslim theologians understand that the Qur'an has two distinct parts. Early in his career, while in Mecca, Muhammad recited verses that were kind to non-Muslims. He called Christians and Jews "people of the Book" and gave them respect and honor. Muslims claim that this was the period when he was politically weak and was striving to gain support. Thus, he turned to the monotheists, thinking that they would support him. Two verses found in the Meccan Qur'an are as follows:

Those who believe [in the Qur'an], and those who follow the Jewish [Scriptures], and the Christians and the Sabians,—

any who believe in Allah and the Last Day, and work righteousness, shall have their reward with them or on them shall be no fear, nor shall they grieve. (*Surah* 2:62)

Let there be no compulsion in religion: truth stands out clear from error; whoever rejects Tagut and believes in Allah hath grasped the most trustworthy hand-hold, that never breaks. And Allah heareth and knoweth all things. (*Surah* 2:256)

These verses and others from the early writings of Muhammad can easily be understood to say such things as:

1. Anyone who believes in one God (Allah) should be respected and left alone.
2. There should not be an attempt to force people (especially Christians and Jews) to convert to Islam.
3. Christians and Jews have nothing to fear from Islam.

Muslims quote these and similar verses to Westerners to show that Islam is a religion of peace, love, and forgiveness.

However, the second part of the story is that a section of the Qur'an was written in Medina. By the time Muhammad arrived in Medina, he was accepted as both a political leader and a military general with great talents in leading men. In Medina he fought many battles, including several against Jewish tribes where reportedly all the men were killed and their possessions taken by the victors. At this stage in his life, he no longer needed the Christians and the Jews who actually did not have much military strength (though the Jewish tribes were rather wealthy). His dreams of an influential movement were now being recognized. Now he turned on those he had been courting and began to write such words as:

Then fight and slay the Pagans wherever ye find them, and seize them, beleaguer them, and lie in wait for them in every stratagem [of war]. (*Surah* 9:5)

If anyone desires a religion other than Islam, never will it be accepted of him; and in the hereafter he will be in the ranks of those who have lost. (*Surah* 3:85)

O Prophet! Strive hard against the unbelievers and hypocrites, and be firm against them. (*Surah* 66:9)

Those that make war against Allah and his apostle and spread disorders in the land shall be put to death or crucified or have their hands and feet cut off on alternate sides, or be banished from the country. (*Surah* 5:33)

It is not for any prophet to have prisoners until he has made wide slaughter in the land. (*Surah* 8:68)

Muhammad's language had changed. His latter words commanded harm to non-Muslims. Only non-Muslims who convert to Islam and practice required religious duties will escape the horror of his wrath. No matter how Muslims try to explain away the second set of verses, terrorists use them, indicating that the end justifies the means. Verses like these form the basis of a fundamentalist's definition of *jihad*.

According to Qur'anic statements, Islam's ultimate goal is to enforce worldwide submission to the Qur'an—whatever the cost. Those that the West labels as terrorists are often people seeking to obey the Qur'an. What makes things more complicated is that Muslims in the world today are either ignorant of or hide their knowledge of the teachings of the whole Qur'an.

FOUR IMPORTANT QUESTIONS

Since the definition of *jihad* is so germane to our understanding of how Islam plans to change the world, it is important for us to look at four important questions that need to be answered. Each has to do with relations between Islam and the West, and each shows the immense difference in worldview.

Question 1: Is *jihad* defined in the same way by Muslims in different parts of the world?

Often geography has much to do with one's theology. Western Christian nations, for example, look at the Bible differently than those living in underdeveloped nations. Christian missions have often been accused of cultural imperialism, of trying to force their values upon those living in other parts of the world. The same can be said of Islam. The world of Islam consists of forty-six countries where more than one-half of the population is Muslim. The majority of these countries use Arabic as either the main or the second language. An understanding of what is being said in various parts of the world is important in answering the above question.

For years, many in the West were at a loss to explain how Israel could accuse Yasser Arafat of being a terrorist. This was the man who had been awarded the Nobel Peace Prize and who frequently and publicly condemned the use of violence. Only recently has the West begun to understand that he would say one thing in English to the media and something entirely different to his own people in Arabic. The lack of good Western interpreters meant that we had to depend on translations provided by Arafat's own people. For years this worked, but only recently has the world begun to hear what Israel has been saying for a long time. Arafat says different things to different audiences.

The same problem exists in our understanding of *jihad*. In looking at the difference between the Meccan and the Medinan Qur'an, we can see that different parts of the Qur'an are used in different areas of the world. In the West, the Meccan Qur'an, which teaches tolerance and acceptance, is used. In the Islamic world, the Medinan Qur'an has a strong presence. Both are Qur'anic but two different messages are sent out. Both are true to the Qur'an, but it's essential to understand the very important Islamic doctrine of abrogation.

Abrogation states that a later revelation from God abrogates an earlier one. In this way, Muslims can say that they accept earlier scriptures such as the books of Moses *(Tawrat)*, Psalms *(Zabur)*, and the Gospel *(Injil)*, as being divinely inspired, yet they view these writings as inferior to the Qur'an because they came earlier. It is even possible that changes made by Muhammad or other writers must be accepted since they came later and God revealed the changes. This explains why Muslims can easily say that their differing Qur'anic account of the crucifixion and death of Jesus is superior to that of the Bible.

In looking at the two parts of the Qur'an, we are told that the earlier verses are inferior to the later verses. Therefore, both ideas of *jihad* are Qur'anic, but when it comes to a final interpretation, those verses advocating violence are more important because they abrogate the earlier, moderate statements. According to this well-known Islamic doctrine, when God replaces a verse, the latter version is a better and improved one, and may even contain opposite instructions. For example, *Surah* 2:106 says: "None of our revelations do we abrogate or cause to be forgotten, but we substitute something better or similar: knowest thou not that Allah hath power over all things?"

Furthermore, man is not to allow this teaching of abrogation to cast doubt upon the reliability of Muhammad. *Surah* 16:101 declares: "When we substitute one revelation for another, and Allah knows best what He reveals, they say 'Thou [Muhammad] art but a forger': but most of them understood not." Thus authentication for the truth of Muhammad's claims is not required.

Geography is a determining factor in one's understanding of *jihad*. I submit that Muslims living in the West will attempt to give a less militant interpretation based upon language and on the fact that they are living in an area where Islam is weak. Those in countries where Islam is strong can and do use the more widely accepted interpretation of *jihad* that calls for a more violent holy war. Newspapers and media outlets in Islamic countries condemn the West and its religion in fluent Arabic while those in the West sound a song of tolerance.

A good example of this occurred when Dr. Jerry Falwell, a well-known Christian evangelist and pastor, made a statement calling Muhammad a terrorist. Newspapers in the Middle East reported that clerics were calling for the death of Falwell. The Iranian cleric Mohsen Mojtahed Shabestari, in addressing his weekly Friday prayers in the northwestern town of Tabriz, said Falwell was a mercenary and "must be killed. The death of that man is a religious duty." Another cleric, Grand Ayatollah Mohammed Hussein Fadhallah, with an eye to the Western media, cautioned against resorting to physical violence against Falwell, saying Islam "is a religion of mercy and love."[9] There are many such examples of world events being reported completely differently in the Middle East media and the Western media.

Question 2: Is Islam prepared to offer equal rights to others and is it prepared to exist side by side with other ideologies?

In numerous conferences with Muslims, I have asked the question, "Why does Islam not allow Christians and other religions to build churches and religious buildings and to have a presence in their countries?" This question is never answered. Instead, it is countered by a question from the Islamic side, "Why do you Christians use the giving of aid to our people as a means to try to convert them?"

But the question remains, Why are Muslims allowed to establish mosques and Islamic centers in the Western world when the same privilege is not granted to Christians in many Muslim countries? For example, there is not a single church in Saudi Arabia. Christians there gather either in embassies or associated cultural centers or military bases. However, in the United States, there are thirty-five hundred mosques, and they are growing at the rate of four to five a week! Wherever Islam spreads it has closed the doors behind it.[10]

If Islam is really a religion of peace, love, and forgiveness, then it should allow for the basic rights of others to have freedom of worship. That is not the case. Once while working in a strongly Muslim country, I visited one of the main cities. On a Friday morning, every one of the known Christians in that country—hundreds of them—were put into prison. I, along with one of our missionaries living in that country, determined that our U.S. ambassador was a strong Christian. We went to him and asked for help, and he arranged an appointment for us with one of the top officials in the Department of Internal Affairs. We presented the official with the details and asked that the Christians be released. He refused to help.

At that point, I reminded the official that his country was a signatory to the United Nations declaration that guaranteed freedom of religion for its citizens. I shall never forget his reply. He said, "That was the Department of Foreign Affairs that signed the document. The Department of Internal Affairs makes its own rules." It was clear that there were two different ways of looking at all matters.

Question 3: Are Islam and democracy opposed to each other, or can Islam exist in a democracy?

Why is there no democracy in the Arab world that ensures action and not simply words concerning human rights? Contrary to what Islamic leaders declare to the West, the voices of Arab Christians and other non-Muslim groups in their countries are not heard. They are persecuted and not given rights on par with Muslims. Even Muslims are not allowed to question or criticize their own religion, and are threatened with severe persecution and death for leaving the Muslim faith. Muslims who have converted to Christianity remain hidden out of fear. Today there is not a single visible church of Muslim converts in any Arab country.[11]

This lack of true democracy removes any common ground for dialogue or constructive cooperation between Muslims and non-Muslims as they face political, social, economic, and religious challenges. Some have even stated that the reason that countries like Saudi Arabia were not supportive of the war in Iraq had less to do with the fact that Iraq was a Muslim country than with the fear of the creation of a democratic country in the heart of the area. In countries run by dictatorship, there is more emphasis on a holy war interpretation of *jihad.*

Malise Ruthven is sympathetic to Islam but expresses deep concerns about the political status of Islamic countries. She writes:

> Most Muslim states are ruled by bloody and repressive dictatorships which, far from satisfying the imperative of social justice exemplified by the Prophet's career, seem to be incapable of granting even the most basic human rights to their citizens. Official murder, arbitrary imprisonment and extralegal government in all its forms can be found in Muslim states from Morocco to Malaysia.[12]

Certain human rights that are recognized and respected in democratic countries are missing in Muslim countries. If Islam is truly a religion of peace, love, and forgiveness, why is there so little positive fruit in places where it has power?

Question 4: Is Islam ready to publicly condemn acts of violence done in the name of *jihad*?

After the attack on the World Trade Center in New York, there was a worldwide outcry against the use of violence—except in Muslim countries where people not only celebrated the attack but also praised those who committed the infamous deed.

The Western world awaited Muslim condemnations, but they received only condolences for those who had died. Why was the Islamic world so silent? Possibly because this was viewed as a part of the *jihad* against the West and thus should not be condemned.

Many have asked Muslim clerics: Are those who committed this crime in paradise since they did it in the name of *jihad*? The clerics' silence has been deafening.

The Four Cs of Christian-Muslim Engagement

There has been engagement between Islam and Christianity since Muhammad's flight to Medina from Mecca in A.D. 622. These two great religions have continually had conflict and war. Each blames the other and sees themselves as the victims. There is no reason to see a cessation of this conflict in the near future.

First C: Increased Contact

As Islam began its explosive growth soon after the death of its founder, the areas that fell first to the sword of Islam were Christian. Within a hundred years, Islam had taken control of an area that covered the Arabian Peninsula and extended all the way to the gates of Constantinople. Their conquests covered much of previously Christian North Africa. Wars have continued between Christians and Muslims from that time up to the present. *Jihad* has been a dominant theme from A.D. 622 to the present. Over the centuries, Muslims saw that it was their Allah-given duty to destroy Christian empires and establish Islamic rule.

Before the fifteenth century, countries and empires fought against each other, but, with time, both Christianity and Islam began to be diffused into the various populations of the world. Globalization gave rise to a new form of multiculturalism, with large minority people groups living in modern countries. Freedom of religion and human rights have each helped give an identity to minority religious groups in most countries of the world. Thus, Christianity and Islam are now living side by side in many parts of the world. This has not brought peace and understanding, only new and different problems.

Both Islam and Christianity are seen as world religions, each claiming over one billion adherents, and both have followers in almost all countries of the world. Contact on a local level is now inevitable.

Civil libertarians will preach community and understanding, both of which are wonderful goals and should be the goals of humanity. But the reality is that this close proximity has brought more problems than solutions. In my research I have discovered that when a minority in a country reaches approximately 12 percent of the population, problems appear as the minority group seeks more recognition and power. While this is natural in most situations, it is intensified with Islam because of the strong doctrine of the establishment of an *ummah*, or Community of God. Coupled with the strong emphasis on Arabic as the language of both heaven and the Middle Eastern culture, separation and resentment escalates in most parts of the world. Muslims see that their obligation to Allah is to help others accept Allah's mercy, whether they want to or not.

Contact need not be negative. Different cultures can learn much from each other while enriching different lifestyles. This is especially true when genuine dialogue takes place. Nevertheless, contact more often affords opportunity for conflict and problems.

Second C: Increased Conflict

Most children in the Western world have heard the classic closing sentence of many well-known fairy tales: "and they lived happily ever after." It would be nice if the history of the Islam-Christianity encounter could end in this way. Many believe this possibility still exists, but they are an ever-decreasing minority. It seems that contact with Islam inevitably leads to conflict. In the past three decades there have been many conflicts between nations, people groups, and individuals. But leading the pack are conflicts between Muslims and their neighbors. Of the many defined conflicts in the world today, most involve Muslims who often declare *jihad* as a basis for their actions. Here is a list of some conflicts between Muslims and others:

Country	Opponent	Results
Israel	Jewish Israel	A continuous conflict marked by the suicide bombings of men, women, and children
Chechnya	Russia	Formation of a terrorist movement that has engaged in bombing of apartments and taking hostages in theaters and other public places

Country	Opponent	Results
Philippines	Philippine Government	Terrorist movement has bombed civilian areas and taken foreign hostages
Nigeria	Protestant Churches	Burning of Protestant churches and killing of Christians, including pastors in the north
Bosnia	Orthodox Christians	Burning of churches and killing of Christians
Indonesia	Christians	Terrorism against tourists from the West, the killing of Christians on many of the islands, and bombing of churches all over the country
Pakistan	Christians	Terrorist attacks on Christian schools and churches and assassinations of leading Christians
China	Chinese Government	Terrorist attacks in the western part of China
India	Hindus	Attacks on a train loaded with Hindus, killing most on the train; terrorist attacks in various parts of the country, including on hotels
Kashmir	India	Constant terrorist attacks against the Indian forces in their part of Kashmir
Sudan	Christians	Genocide against the Christians and animists in the south, including bombing of hospitals and schools; more than two million Christians have been killed
Egypt	Tourists	Terrorist attacks on tourists and on the Coptic Christian minority
Algeria	Moderate Muslims	Killing of more than thirty thousand citizens who do not agree with the establishment of an Islamic Republic
United States	Civilians	Terrorist attack on the World Trade Center and the Pentagon, killing nearly three thousand civilians, and other smaller attacks

In all parts of the world, contact with Islam has led to violence. Many in the Muslim world blame others for the conflict, saying they are only trying to defend their rights or territory. However, it would appear to the educated person that the number and scope of these conflicts point to a well thought-out plan for world dominance, which includes conflict under the theological protection of *jihad*.

One would think that, after a war in which an Islamic country is defeated, others would be discouraged from continuing their *jihad* against the conquerors, but the opposite seems to be true. Rollin Armour states, "For non-Muslims to take over land sacred to Islam is a violation of fundamental Islamic belief and tradition and one of the classical justifications for Islamic *jihad*."[13] Defeat of a *jihad* only breeds other *jihads*.

Third C: Increased Conquest

The history of Islam in its first thousand years is a history of conquest, of Arab holy warriors sweeping into surrounding areas brandishing the sword against those who would resist. Many different explanations have been given for the rapid success of the Arabic hordes. Perhaps the cruelty of the attacking Arab legions threw their foes into panic. Some say that internal fighting had weakened the surrounding Christian empires. Others say that Christians had taken seriously the teachings of Jesus Christ against using the sword, even in defense. The fact remains that during this period, Islam continued its conquests to the north, east, and west with startling successes.

Ahmed Rashid said of this expansion: "Since the seventh century, followers of The Prophet Muhammad have fanned out to spread His message throughout the known world." The author continues with this evaluation:

> The conquerors would transform the vanquished empire, but in time their empires would change and become urbanized, until each was in its turn conquered by new nomadic Mus-

lim tribes. The changes the conquerors wrought—religious, political, social—have often been driven by the concept of jihad.[14]

With time, most Muslims ignored the greater *jihad* advocated by the prophet and adopted the lesser *jihad* as a complete political and social philosophy.

Rashid goes on to say that "it is this perversion of jihad—as a justification to slaughter the innocent—which in part defines the radical new fundamentalism of today's most extreme Islamic movements."[15] It is impossible in this short space to review the history of the expansion of Islam, but there are several overall statements concerning their conquests:

1. Most of the areas now controlled by Islam were conquered by the sword.
2. Soon after Islam took over an area, a majority of the peoples converted to Islam.
3. No major areas of the world today have reconverted to their previous religion after being forced to accept Islam.

Fourth C: Increased Condescension

An article in the *Muslim World League Journal* written by Hussein K. al-Hussein, "Islamic Jihad: Some Misconceptions," stated:

Jihad is not a defensive war only; but a war waged against unjust regimes. It should be pointed out that the war in this case is waged against the leaders and their forces and not against the people ruled by such regimes. People should be freed from the unjust regimes and their influences so that they can freely believe in Allah. Not only in peace but also in war Islam prohibits murder, terrorism, kidnapping, and hijacking when carried out against civilians. Whoever commits such violations is considered a murderer in Islam, and is to be punished by the Islamic state. Islam did not spread by the sword, as it is taught in the west. The state may have spread by the sword, which is always the case, but the people freely accepted Islam.[16]

The author is trying to show that, in reality, most people want to live under Islam, and *jihad* simply affords them the opportunity to achieve this goal. Understandably Muslims believe they are right and so all people must truly desire this religion. It is hard for them to see that many are not interested in being liberated, especially as defined by Islam.

Al-Hussein made an obvious error in stating that Islamic faith did not spread by the sword. There were two categories of vanquished peoples. The first were the Christians and Jews who still were considered to be the people of the Book, and the second were the animists and others who did not accept monotheism. History shows that those people who were conquered by the forces of Islam had a choice to make. Rollin Armour states, "The Islamic practice of permitting Christians and Jews ('the people of the Book') and others to continue in their own religion, if under restrictions, has been a striking feature of the Islamic faith. Islamic law viewed idol worshipers differently and allowed them only two choices, conversion or death."[17]

The treatment of the Christians and the Jews who had been conquered was determined very early. The *Pact of Omar*, which is discussed later in this book, spelled out how they were to be treated. Among the restrictions was a yearly tax based on population of the land. The vanquished could not try to convert Muslims to their faith and were simply tolerated. In some countries they took on slave status, as we see in Sudan today.

Conclusion

Many different definitions of *jihad* are used. Beyond the normal academic definitions, one fact remains. A large number of Muslims in the world today see *jihad* as not only permissible but as necessary in order to create a worldwide *ummah. Jihad* is thus an essential part of the Islamic faith. Muslims must admit that *jihad,* as practiced by the extremists, violates several fundamental principles.

Christians must understand that the explanation of *jihad* as only an inner struggle is no longer valid. Christians must take into account that the violent form of *jihad* is very much alive. *Jihad* forms an important part of Islam's search for world dominance.

Mosques are placed in highly visible areas in many cities worldwide.

chapter **four**

If You Build It, They Will Come

The Importance of the Mosque in Islam

The first time I entered North Africa, I crossed the Straits of Gibraltar from Spain and headed for the Moroccan city of Tangier. The outline of the city from the boat was spectacular. A long train of hills forms a backdrop for the city. Toward the elevated western part of the city, the two spires of an old Roman Catholic cathedral reach into the heavens. Not far to the east looms an even more spectacular edifice: a new mosque with its minarets towering over both the mosque and the city.

After my friends met me, I mentioned the two very beautiful buildings that gave a magnificent backdrop for Tangier. One of my friends then proceeded to tell me the story of these two houses of God on the hill. The church was built by the French during the time of its colonial occupation of Morocco. A wealthy man from Saudi Arabia came to visit Tangier and saw that the tallest building in town was the church. He promised to give the money needed to build a mosque next to the church—but the new mosque not only was to be bigger than the church, but its minarets needed to be higher than the spires of the church.

I chuckled at the story and the human foolishness it revealed. Only later I learned that, far from being simply a humorous story, it was a serious display of an important part of Islam's strategy.

The Importance of the Physical Structure

In Christian missiology, the "presence" philosophy emphasizes the importance of having at least one believing person in a given area so that Christianity has a presence. The next step is to build a building, so all can see that it is not just a few believers but a building that would outlive any who came to worship there.

The greatest missionaries in the history of the Christian faith were the Celts who brought Christianity to northern and central Europe as well as to many other areas. One of their favorite methods was to locate the important river in the area, and to begin at the mouth of the river and build a church, and often a monastery with it. After the area around the church became Christian, they would sail up the river to an area not yet covered and then build a church and a monastery. This continued for many years until most of northern and central Europe converted to Christendom. Tourists who take a Rhine cruise in Germany are met with churches and monasteries at intervals on the river. This is proof of the success of the Celtic strategy.

Christian missions have gradually changed their philosophy and now see the church building as more of a liability than an asset. The emphasis is more on house churches that can be mobile and are much less expensive. Thus it is difficult for the Westerner to understand why Muslims put so much value on the building of new and beautiful mosques all around the world. The typical Western attitude is that these excesses are being carried out by wealthy oil sheiks playing out fantasies by leaving a physical memorial to their lives. Nothing could be further from the truth. Islam has incorporated the building of mosques into their intentional mega-strategy.

A New Paradigm of Islamic Missions

As a background for this idea, let us compare the historical development of Islam and Christianity. MARC, which is the research arm of World Vision, has organized the history of Christian missions into six paradigms of thinking. Recently, while teaching about the historical development of the Christian church, I became interested in the third period, which can be described as follows:

Period of time:	A.D. 600 to A.D. 1400
Scriptural basis:	Compel them to come in (Luke 14:23)
Goal of missions:	The expansion of Christendom
Who did missions:	Monks and conquistadors
Purpose of the church:	To promote the centrality of church, state, and culture
Identity of church:	Church as a powerful institution[1]

As I studied this paradigm, it became evident that this is the developmental period Islam is at today. Interestingly, according to the Islamic calendar, we have just passed the year 1380. Islam is now going through the same developmental stage that Christianity went through up until six hundred years ago. Not surprisingly, *Da'wah* has been described as a "come" philosophy (while today Christianity is a "going" religion). Also, Islam does not separate politics and culture from religion.

The construction of many of Christianity's most valued cathedrals and church buildings took place during the third period. When a religious movement seeks to be powerful politically, one of the important attributes contributing to these phenomena is the building of a physical presence. This is where Islam is today.

The Functions of the Mosque

Although Muslims pride themselves on being multicultural and having a presence in most countries of the world, they are still rapidly identified by their Middle Eastern heritage. They are trying to address this problem by what they term the "Built Environment of Muslims."[2] The look of new mosques often is anything but Middle Eastern. As the Islamic faith expands into new areas of the world, there are those who seek to impose foreign imports of models of architecture; however, an article on the subject states, "A reading of the Qur'an or a study of the *sunna* will not give instructions on how to design a house in Morocco or Indonesia. Those who have tried to derive specific examples from these sources are doing both themselves and the sources a disservice."[3]

While there are no Qur'anic dictates that prescribe the architecture used, Islam's urban ethos does encourage designers to create public spaces that promote social interaction between individuals.[4]

As the mosque became the center of society, it began to take on many different functions, the basic and foremost function being a house of prayer. With time it became a social center, a marketplace, and the political center of the local area. John Esposito writes:

> Mosques throughout the world, such as the Umayyad Mosque in Damascus and the magnificent mosques of old Cairo and Tehran, are often adjoined by magnificent bazaars. Traders and businessmen were among the most successful sectors in society and were responsible for the spread of their faith.[5]

Just as Islam prohibits the separation of the political, social, and religious aspects of life, the mosque physically brings the same elements together as glue for the society.

The History of the Development of Mosques

To better understand the place of the mosque in Islam, it will help to look at the history of its development. Martin Frishman, in "Islam and the Form of the Mosque," argues, "From their beginnings, the monotheistic religions were opposed to the use of buildings specially designed to house the faithful at prayer." This opposition was based on both a desire for humility in the presence of the divine and a fear of "idolatrous worship of an object or edifice." He goes on to suggest that the need for converts drives the religious establishment to build facilities that became more elaborate and impressive as the status of the religion grows.[6]

In the early years of Islam, little importance was placed on the mechanics of worship. The mosque existed wherever the worshiper prayed—a similar idea to the Christian concept suggested by Matthew 18:20: "For where two or three come together in my name, there am I with them."

The first "mosque" was the home of the prophet in Medina. Built in the standard Arabic fashion, the home featured a large walled courtyard, with living accommodations forming two walls of the structure. A large portico constructed out of palm trunks and branches formed the *zulla,* which was "a place for deliberations on community affairs,"[7] in addition to being a comfortable place of worship in hot or inclement weather. This combination of courtyard and sanctuary, the *zulla* and *harem,* became the model for later mosques.

Some basics in mosque design have remained the same since the earliest periods of Islam. The prayer hall of any mosque should have one wall facing Mecca. Shortly after the time of the prophet, the place where Muhammad preached in his mosque was marked with a stone called the *qibla.* While initially referring to the stone itself, the *qibla* came to refer to the direction of prayer. Thus, even to this day, the wall aligned with the direction of prayer is called the *qibla* wall and is marked by the *mihrab,* a niche directly in the center of the wall, often elaborately decorated, which serves as the visual focus for prayer.

Another mosque architectural feature that can be traced back to Muhammad is the development of the *minbar,* a pulpit used for Friday prayers. Initially the prophet addressed the congregation while leaning against a pillar. However, as the crowds of worshipers grew, a rising pulpit with steps was developed to enable the followers to better hear the prophet. The *minbar* soon became an essential part of larger mosques. *Minbars* have also developed into ornate works of art. The original three steps of the prophet have been extended into grand staircases, often capped with a covered platform. Traditionally, the *imam* delivering the Friday prayers will stand one step below the platform, leaving that space reserved for the prophet.

Local officials have used the *minbars* as a pulpit for preaching, as well as a place of government pronouncements. Unlike Protestant

Christianity's division between church and state, the mosque and state do not operate in separate realms.

Many larger mosques also feature a *dikka,* a wooden platform aligned with the *mihrab,* allowing one respondent, or *qadi,* to lead the congregation in following the positions of the *imam.* Frishman suggests that the role of the *imam* is not unlike that of the cantor of the Greek Orthodox tradition. Next to the *dikka* is the *kursi,* a lectern on which the Qur'an is placed for recitation during the service.

Another common pattern in mosque architecture is a pool that includes fountains and can be used for the ritual washing of religious participants, or sometimes for purely decorative purposes.

Perhaps the most universally recognized symbol of the mosque is the *minaret.* These large towers serve as commanding local landmarks in indicating the presence of Islam and are the place from which daily calls to prayer are issued. It is important to note that the adoption of the minaret was a slow process. The call to prayer during the prophet's lifetime was given from the roof of his home in Medina. It wasn't until the fourteenth and fifteenth centuries that minarets became an obligatory part of mosque design.

Architecturally speaking, the use of towers was common throughout the Near East. Frishman suggests that minaret adoption could have been based on a variety of traditions from "Zoroastrian symbolic fire-towers to Roman watchtowers, coastal lighthouses or church towers."[8] Dogan Kuban suggests that since the first minarets were used when the mosque of *Amr al Fustat* in Egypt was replaced, the form was most likely influenced by the many Syrian church towers of the area.[9] Additional evidence for this view may be found in Damascus, where Muslims were using an old pagan temple prior to the construction of their own mosque. This building had four corner towers dating to the Christian period.

In time, the architectural development of the mosque began to take on regional traits. Outside the Middle East some beautiful examples of architecture are found in Africa, India, and Central Asia. As Ismail Serageldin explains it, "Societal specificities are defined by local geographic, climatic and morphological features and social practices that give a 'sense of place' to particular locations and 'character' to an environment."[10]

Today there is a debate going on in architectural circles concerning the design of newer mosques. Some advocate newer and more modern design while others seek to return to the basic design of yesteryear. Those who purpose innovative additions to the traditional design appear to be the winners. However, most new mosques will immediately be recognized as mosques due to the basic design.

THE DESTRUCTION OF CHRISTIAN CHURCHES

A trip through the beautiful countryside of modern-day Turkey made me remember my studies of the journeys of the apostle Paul two thousand years earlier. It was Paul and his coworkers who started churches that flourished and formed the foundation for the Holy Roman Empire. In looking for churches, I spotted numerous ruins, but no churches actually being used. One guide stated that most of those I saw were Armenian churches. Since most of the Armenians had left, the buildings were left to deteriorate. I accepted this explanation.

Later, I decided to look into this further to see if it would be possible for modern-day Christians to buy the ruins and rebuild the churches. In doing so, I discovered that there had been a war of genocide against the Armenians in which almost two million Armenians were slaughtered. Turkey has repeatedly denied that this genocide took place, but many Western historians accept it as fact.

During the actual battles many Christian churches were destroyed. As a sign to later generations that Christianity was a dead religion, it was forbidden to remove the ruins or rebuild the churches. The ruins still remain as a reminder that Islam rules in Turkey, and that Christianity, with its rich history in that part of the world, is no longer welcome.

This is not an isolated instance. Not only do Muslims seek to build mosques, but they also seek the destruction of Christian churches in most parts of the world. On one of my trips to a Middle Eastern country, I was invited to preach in a large Protestant church in the capital city. The building had been built during British rule in the 1930s. The building was large and well built, but it was sadly in need of renovation. Some windows and doors were broken, parts of the floor needed to be replaced, and an overall paint job was greatly needed. I suggested to the pastor that it would be simple to organize a team of Christian laypeople who would be happy to come and renovate the church free of charge. He thanked me for the offer but told me that the law of that country considers it a crime to repair a church without permission, and this permission could only come from the leader of the country. It was really impossible to get permission to fix up the church.

This same pastor told me of another church in the city whose large cross on the top of the church blew down in a windstorm. In its fall it broke a large hole through the roof. The hole remains today because they cannot get permission to do any repairs on the building. Several streets away stands a magnificent mosque.

Later in the week, I visited a small church in the countryside. Again, the church building was built about the same time as the one in the capital city. Again it was run-down, and I noticed a large hole in the front of the church. The pastor told me that previously there had been a window there. Its wood frame had deteriorated, and so he had put a coat of paint on it to prevent further damage. After he painted the frame, the authorities came and tore out the window because he had not gotten permission to paint the frame. Today the church still has a hole in the front.

Journeys into most of the Middle Eastern countries will show either a lack of Christian church buildings or ruins where they once stood. In Port Said, Egypt, a trip around the old town will show several previously large and beautiful churches still in ruins. The plan seems to be to show that Christianity is a dying religion while Islam is alive and growing—a plan that seems to be working.

A student of the present-day Muslim-Christian encounter will see an interesting pattern. The news will report that there are conflicts between Christians and Muslims, and as a part of this conflict, churches were burned. These reports are abundant from many areas of the world but come especially from Nigeria, the Philippines, and Indonesia. One example comes from Indonesia, where there was a change in the political leadership. The president of the country, a conservative Muslim, was being ousted by his vice president, Mrs. Megawati, who is also a Muslim but somewhat more moderate. When the changeover took place, the police were in the streets to help deter violent demonstrations against the government. To the surprise of many, the changeover was quiet, except for the bombing of two Christian churches in Jakarta. In asking why churches were being bombed because of such a change in government, I was told that the more radical Muslims are always looking for a good excuse to destroy churches, therefore, "why not?"

An older and lesser-used system is confiscating churches in conquered areas and then turning the churches into mosques. Anyone who visits Istanbul, Turkey, must go and see the magnificent Haghia Sophia Mosque. The guide will explain that it was originally the Saint Sophia Church but was later turned into a mosque.

The same scenario will be found in Damascus. I was told that the fourth holiest location in Islam after Mecca, Medina, and Jerusalem is the mosque in Damascus. A look at the conglomerate of sections will show that some of it was built earlier than the beginning of Islam. Again, we are told that part of it used to be a church. On the south side of the mosque, on the upper beam of a little-used but magnificent doorway, is an inscription in Greek, which reads: "Thy Kingdom, O Christ, is an everlasting Kingdom."[11] Three lofty towers and a multitude of graceful smaller minarets surround the mosque itself. One of the taller minarets is called the "Minaret of Jesus," for Muslim tradition says that Jesus will return to this minaret and preach about Muhammad.

There seems to be a definite philosophy within Islam concerning the existence of churches in Islamic countries. In a few countries the building of churches is tolerated, while in most others, such as Saudi Arabia and Egypt, it is forbidden. Before the Taliban takeover in Afghanistan, permission was given for a church to be built in

Kabul—a contemporary forty-nine-foot-high A-frame to attract the international community of that city. It was dedicated in the spring of 1970 after much prayer, planning, and endless negotiations with the government. After three years, government forces came in and completely demolished the building. J. Christy Wilson, the founding pastor of the congregation, writes:

> Government leadership was split into two factions. There were the hard-core Muslims who determined to keep the country pure of non-Islamic influences. A second faction saw the value of close relations with Westerners. . . . Sometimes the government would say one thing and then do another and visa versa. We were never quite sure what would happen.[12]

It should be noted that shrines and buildings of other religions have also been desecrated or destroyed, such as the 2001 Taliban destruction of massive, centuries-old Buddhist statues in Afghanistan.

THE LOCATION OF MOSQUES

As already stated, the construction and location of mosques are an important part of the overall Islamic strategy. Islam focuses the construction of mosques first in the major cities of the world. Expansion of Islam into the West is predominately in the urban areas. Much of their major growth is among refugees, who go to the cities where jobs and accommodations are more plentiful. After establishing themselves, these Muslims come together and rent a building for a mosque. With time, numerous mosques are founded in the urban area. A leading Muslim convert to Christianity told me, "If Islam is to win the West to their faith, they first must win Western Europe. If they are to win Western Europe, they first must win England. If they are to win England to Islam, they first must win London." In 1960 there was only one mosque in London and today there are more than six hundred.

In most of the major cities in Europe, you will find a beautiful mosque located on a prime piece of property, sometimes even in a major park. Officials often will say that oil-producing countries have pressured them for use of the land that could never be used for anything else. One of their arguments is that, in the name of brotherhood, it is right to allow them entrance into the historically Christian centers. The spirit of Christianity is such that many church leaders are bending over backward to help the Muslim community when they are seeking to locate a mosque.

As Anglican churches in England die due to nonattendance, the buildings are put up for sale. In a few cases, when evangelicals or another Christian group has offered to purchase them or rent them, the request was met with hostility, though the building may then have been given or sold to Muslims for a reduced price.

In the West, Muslims will often buy the property under a false name for fear that the owners will not sell to Muslims. Such was the case in a trendy village of Mill Valley, California. A small Baptist church disbanded and their property was put up for sale. A local businessman wanted to purchase the building to be used as a warehouse. After the sale, the building was made into a mosque. It was in this mosque that American Taliban John Walker Lindh was converted to Islam and began his journey to extremism.

The process of establishing mosques also follows the old Celts method of missions. In Africa there are many examples of Muslims building mosques on a road that leads to an area they desire to win. For example, northern Nigeria is Muslim while the southern part of the country is mostly Christian. Beginning in the north and going southward, the Muslims are building a mosque every mile along the main highway. They build in the direction of the south as a symbol of their strategy to bring Islam into the south. I have heard of this being done in many other countries of Africa.

Of course, Muslims are encouraged to build a mosque wherever there is a group of Muslims gathered together and have a need of a place of worship. This is a natural and spontaneous expansion of their faith. It is when a mosque is built in an area where there *are* no

Muslims that it evidences a strategy. Far from being needed, many mosques are built and stand empty, in hopes they will be used later. Generally, the financial costs involved in the upkeep of an empty building do not seem to be a problem for those who are ready to spend the money to build the building in the first place.

THE FINANCING OF MOSQUES

The main reason Christian missionaries do not build more churches where they are working is a lack of financing, especially in the cities. The high cost of land and construction make it impossible and impracticable to build. This has been the number one reason for the change of strategy among missionaries leading to an advocacy of house churches. This does not seem to be a problem with Islam. New, beautiful, and costly mosques are being built all over the world. The financing of these is coming primarily from Saudi Arabia and other oil-producing states in the Middle East. One report on Nigeria states, "The Saudi government has been directly involved in the construction of several large and elaborate mosques in the country."[13]

A physician friend who had worked for five years in Saudi Arabia stated that all one needed to do was a little mathematics to see the enormous wealth that countries like Saudi Arabia have. He stated that there is a minimum of eight million barrels of oil a day produced by Saudi Arabia. They receive at least twenty dollars a barrel for their oil. This goes on every day of the year with the revenues flowing into a country with only six million citizens.

The exact amount spent for the building of mosques and for their overall mission work is kept secret. One author, Marsha Haney, stated, "The Saudis donated most of the $8.5 million to build a mosque for south-central Los Angeles, and five other major mosques across the country."[14]

Paul Johnson wrote in *Forbes* magazine, "They [Saudis' royal family] use their vast financial resources to back subversive Islamic movements of all kinds as one way of protecting their family empire.

They are currently, for example, paying for the building of what is rumored to be 400 new mosques in Bosnia."[15]

Another proof of Saudi Arabian involvement in the financing of mosques was given in a *Time* magazine article on that country. The article stated:

> In March 2002 *Ain al-Yaeen,* an official Saudi magazine, wrote that the royal family wholly or partly funded some 210 Islamic centers, 1,500 mosques, 202 colleges and 2,000 schools in countries without Muslim majorities.[16]

The same article reported, "According to a Western intelligence report, the Saudis are spending about $1 million a year in Tanzania to build new mosques and buy influence with the ruling Chama Cha Mapinduzi Party."[17] If there were a complete accounting of the total funds that have flowed from the Arab states to the building of mosques, the amount would be staggering.

As mentioned before, many have estimated that the *Wahabi* movement, centered in Saudi Arabia, influences approximately 80 percent of all mosques in the United States. The Saudis are willing to financially help mosques in the United States if they agree to accept the basic beliefs of the *Wahabis.*

MOSQUES IN THE UNITED STATES

On April 26, 2001, a national Islamic advocacy group, the Council on American-Islamic Relations (CAIR), released the results of a major study of the Muslim community in the United States. The report, "The Mosque in America: A National Portrait," indicates that mosques in America are becoming dynamic centers for social and political mobilization. Nihad Awad, the executive director of CAIR, said, "Mosques are not only centers for spirituality, they are now bases for political and social mobilization."[18]

Muslims have made a study of the number of mosques and their activation in the United States. Dr. Ihsan Bagby, the report's primary researcher, said, "One of the most significant findings in this survey is that mosques are quite ethnically diverse." Bagby noted that more than one ethnic group attends 93 percent of all mosques.[19]

During a news conference at the National Press Club in Washington, D.C., the council outlined some major findings in the survey. Some of them are as follows:

- There is tremendous growth both in the number of mosques and in the number of those who take part in mosque activities. On the average, there are more than 1,625 Muslims associated in some way with the religious life of each mosque. The average attendance at Friday prayer is 292 worshipers. Some two million American Muslims are associated with a mosque.
- Report findings support conservative estimates of a total American Muslim population of seven million.
- The number of participants has increased at more than 75 percent of mosques during the past five years. Growth is witnessed across the board but suburban mosques have experienced the greatest increases.
- Conversion rates are steady. On average nearly 30 percent of mosque participants are converts. The average mosque has sixteen conversions per year.
- Mosques are relatively young: 30 percent of all mosques were established in the 1990s and 32 percent were founded in the 1980s.
- Four-fifths of mosques are located in a metropolitan area, most often a city neighborhood.
- At the average mosque, 33 percent of members are of South Asian origin (India, Pakistan, Bangladesh, etc.), 30 percent are African-American, and 25 percent are from the Arabic-speaking world.
- Most mosques are involved in some outreach activities. During the past twelve months, a majority of mosques have done each of the following activities: visited a school or a church to present Islam, contacted the media, contacted a political leader, and participated in an interfaith dialogue.

- Almost 70 percent of mosques provide some type of assistance for the needy.
- More than 20 percent of mosques have a full-time school.
- More than 90 percent of respondents agree that Muslims should be involved in American institutions and should participate in the political process.
- In general, mosque leadership does not appear to be highly formalized or bureaucratic. At the majority of mosques, the leader is a volunteer, works part-time, and is employed outside the mosque.
- In a majority of mosques, final decision-making authority rests not with the leader but with a Majlis Ash-Shura (executive committee or board of directors).
- In most mosques with a board, women are allowed to serve as members.[20]

This appears to be the most complete study made in the United States. It must be kept in mind, however, that those involved in the study could have a hidden agenda. They desire to show Islam in the most favorable light possible. However, the report does show that there is a growing presence of mosques in America and that they are gaining power. The building and use of the mosque in the United States have proven to be a very effective strategy, indeed.

An important question that needs to be asked is this: Is there a tendency for a community of Muslims and their mosque to change to a more conservative position after they attempt to blend in to the Western society? The answer to the question seems to be yes. An example of this would be the *Dix* mosque in Dearborn, a suburb of Detroit. Nabeel Abraham's ethnographic study of this community reveals a tension between the culturally assimilated Arab-Americans and more recent immigrants. Abraham relates that one Friday in 1976 a group of Muslim immigrants gathered at the mosque for prayer. When they found the door locked, they simply forced the door open and performed their midday rites. Traditionally the mosque was opened only on Sunday, in an effort to fit in with the predominant culture, but this was scandalous in the eyes of the more conservative immigrants.

This tension culminated two years later with a divisive court battle in which the immigrants wrestled control of the mosque away from the more assimilated community. They immediately began to "reform" the mosque, disallowing weddings, dancing, and other social activities within the structure. The position of women was also dramatically altered. Previously, women were allowed free use of the mosque without restrictions; however, the newcomers believed that women ritually polluted the sacred space, and they sought to "replicate in Dearborn the public forms of female segregation and subordination they were accustomed to in their countries of origin."[21]

IMPORTANT MOSQUES WORLDWIDE

1. The Grand Mosque in Mecca

This mosque is one of the largest buildings in the world and the largest mosque in the world. In the center courtyard is the *Ka'aba* of the large black rock that is contained in a square building. It is this spot that Muslims believe was both the garden of Eden and the place where Abraham was ready to sacrifice Ishmael.

2. The Islamic Center of Washington, D.C.

By 1957, it was determined that there needed to be a mosque in the capital city of the United States. The incentive came from a group of ambassadors stationed in the capital. Through diplomacy they obtained a favorable piece of land prominently located in the heart of the embassy quarter on Massachusetts Avenue. Finances for the mosque came from a number of Muslim countries, with considerable help from Egypt and Turkey. A 160-foot Mamluk-inspired minaret overshadows the whole structure. The square prayer hall was designed for eight hundred persons and is covered by a large dome. At the time of construction, the question of whether to admit women to prayer was in question, but today a small curtained space is provided for female worshipers in the southeastern corner of the hall.

3. The Mosque in Rome, Italy

For many years Islam desired, as a statement of their expansion, to build a large mosque in the city that was considered the center of Christianity. There was strong opposition from the Vatican, especially since some of the builders wanted it to be larger than St. Peter's. In 1963 the Vatican Council agreed that it would allow the building of a mosque in Rome, on condition that it not be in sight of St. Peter's Basilica and that its minaret be no taller than St. Peter's dome. A committee of thirteen ambassadors sponsored the project, and funding came from twenty-four Muslim countries. The building is on six acres of land, and the building itself covers most of this area. It was designed to accommodate twenty-five hundred worshipers. A gallery covering about 10 percent of the prayer area is designated for women.

4. The Mosque in Cordoba, Spain

Here is an example of a mosque being turned into a church. When the Moors were driven out of Spain in 1492, most of the mosques were converted into churches. The most dominant of those was the Cordoba Mosque, which became a cathedral. There are continued attempts by Muslims to retake the building. An Islamic news organization reported an incident where fifteen Muslims entered the cathedral and prostrated themselves on the floor. When the guards surrounded them, the Muslims shouted, *"Allahu Akbar"* ("God is the greatest") and started reading aloud Suret [*Surah*] Al-Fatiha (the first chapter of the Qur'an).[22] Such attempts to retake buildings that were previously mosques are more frequent today, especially in Spain.

5. The Central Mosque in London

The first attempt to build a mosque in London was made in 1940 by the Egyptian ambassador to England. By 1974 construction began on the Central Mosque of London that was built for $4.5 million, the bulk of which was provided by the Mosque Trust, which receives funding from a number of Muslim governments. The site, provided by the British government, is in the city's much-beloved Regents Park. An Islamic culture center stands alongside the mosque. The prayer hall was designed to hold approximately one thousand people.

6. The White Mosque in Nazareth

The most important mosque in Nazareth is the White Mosque, which was completed in 1808. Its cream-colored wall and green trim are similar to other buildings built during the Ottoman period.

In 1990, there was a movement to build a new mosque in the city next to the Basilica of the Annunciation church. The state had given permission to build a small mosque, but the plans were changed to build a much larger mosque. This led to tensions in the area with Christian leaders. Many saw the building of the mosque as an attempt to drive Christians from Palestine. In 2002, Israel's cabinet decided to halt the construction and one year later the foundations were razed.

Today, there are seven mosques in Nazareth. The percentage of Christians has significantly dropped from 10 percent to 3 percent in the last fifty years. (Like Nazareth, where 35 percent of the sixty thousand inhabitants are Christians, Bethlehem has lost a large number of Christians. A mere thirty years ago there was only one mosque in Bethlehem; today there are eighty-nine.[23]) Once again it is apparent that Muslims desire to use the mosque as a way of graphically showing Islam's superiority to Christianity.

7. The Mosque in Abiquiu, New Mexico

In the early 1980s Muslims built a mosque and training center in the isolated village of Abiquiu in northern New Mexico. The mosque became the headquarters of Dar-al-Islam, an organization "dedicated to the betterment of our society [which] strives to achieve its purpose through education in the broadest sense . . . and through programs which benefit both Muslim and non-Muslim people of North America."[24] The mosque was built using an Indian pueblo form of architecture. I attempted to visit the adobe-style mosque but could not due to a "No Trespassing" sign. I asked the local people why they had such a big mosque in such a small village. I was told it was to school the children of Muslims. Later, I learned that it contains a major training center.

CONCLUSION

A well-known statement says, "Man molds the buildings and the buildings mold the man." Apparently it is very difficult to divorce Islam from the mosque. Far from being a simple relationship, the mosque is also an important part of Islam's search for world dominance. In summary, several observations can be made:

- The mosque in Islam is more than just a building; it is the center of community and has many uses.
- The physical presence represented by the mosque is very important to those who are planning the strategies for Islam's growth.
- Large amounts of money are being invested into the building of mosques, not only in Muslim countries but also in Western areas.
- The burning of churches and the building of mosques go hand in hand within the overall Muslim strategy.
- New mosques reflect the architecture of the host country but still retain traditional Middle Eastern forms.

The Qur'an is taken very literally by most Muslims.

chapter **five**

Changing Demographics

The Web of Immigration

When the final history of the last century is written, a very big chapter will deal with immigration and the mass movement of people, especially in the last half of the century. The direction of the flow of humanity was generally from the more destitute countries of the south to the more prosperous north. Australia and New Zealand, among other countries, have experienced population growth due primarily to immigration.

When Richard Nixon was in office in the latter part of the 1960s there were nine million foreign-born persons living in the United States. When George W. Bush took his first oath of office, the number was nearing thirty million.[1] Many of these are illegal immigrants that have migrated north, mostly from the Spanish-speaking countries of Latin America. The adjusted census of 2000 put the number of illegal immigrants in the United States at nine million. Some have estimated that this number is now well over twelve million. Most of those coming to America are Roman Catholic by birth and they bring with them a dedication to the Christian faith.

On the other hand, the immigrants coming to Europe are mostly Muslim and they are bringing with them the Islamic faith. Is this migration of Muslim peoples just an economic reality or is it part of a well orchestrated strategy to attempt to change the religion of Western Europe? The answer is clearly *both*.

Realizing that world immigration consists of many different peoples going to numerous countries, only the migration of Muslims to Western countries is under discussion here.

WHY DID THEY COME?

For all practical purposes it can be said that the mass migration of people began after World War II. There were many reasons for a family to pick up and move to a new country, including:

1. **Economics**. Family fathers and young people saw that moving into the countries of the north would give them a better chance for a more comfortable life. The majority of immigrants came from countries with a low gross national product, thus the poor there could not count on increasing their standard of living. A change would afford them and their loved ones a better life.

2. **Colonization**. After the war many of the older colonies of the Western European countries were granted their independence. Because of this close affinity, citizens of the former colonies felt they could do better in the mother country than on their own. This was true in regard to the relationship of North African countries to France as well as South Asian countries to Great Britain. In fact for many years France refused to grant Algeria its freedom but rather considered all the citizens of Algeria to be French citizens.

3. **Search for Work**. After the war the economies of the Western European countries began to boom and there was a real need for lower cost labor. This was the situation faced by Germany. In looking to the south they saw Yugoslavia and then Turkey. Many men from these countries came to Germany to find work. Later they brought their families and many decided to stay and seek citizenship.

4. **Strategy**. In the later part of the 1980s and the 1990s strategists

for Islam saw a real possibility of bringing many citizens to Europe so as to increase their numbers. Immigration became a part of their strategy for global domination and the eventual conversion of the world to Islam.

5. **Openness.** There was a general openness exuded from Western countries to those peoples who were deprived of the bare essentials. Americans and Europeans are generally very compassionate, and thus they extended an open invitation to immigrants to come and find a better life. This was especially true during the Great Wave of immigration from 1890 to 1920. During this early period the welcome sign was very visible and many from around the world took advantage of this openness.

6. **Extended Families.** When the first generation came for the described reasons and were pleased with their new home, they invited other members of their extended family to come. In the case of Muslims, the extended families were rather large. Also, most of the Western countries had very lax immigration rules toward family members since they did not want to divide families.

Not all came because of these six points but most fell into one or two of the above mentioned categories. Often the impetus for changing countries was a combination of several factors. For example, it is possible that the first generation came simply out of a need for a better life. However it is also possible that after arriving they became more dedicated to their religion and began to ask relatives to also come and help create a large bloc of their religion in the area where they lived. This is happening more and more in our contemporary world.

The Decline of the West

As stated earlier, the migration of those from the poor countries to the richer northern countries in the thirty years before World War I was significant. But what problems did this movement bring with it? Many contemporary writers are looking at the decline of the West in terms of population, influence, natural resources, and so on, so these issues deserve a closer inspection.

What is happening with the populations of the northern countries? Conservative political commentator Pat Buchanan states:

> In 2000, the total population of Europe, from Iceland to Russia, was 728 million. At the present birthrates, however, without new immigration, her population will crash to 600 million by 2050. That is the projection of World Population Prospects as given in the 2000 Revision Highlights released by the authoritative UN Population Division on February 28, 2001. Another study has Europe's population plummeting to 556 million by mid-century.[2]

In looking at these figures, it is apparent that the loss in population of the ethnic Europeans presents a major problem. The combination of the thirty years of wars and the Black Plague during the Middle Ages in Germany lowered the population at a greater rate. It has been estimated that during this period in the Middle Ages possibly over a third of all Europeans were wiped out. There have been many reasons given for this present decline, some of which include: (1) the desire of the Europeans to only have one child; (2) abortion that is killing off the next generation; and (3) a philosophy of life without children. The decline of the ethnic European population combined with the influx of migrants from other countries presents a picture of a continent with a real problem.

At university, I was taught that a country could absorb up to 12 percent of its population with a minority culture without any real significant lasting effects. Beyond that point, significant problems would begin to occur. In looking at the United States in the early days, most families were first or second generation residents, so immigration was not an issue. In fact, there were good faith attempts to make the new peoples feel at home and to integrate them into the existing culture. This was the goal and it was largely successful. A popular concept in the mid-1900s was of America as a melting pot. This meant that people from all cultures of the world could come and join with others and soon become a pot of one great culture that could be called American. In the early stages this appeared to be the case. Later some changed the description to say that it was more of a mosaic. Each culture retained its own small ways of life but when you put them together they became a beautiful picture. Later others said that it really is more of a stew. Each culture retained its own identity but at the same time it contributed to the whole, somewhat like a potato or a piece of meat kept its identity but added to the whole. Other words and phrases have been suggested but the overall goal was the same: a homogenization of all cultures so that they could all live together in one country peacefully. In the early stages of the Great Migration it looked as if the goal was in reach, but a very significant problem began to occur. This problem was Islam.

ISLAM AND INTEGRATION

Early Muslim immigrants after World War II appeared to desire integration in the new culture. Great efforts were made to both learn the language of the country and to conform to the accepted norms of the culture. Even when it came to religion some attempts were made to become acculturated. There were mosques in the United States that even allowed their members to have chairs for the services and to allow women to attend all services. In many mosques the services resembled more of a Christian service than the traditional Islamic service. These mosques no longer exist. Either they changed because of a desire to conform more to their traditions, or they were taken over by more radical groups that would not allow such a compromise.

With time, the prevailing attitude of most Muslims in the new countries turned from acceptance of the new culture to one of alienation. It became very necessary to continue to practice the old orthodox habits rather than adjust. This attitude has become the norm. In trying to understand what implications this holds, several high-profile customs of Islam are examined.

Freedom of Speech

In recent years the debate of freedom of speech among Muslims in Europe has intensified. For the most part, freedom of speech for Muslims living in Europe is accepted if it means that European Muslims are allowed to criticize Christianity, but it does not work both ways. The case of Salman Rushdie was the high point of the recent debate. In 1988, Rushdie wrote *The Satanic Verses*, a novel depicting Muslims and Islamic theology in a bad light. Immediately there were *fatwas* coming from many directions, each calling for the death of the author. In fact, Rushdie had to go into hiding and receive protection from European police. It is said that he still needs protection from those who are trying to kill him.

A second person who dared to criticize Islam in his practice of free speech in Europe was Dutch movie producer Theo van Gogh. He produced the 2004 film *Submission*, an exposè on the treatment of women in Islam. He was killed in November of that same year in the Netherlands by a Dutch citizen named Mohammed Bouyeri, who left on the body a letter threatening Western governments, Jews, and van Gogh's production partner Ayaan Hirsi Ali, a Dutch writer known for his critical views of Islam.

A third case was the Danish cartoon controversy. In September 2005, the Danish newspaper *Jylland-Posten* published cartoons of Muhammad as a way of showing defiance against Muslim-related censorship. The voices of Islam over the cartoons were loud and clear. Many Islamic organizations and leaders called for the prosecution of *Jylland-Posten,* claiming that regardless of freedom of speech the Danish must be punished. The problem is one-sided and it is apparent that it has become an issue with most ethnic Europeans.

Honor Killings

Traditionally honor killings of family members who go against the wishes of their families are allowed in Muslim countries and even condoned in Sharia law. Types of honor killings include the killing of young girls who have an affair before they are married or those who are pregnant out of wedlock. Others are killed because they have converted from Islam to another religion. Examples of such killings are often reported in the news in Muslim countries. "The Turkish women's organization, Papatya, has documented forty instances of honor killings in Germany since 1996."[3] This is only the tip of the iceberg. Although perpetrators of such honor killings would face criminal charges in the West where the law states that those responsible must be brought to justice, family members who commit these violent acts seldom face punishment in Muslim lands. In many cases their actions are condoned and even praised by members of their society. A 2006 BBC poll for the Asian network in the United Kingdom found that 1 in 10 of the five hundred young Asians polled said that they could condone the murder of someone who dishonored their family.[4] (A high percentage of Asians living in Great Britain have come from Muslim countries.)

Women's Rights

Many immigrant young girls are punished because they want to adopt the culture of their new country. They are not allowed freedom of choice. Much of this is a question of culture rather than religion. Even though some of the younger generation want to conform to the society in which they live, the older people generally want to retain their Islamic culture but often in so doing they disregard the rights of their own. Such issues as forced marriage, a lack of higher education, and strict dress codes among women from Muslim countries create tension between westerners and those of Muslim backgrounds.

Sharia Law

In several European Union countries, such as Sweden and the United Kingdom, Muslim groups have asked to apply certain laws on their people such as Islamic inheritance, marriage, and divorce laws as defined by the Qur'an. These requests have created great controversy in those countries. At one time, a province in Canada worked toward passing a law that would give Muslims the right in some instances to live under Sharia law and not under the law of the land. At the last moment this law was not passed.

I have a close relationship with a high judge in a Middle Eastern country who secretly converted from Islam to Christianity. In a long discussion, he stated that if the Western countries ever granted Muslims living in their countries the right to live under their own laws, then the battle is lost. He strongly stated that people must have only one legal system in a country. This also goes for Sharia courts. However, the United Kingdom has officially sanctioned Sharia courts that pass legally binding Sharia judgment. Legal Muslim tribunal courts started in August of 2007 and the first official Sharia court was opened in September 2008. By 2009, the existence of at least eighty-five official Sharia courts was revealed. These courts are not open to outside observers. Among the rulings that have been made:

- No Muslim woman may marry a non-Muslim man unless he converts to Islam.
- Any children of a woman who does marry a non-Muslim should be taken from her until she marries a Muslim.
- Polygamous marriage has been approved.
- A woman's duty to have sex with her husband on his demand has been enforced.
- A male child belongs to the father after the age of seven, regardless of the circumstances.[5]

This type of dual legal system can be witnessed in many areas of strong Islamic influence. Even though these laws may contradict Western laws, they are often practiced alongside and parallel to Western laws.

The Effects of Immigration

Immigration has always been a part of Western life. Between 1821 and 1924, about fifty-five million Europeans migrated overseas with thirty-four million coming to the United States.[6] Mass movements of peoples were not only an accepted concept but a desirable one. Between the two great wars in Europe a large number of people uprooted by the fighting became refugees. After the war there were many reasons for a new wave of immigrants. Sometimes it was the product of decolonization, and sometimes political reasons rising from the establishment of new states. Also, advances in transportation simply made such travel much easier.

Persons living in the West began to create very definite political ideas, especially during the Cold War period. But when it came to immigration, most were ambivalent. Their roots supported what was happening; at the same time the numbers of new people living in their country was a concern. Eventually a spirit of hospitality and openness of the Western Christians won out and there was practically an open door for all to come. In fact, some countries—Germany and Switzerland among them—encouraged immigration because of their labor shortages.

By the 1980s there seemed to be a shift away from this open attitude. I remember that in the 1970s when the Baptists wanted to find a new building for a church, they approached the Anglicans who had several buildings they were no longer using. The Anglicans refused to sell their unused churches to the Baptists but then gave the same buildings to the Muslims as a sign of their hospitality and friendship. Soon, however, the reception of Muslim immigrants by Westerners began to erode.

There were several reasons for this change. One was the growing unemployment rate. This, combined with the overwhelmingly "non-European" character of many refugees, created new tensions between the new and old inhabitants of various countries. Also by this time there was an emphasis in the Muslim community to cease their philosophy of integration and to embrace one of separation. Instead of helping their cause in the West, this hurt it.

Muslim immigration was the most important part of the European migration scene. "By the early 1990s two-thirds of the migrants in Europe were Muslim, and European concern with immigration is above all concern with Muslim immigration. The challenge is demographic—migrants account for 10 percent of the births in Western Europe, Arabs 50 percent of those in [the capital of Europe,] Brussels."[7] As stated elsewhere, the United Nations has reported that with the current rate of growth, 50 percent of all young people under the age of twenty-one in the world will be Muslim by 2050. This exponential growth threatens the well-being of Europe.

Despite the concern shown by their people, most political rulers did not take strong stands against the new movement of peoples. The leaders in England, Germany, and France in particular realized that the Muslims in their countries presented an ever-increasing potential bloc of voters. Not wanting to alienate a large bloc of voters, they only granted lip service opposition to what was happening. In France, the Prime Minister did approve a ban on girls wearing the traditional Muslim garb in schools, but the intimidation tactics of the Muslims proved to be so successful that most politicians backed down.

A case in point is the events surrounding the proposal to build a large mosque in the city of Duisburg-Marxloh, Germany. There were numerous changes in size of the new structure that would have been forbidden in a church but as the mosque was coming to completion (with a large grant of over three million euros from the State of Nordrhein-Westfalen), a dedication service was planned. The governor of the state was asked to bring greetings and to speak. This high-ranking politician contacted an expert on Islam in Europe and asked what he should do. The expert asked for the name of the mosque to be dedicated. The politician's answer was: "I don't know, why?" The expert explained that in most European cities the mosques are named after Muslim men who were known for fighting Christians. In checking for the answer it was learned that this particular mosque was named after Ottoman Sultan Mehmed II, the man who slaughtered Christians after the fall of Constantinople. Even with this knowledge the *Stadtpresident* said there was nothing he could do but to take part in the celebration.

One of those who stood up to the intimidation of the growing power of the new immigrants was an investigative reporter in Germany—Udo Ulfkotte. He wrote several best-selling books about the dangers of Islam in Europe. The first book, *The War in Our Cities*, earned him a reputation among the Muslims. For a short period of time there was an injunction on the sale of the book in Germany but it was then lifted. However, soon after the book appeared, the Internet was full of *fatwas* that put a price of fifty thousand euros on his life. The pronouncement stipulated that anyone who killed him could collect this amount. This was not the end of the intimidation. Soon a younger German lady claiming to be Doris Ulfkotte, the wife of Udo, appeared on YouTube and then proceeded to run down the Turks, Muhammad, and the Qur'an. This so infuriated the Turkish community that they also placed a bounty equivalent to fifty thousand euros on her life. It did not seem to matter that the lady in the YouTube video was, in fact, not Doris Ulfkotte. Udo has stated that both he and his wife live a life of exile in their own country. As the immigrants grow in numbers, their ability to intimidate grows with it.

Another European who has taken a stand against the growing power of Islam in Europe is the Dutch politician Geert Wilders who is a Dutch member of parliament. He has strongly spoken against the growing influence of Muslims in Europe. His reputation has grown to the point that the government of England forbade him to enter the country. He had broken no laws but he is so vocal on his criticism toward fundamentalist Islam that European politicians fear the Muslim backlash his visit would bring. Wilders's message is very simple: Europe is in danger of losing its identity. He quotes such statistics as:

- There are thousands of mosques throughout Europe. Many European cities are already one-quarter Muslim—just take Amsterdam in the Netherlands, Marseille in France, and Malmo in Sweden.
- In England, Sharia courts are now officially part of the British legal system.
- A total of 54 million Muslims now live in Europe.

- In the Netherlands, 60 percent of the population identifies the
  mass immigration of Muslims as the number one policy mistake since World War II.[8]

The Many Faces of Islam

Many who live in the West see Islam as simply a religion much the
same as Buddhism, Hinduism, or Christianity. In looking at Islam
through these glasses, they fail to see the real Islam, but even the
Muslims reject this notion that their faith is only a religion. They
claim that it is much more than just a religion but rather a complete
way of life that encompasses 100 percent of the Muslim's existence.
It is an economic system, a social system, a political system, and a
religious system all rolled into one.

But why does Islam present a different face in different countries of
the world? It must be remembered that many of the leaders who created the Islamic strategy to take over the world have by necessity instructed their followers to act differently in various parts of the world.
When looking at the situation more closely, this becomes apparent. I
have traveled in over one hundred countries of the world and in most
of the Muslim countries. I have seen firsthand how the number of
Muslims living in a country tends to influence the social and political
order of that country. In their attempts to Islamize a nation, they act
quite differently depending on how many of their people live there.

For example, in countries where Muslims are only a small percentage of the overall population, such as the United States and Canada, they are seen as friendly, loving people who obey the laws and
seek only to contribute to the well-being of the country.

When Muslims have between 3 percent and 10 percent of the population, they begin to demand certain rights such as the introduction
of *halal* food (clean by Islamic standards) into school cafeterias. There
will be the beginning calls to allow Muslims to live under Sharia law
instead of the law of the land. Muslims are in a place to have the ability of turning an election for those who comply with their wishes,
thus exerting an influence on the political scene that goes beyond

their small presence in the population. This can be seen in countries like Germany, the Philippines, Great Britain, and Thailand.[9]

When the Muslim population grows beyond 10 percent, there begin to be the first signs of aggressive unrest in the Muslim population. There can be the burning of cars and violent uprising, particularly when there are any signs or actions that offend the Muslim psyche. Examples of this can be seen in the reactions to the Danish cartoons (see "The Strange Case of Denmark" below), and to the burning of a Qur'an by one man in the United States. This can escalate to sporadic killings and the burning of Christian churches and Jewish synagogues, as is happening in such countries as India, Kenya, and Russia.

When the Muslim population nears and surpasses half of the population, citizens can expect widespread massacres, chronic terror attacks, and the beginning signs of civil war. Also at this level, there is unfettered persecution of those from other religions, especially Christians and Jews. When Muslims are in power, there is often a tax (*jizya*) imposed on non-Muslims and the imposing of Sharia law, which must be obeyed by Muslims and non-Muslims alike. This is now happening in countries such as Sudan, Uzbekistan, Nigeria, Malaysia, Lebanon, Ethiopia, and Bosnia-Herzegovina.

In Muslim nations (where 80 percent or more of the population is Muslim), you can expect continuous intimidation, arrests, burning of stores of non-Muslims, and ethnic cleansing. This continues on a daily basis and only occasionally is reported in the Western press. Such is happening now in countries such as Pakistan, Turkey, Iran, Egypt, and Indonesia.

Of course the goal of Islam is to have the country reach 100 percent Muslim population. This ushers in the peace of "Dar-es-Salaan," the perfect society in which everyone is a Muslim, Sharia is the only law, and the Qur'an is the only true word. Non-Muslims have great difficulties even visiting these countries, which include Afghanistan, Saudi Arabia, and Yemen.

As Islam grows in any particular country, it can be expected that the actions of the Muslims living there will also change and become much more aggressive. Those who see Islam as a peaceful religion have not yet taken a good look at what is happening worldwide with the growth of Islam.

A Target City—Cologne, Germany

When Christianity was founded, it flourished in the cities of the Mediterranean basin. Urban areas such as Rome, Ephesus, Corinth, and Antioch saw rapid spread of the new faith. Islam, on the other hand, grew and flourished in the more rural areas of Arabia and only became urban after the conquest of larger cities. One might expect this rural-urban divide to continue up to today. In fact it has, but with the opposite effect; it is now Christianity that has its major growth in rural areas and Islam that is growing more in the major cities of the world. Many Christian strategists have sought to send more missionaries to the cities and also to spend more resources for missions in the cities. While their efforts have been less than successful, Islam has flourished in the cities.

There are many reasons for this. Here are but two of the more important ones. First, Islam is an easy religion both to follow and to understand. It is a legalistic religion and any doubt about whether a certain activity is allowed or not can be addressed by a rule generally found in their Sharia law. Also their basic belief system is easy to grasp. Over the years I have sent out classes of students to ask citizens of many Christian countries to define both Christianity and Islam. As the common person tried to define Christianity the answers were varied and seldom concrete. However, when Muslims were asked to define Islam, the answers were simple, to the point, and usually included the five pillars of Islam. Muslims know the simple basics of their faith.

A generalization can be made here. As Christian pastors encourage believers to examine the faith critically, there remains little common ground (although some have suggested the Apostles' Creed as a starting point). The average Muslim, however, is required to stay with the basics and is not encouraged to question their faith. Islam's simplicity of belief and faith appeals to the city's working masses.

Another reason has to do with a strategy that has been developed by the Muslims. In the beginning of the last fifty years, Muslims who migrated to European countries simply went to where they could find work. This was generally in the cities. Later, Islamic strategists began to plan their migration so that the movement of their peoples would have the greatest effect. A good example of this plan of winning the cities can be seen in the German city of Cologne, where I spent a great deal of time talking with citizens, both Muslim and Christian.

The Turks who first came to this city simply came to the center and rented the buildings of the Germans who had moved out to the suburbs. The center of the cities was a natural place for them to live. They were close to their work and housing was cheaper. Later Muslim strategists looked at Cologne and determined that they would target a certain quarter of the city. Instead of just leaving the growth of the Muslim community to chance, they developed a six-step plan:

1. Identify the section of the city that should become Muslim.
2. Create a well-defined core in this section of the city for Muslim believers.
3. Purchase property in this core for both apartments and small businesses. Funding would be available either as a gift or through a zero-interest loan from Islamic sources.
4. After a small business or a store has been in existence for a while, the proprietor invites a relative to come to the same city. They then would go several blocks away, encroaching into the German area and begin the same type of business. This would be repeated time and time again. The core would begin to expand.
5. As the Germans in this core area begin to feel hemmed in, they would move out and then their property would be purchased by Muslims for a reduced price.
6. They would be sure that all their signs would be in the Turkish language. Their women would wear burkas and anyone who is not a Muslim would feel uncomfortable. Soon they would have control of the designated area.

The basic idea was that Muslims would move to another area of the city and repeat the six steps. Once the area became Muslim they would build both a mosque and a school for their children. After a certain part of the city was Islamic then they would build a large mosque in the center of the city as final proof that they had arrived.

This strategy has been successful. At the present time Cologne has 120,000 Muslims who make up 12 percent of the city's population and who worship at one of the thirty mosques in the city. The biggest battle in the city is over the construction of a new large mosque. As stated in chapter 4, the Muslims want to build significant mosques, often in areas of historical value, as a way to show their advances and superiority.

This pattern of growth is being practiced all over Europe today with great success. It should be noted that there is a final step in their plan—one that has not yet been successful in Germany but has been used in England—the creation of Sharia courts in the Muslim sections of cities. Because they have so completely taken over certain sections of cities, such as Birmingham and London, there have been no-go zones set up for British policemen. English rules of law do not apply in these area but rather the people police themselves and those who are brought to court appear not before a British court but the locally established Sharia court. This implementation of a foreign legal system in the larger cities of Europe will be forthcoming in the near future.

What is taking place in one of the largest cities in Germany, Cologne, is taking place all over Europe today. Immigration has become a valuable tool in helping this strategy move forward.

The Strange Case of Denmark

Denmark has always been seen as a peaceful little country with rather liberal laws in respect to human rights. Due to its small size, it did not present a threat to any other country. In fact most of Scandinavia was seen as being progressive and liberal in its immigration policies. Because of its distance from the south and a limited history of colonization, there was not a flood of migrants from the south wishing to get in. In the 1970s and 1980s only a few isolated Muslims could be spotted because of their Middle Eastern dress. The Danes in general were oblivious to the presence of Islamic forces building in their country.

In the summer of 2005 all of this seemed to change. Cartoons that poked fun at both the prophet Muhammad and Islam appeared in a Danish newspaper. These seemingly harmless drawings sparked riots and rebellion in many Muslim countries around the world. Dozens were left dead on streets, European embassies were attacked, and Danes were considered "unwelcome" in many countries. Denmark's attempt toward multiculturalism had failed and now the Danish people had to wake up to the fact that the growing numbers of Muslim immigrants were not as peaceful as first thought.

In the 1990s it began to be apparent that Muslims had taken up residence in Denmark. At first they seemed to keep to themselves and did not attempt to integrate into Danish life. But by the time the cartoon appeared it was apparent that Denmark had a colossal problem on its hands.

A 2002 *New York Post* article by Daniel L. Pipes and Lars Hedegaard forecasted accurately that the growing immigrant problem in Denmark would explode. It stated: "Muslim immigrants constitute 5 percent of the population but consume upwards of 40 percent of the welfare spending." They went on to comment on public safety issues, saying, "Muslims make up a majority of the country's rapists, a combustible issue given that practically all the female victims are non-Muslim. Similar, if lesser, disproportions are found in other crimes."[10]

When the 5 percent mark was reached, there was a push for the Danes to make concessions in many areas of life without the Muslims giving an inch. They sought the institution of their holidays in the calendar, acceptance of the *burka* for their girls. Even Muslim leaders openly declared their goal of introducing Sharia law. The patience of the Danish people began to wear thin and there was an increasing stress between the two sides, but it was apparent that the citizens of

Denmark could do little to stem the tide. The Pipes and Hedegaard article cited one sociologist who estimates that every third inhabitant of Denmark in forty years will be Muslim.[11]

As the Danes wrestled with this problem, they moved to tighten up their immigration laws, a move that was condemned by more liberal European nations. In order to become a Danish citizen you now must:

1. Attend three years of language classes
2. Pass a test on Denmark's history and culture
3. Pass a Danish language test
4. Demonstrate intent to work and have a job waiting

There are other restrictions including one that states if you wish to bring a spouse into Denmark, you must both be over 24 years of age. It is no longer possible for one immigrant to enter into the country and then bring in their extended family. It is also forbidden to build a mosque in the capital, Copenhagen.

Susan MacAllen, in an article entitled "Salute the Danish Flag: It's a Symbol of Western Freedom," writes that a large thorn in the side of Denmark's *imams* is the Minister of Immigration and Integration, Rikke Hvilshoj. Ms. Hvilshoj writes, "There is an inverse correlation between how many come here and how well the country can receive the foreigners." She is open to multiculturalism but sees a problem with the rise of those who do not seek to integrate. She paid a price for her stance. MacAllan relates:

> Perhaps to test their resolve, the leading radical imam in Denmark, Ahmed Abdel Rahman Abu Laban, demanded that the government pay blood money to the family of a Muslim who was murdered in a suburb of Copenhagen, stating that the family's thirst for revenge could be thwarted for money. When Hvilshoj dismissed his demand, he argued that in Muslim culture the payment of retribution was common, to which Hvilshoj replied that what is done in a Muslim country is not necessarily what is done in Denmark. The

Muslim reply came soon after: her house was torched while she, her husband and children slept. All managed to escape unharmed, but she and her family were moved to a secret location and she and other ministers were assigned body-guards for the first time—in a country where such murder-ous violence was once so scarce.[12]

Another account of the radicalism now prevalent in Denmark was an article in a Danish newspaper stating that in Arhus, the second-largest city of Denmark, several Christian churches now have Mus-lim guards at the doors of the churches when they hold their worship services. This arrangement was made after some Muslim leaders vis-ited the pastors and told them that their churches would be in danger of being torched but they would be provided Muslim guards for a fee. The pastors were told that only then would the Muslim com-munity post guards so as to guarantee that no harm would come to the church and its members.[13] All this is taking place in a dominant European once-Christian country.

Many other countries of Europe are looking at Denmark. Some have experienced many of the same activities, but today there is a real awakening as to the problems that the ever-increasing number of Muslims in European Christian countries can bring and are bringing.

A Possible Solution for the Problem

Numerous politicians and leaders in Europe are very much aware of the problems presented them by the increasing number of Mus-lims in their country. But how to approach the problems and find solutions that will be acceptable to all sides is a debated question. Many attempts are now being made. Some suggestions have been put forth in political circles in Europe as they wrestle with the increasing problem of Muslim growth.

In 2006 some members of the European parliament from London commissioned a well-known expert on Islam, Mr. Sam Solomon, to help develop a "Charter of Muslim Understanding" in order to find a way that Muslims and Western Europeans could live and work together in harmony in the countries of the European Union. The introduction of the proposed charter states:

> If Islam is a religion of peace, as portrayed by the Muslim community and its clergy, and those acts of terrorism committed in its name are the acts of a few misguided individuals who have misunderstood and misinterpreted its teaching, then Islam is completely innocent of the violence and the terrorism that is sometimes attributed to it.[14]

A foundational principle of the charter was that if terror and violence could be set aside then reasonable men and women of faith could find valid solutions to the multiple differences. The charter drew heavily on such documents as the United Nations Universal Declaration of Human Rights (1948) and their International Covenant on Civil and Political Rights (1966). The final proposed charter consisted of ten articles each with three to fourteen sub-points. The complete charter is too long to reprint in its entirety, but a brief summary of the ten articles follows:

Article 1: Muslims will respect all other non-Muslim religions in word and deed by issuing a clear *fatwa* forbidding violence and force against them. This includes targeting and killing of any civilians.

Article 2: Muslims will introduce a clear educational program through Islamic institutions promoting brotherhood, declaring the equality of all men and women, and teaching the validity of the national domestic law over Sharia law.

Article 3: There will be no recriminations against any Muslims or non-Muslims who choose to change their religion or adopt another faith.

Article 4: Any *fatwa* would be null and void that promotes violence against individuals or institutions. The Muslims in Europe would disregard as unlawful such statements.

Article 5: Since Islam is a peace-loving religion all parts of the Qur'an that seem to promote physical violence, whether implicit or explicit, would be subject to new interpretation or else be considered invalid and non-Islamic.

Article 6: All acts of terrorism are prohibited, shunned, and outlawed. No violent physical *jihad* operations will be regarded as sacred and no one who chooses to die in such will be regarded as a martyr.

Article 7: In full cooperation with the local police and intelligence services we will help to monitor mosques who seem to teach violence including books, CDs, DVDs and all other media that serve the cause of militant Islamists so as to decrease this negative influence.

Article 8: We will foster a better relationship with non-Muslims and promote peace by issuing regular *fatwa*s promoting peace and brotherhood. There will be a direct attempt to forbid any anti-Jewish or anti-Christian supplications at all times.

Article 9: To discard all Islamic texts that discriminate with impunity against Christians and Jews by describing them as *kaffirs*, apostates, polytheists, or other negative terms. Also the leadership will refrain from declaring persons as *takffir* since the Muslims must then see that this person is eliminated.

Article 10: Request all officially constituted Islamic bodies and institutions to revise and issue new interpretations of those Qur'anic verses that call for *jihad* and violence against non-Muslims. (At this point there is a list of seventeen Qur'anic verses that appear to call for violence and that have been used to prove to Muslims that terrorism and *jihad* are valid.)[15]

This charter was given to a number of Muslim leaders to examine and to comment upon. Instead of it becoming a solution for the problem, it only served to intensify the difficulties. As could be expected most Muslim leaders who read the document universally rejected it. The reason being that such a charter would have precedence over their holy literature and that this charter would allow nonbelievers to interpret the Qur'an. This could not be allowed. Also many saw it as having the effect of limiting their rights in Europe. When Christian and Jewish Europeans read the charter there was a consensus that such a charter should be accepted. Once again, the scope of the problems between the new immigrants from Islamic countries and the host Europeans was seen. What had been designed as a solution only continued the division between host and guest.

CONCLUSION

The size and scope of the immigration issue in Islam's strategy to take over the world cannot be sufficiently covered in one short chapter. The best that can be done is to show that immigration is every bit as much a danger for the West as *Da'wah*, *jihad*, and the building of mosques. This chapter has simply introduced the problem. Only a few examples of Islam's use of migration to assume control of areas of Europe have been provided; I personally have researched the situation in the city of Cologne and in Denmark. The question of immigration is one of the more pressing problems in the American political scene today, as well as that of most European countries. Understanding the problem is halfway to solving it. Immigration must be seen as only one part of their overall strategy. Let us all continue to work on the problems in the hopes that valid solutions can be found to allow all to live peacefully on planet earth.

chapter six

It's the Law

The Social Implications of Islamic Law (Sharia)

In reading the story of the Arab and the camel, one assumes that the camel did not belong in the tent, but one could also ask, Why not? The answer is clear: The size of the camel was such that the Arab would lose freedom of movement and the ability to exert his will within his own tent. Once the camel was in, the Arab had no control over what went on in the tent—or even whether he was allowed to stay! There is a fear in the Western world that the same thing would happen if Islam were to be successful in dominating the world. The camel would be in the tent and nothing could be done about it.

Sharia law could be compared to the camel. Most Americans cannot imagine that their lifestyle would change if the United States became Islamic. There is a real ignorance among most Americans concerning the social implications of an Islamic takeover. One of the most observable results of such a change would be the implementation of Sharia law.

For Muslims, Sharia law is not considered an option but rather an obligation. If a country becomes an Islamic Republic, then this Muslim legal system becomes the law of the land. All living in the country, Muslim and non-Muslim alike, are under its rules and regulations. Again, even if the Arab did not want the camel in the tent, once it was in he had to live with its realities. If Islam takes over a country and it becomes an Islamic Republic, its inhabitants must live with Sharia law since it is a crucial element of the whole Islamic way of life. In this chapter we will try to better understand Sharia and its implications where it is practiced in contemporary societies.

DEFINITION OF SHARIA

The literal definition of the term *Sharia* is "a path or way to a water hole in the desert." For early Muslims it was seen as a utopian way of life that was given to prepare men for the heavenly society. The term defines what Muslims believe is the divine and eternal law and the perfect way humanity should live. But since perfection is not possible, Muslims have another term that relates more closely to the way that this divine law is practiced here on earth: *fiqh*. Despite these delineations, the term *Sharia* is used to refer to Islamic law as practiced by Muslims.

Another explanation is given by Ghulam Sarwar in *Islam: Beliefs and Teachings*, a book used in England to teach Muslim schoolchildren the basics of their belief. Sarwar writes:

> Sharia is the code of law for the Islamic way of life which Allah has revealed for mankind and commanded us to follow. . . . Sharia or Islamic law consists of the code of conduct for Muslims and is based on two main sources: The Qur'an and the *Sunnah* of the prophet. It aims towards the success and welfare of mankind both in this life and life after death.[1]

Muslims see Sharia law as having come down to humanity from God, while they see all other legal systems as being "man-made laws." They claim that it is a complete and perfect system that guarantees success, welfare, and peace in this life on earth as well as life after death. In understanding how Muslims compare Sharia to other legal systems, let us turn to A. H. Qasmi's *International Encyclopaedia of Islam*, composed for those trying to understand the basics of the Islamic faith. He compares the two in the following chart:

Man-made Law	Shariat [Sharia] or Allah's Law
1. Men make laws when they feel the need; these laws start from a few and then grow in number over the years.	1. Islamic law is complete and perfect, and covers all aspects of human life. Men of learning explain and clarify Shariat for the benefit of ordinary people.
2. Laws made by men are not permanent; they can be changed to suit people's wishes and desires. For example, in a particular country at a particular time, drinking alcohol may be banned; but this can change when public pressure grows. The American Government once banned all alcoholic drinks, but removed the ban after a time because it could not be enforced.	2. Shariat is permanent for all people all the time. It does not change with time and conditions. For example, drinking wine and gambling are not allowed under Islamic law. No one can change this; it is law that is valid for all time and for all places.
3. Man does not have knowledge of the future. Hence, man-made laws cannot stand the test of time.	3. Allah is All-knowing and All-powerful; He is the most Wise; His laws are the best and are complete.
4. Man is a created being. His laws are the creation of the created.	4. Allah is the Creator and His laws are for Man, His creation.
5. Man-made laws may be suitable for a particular nation or country. They cannot be universal.	5. Allah's laws are for all nations, all countries, and for all time. They are universal.
6. Men make laws to suit their own needs. If members of parliament want to decrease the rate of tax on the rich, they can do so, even if the majority of people suffered and there was high unemployment in the country.	6. Allah is above all needs. He is not dependent on anything, so His laws are for the good of all people and not for a few, selfish people.[2]

Muslims believe their legal system is far superior to that of the West, thus it is understandable that they would do all possible to seek to institute Sharia as the one universally accepted system. In other words, within an Islamic state the law is equal to Sharia.

THE FIVE MAIN SCHOOLS OF JURISPRUDENCE

In understanding Sharia, it should be noted there is not universal agreement on the details. Over the fourteen hundred years of the existence of Islam, five definable schools of Sharia have developed:

Hanafi School: Created by Abu Hanifah, considered the most tolerant of differences of opinion. Most influential in Turkey, the Balkans, Central Asia, Chinese Turkmenistan, Afghanistan, Pakistan, and India.

Malikis: Centered on customary and legal practices in Medina. Mostly in Spain, and in North and West Africa, where it remains the most important Islamic legal school.

Shafi'is: Use of *Hadith* and analogy. Observed in Egypt and Arab states in the Middle East, as well as by the Kurds and Muslims in the Indian Ocean and Southeast Asia. Founder was a student of Ibn Anas.

Hanbalis: Based on the use of authentic *Hadith* in preference to analogy. Dominant in the Arabian Peninsula. Associated with Islamic fundamentalist Ahmad ibn Hanbal.

Jaf'aris: Followed by most Shii'as.[3]

They all agree on the Qur'anic basis for their legal system, but they differ in their interpretations. One example would be in determining the time for the start of Ramadan. Sharia defines this event as beginning at the start of the new moon. The problem is, who determines when the new moon becomes visible? In the early days this could be accomplished by looking at the sky; when a small sliver of the moon could be seen, then the start of Ramadan was declared. But what do you do if the sky is cloudy or the *imam* has poor eyesight or if one person claims they can see the moon while others disagree?

Each of the legal systems has defined exactly how to determine which first sighting of the moon is acceptable. One system says that if three men see the new moon, this is sufficient. Another says that since the testimony of two women equals that of a man, the combined testimony of men and women (with two women being equal to one man) is acceptable. Another system states that it must be the leader of the community who makes the determination. There are differences in the details, but the fact remains that Muslims must adhere to the month of fasting or be in danger of punishment.

THE PACT OF UMAR

The Pact of Umar (sometimes called the Code of Umar or the Covenant of Umar) was an agreement with the Christians of Jerusalem that concluded on the occasion of the conquest of that city by the Muslims. During this time Umar rescinded the Roman decrees that had banished Jews from Jerusalem and accorded Jews all the rights granted Christians. Umar supposedly saw both the Christians and the Jews as "people of the Book" and desired to treat them the same. It is claimed that the pact allowed the people of the Book who had been conquered by the Muslims to be treated equally.

Historically, Muslims have claimed that this pact shows how tolerant Islam was in dealing with non-Muslims in newly invaded territories. Contrary to this claim, both Jews and Christians have been severely oppressed and made second-class citizens of their own countries. Christians living under Islamic rule today expect to be treated the same as those of earlier periods. In fact, millions of Christians who currently live in Muslim countries live as second- or third-class citizens.

The Pact of Umar was made by the Caliph Umar Ibn Khatib soon after the death of Muhammad in A.D. 638. It was purportedly written by the conquered Christians themselves since most statements begin with the statement "We shall . . . ," but the pact was forced upon them by the Muslim conquerors. In exchange for agreeing with the pact's conditions, the non-Muslims were allowed to live in the country where they had the benefit of limited protections. Among the laws restricting non-Muslims were:

- Non-Muslim males to pay a poll tax plus a land tax
- Non-Muslims not allowed to be engaged in military service
- No new churches or synagogues to be built; existing ones can only be renovated with permission
- No display of crosses and no religious processions
- A Christian's house could not be built taller than those of Muslim neighbors
- Clothes must be different from those worn by Muslims
- Non-Muslims forbidden to ride on horses and had to ride on mules or donkeys or walk if Muslims were walking
- Non-Muslims had to show respect to Muslims, i.e., by giving up their seats to them
- The testimony of a Christian or Jew could not be accepted against a Muslim in a court of law

DHIMMA STATUS

The Arab word *dhimma* means "protected person" and is directly related to the Pact of Umar. Those under *dhimma* status were the Christians and Jews living in a covenant relationship with their Muslim conquerors. This status is open to many different interpretations and is often ambiguous or contradictory. This status does not define the rights of the person living in this status and also does not always define the penalties for those who break the covenant.

Down through history different rulers have interpreted these *dhimma* laws differently. Leaders from Islam will point with pride when the Muslim leaders have treated the conquered people with dignity. They have a short memory, however, when the people have been treated harshly. Often the conquered believers had only the same choice as that afforded to non-people of the Book: conversion or death.

Dhimma status is based on two important concepts:

> First, that Muslims are superior to any other religious group ("Ye are the best community that has been raised up for mankind" 3:110), and secondly, that Christians and Jews who had not accepted Islam should be conquered, humiliated, and subjected to the payment of the tribute poll tax, the jizya, not payable by Muslims (4:29: "fight against those who have been given the scripture and . . . follow not the religion of truth until they pay the tribute readily, being brought down").[4]

While unification of all mankind seems to be one of Islam's most dominant propaganda themes, when the religion is studied closely a great deal of separation exists between various groups. People are placed in boxes, each afforded its own definition and rights or lack thereof.

ISLAMIC LAW AND RADICAL ISLAM

The social implications of the establishment of a global Islamic state together with the institution of Sharia law are frightening, but this is the aim of many Muslims. Dr. Kalim Siddique, director of the London Muslim Institute, called upon Muslims to murder Salman Rushdie, author of *The Satanic Verses*. He states clearly that the goal of the contemporary Muslim movement is "to eliminate all authority other than Allah and his prophet; to eliminate nationalism in all its shapes and forms, in particular, the nation-state; to unite all Islamic movements into a single global Islamic movement to establish the Islamic State; to reestablish a dominant and global Islamic civilization based on the concept of *tawheed* (the unity of Allah)."[5]

The *Wall Street Journal* on April 15, 2003, published an article titled "A Saudi Group Spreads Extremism in 'Law' Seminars." The article began by saying, "In late February, more than 300 young men from across Europe gathered for a weekend seminar on Islamic Law put on by the Al-Waqf al-Islaami Foundation."[6] The article went on to explain that the most famous graduates from the seminar were half a dozen members of the group of young men from Hamburg, Germany, who plotted the September 11 attacks. The language of the seminar was Dutch, but "the message was imported from Saudi Arabia, via Saudi books and lecturers who taught a strict, orthodox interpretation of Islam." One of those who attended was quoted as saying, "I don't want a separation of state and religion. I want Sharia [Islamic law] here and now."[7]

Financing for this and similar conferences comes from the *Wahabi*-dominated Muslim World League. The leader of the conferences, Mohammed Cheppih, spokesman for the Al-Furqaan Mosque and Al-Waqf Foundation, stated that he does not know how much money the Al-Waqf Foundation spends on its programs in the Netherlands. "He says that the local branch of the Muslim World League, which he represents, spends $50,000 a year to offer courses on Islamic law and beliefs in Rotterdam and Amsterdam, among other activities in the Netherlands."[8]

Time magazine, in an article on Saudi Arabia titled "Saudi Arabia: Inside the Kingdom," stated: "Apart from channeling money to foundations that have assisted terrorist groups, Saudis have for years supported institutions abroad that propagate Wahhabism."[9]

Historically, the teaching of Sharia and radical Islam have been closely related. Al-Waqf and other Muslim organizations have helped to create a world where there is a division between Muslims and non-Muslims. The next step is the separation of governments of the world into two groups: those who have Sharia and those who do not. There will be constant pressure on the non-Islamic states to conform to the Muslim idea of the *ummah*.

Sharia and the Failure of the Islamic State

"Almost the entire Muslim world is affected by poverty and tyranny."[10] This statement comes from the pen of Bernard Lewis, the respected professor of Near Eastern Studies at Princeton University. In his chapter titled "The Failure of Modernity," he speaks about the failure of the Muslim states to keep up with the rest of the world. In statistic after statistic, Islamic countries lag behind. The countries that practice Sharia as the law of the land, such as Iran, Afghanistan, and Sudan, rank close to the bottom in most categories. Lewis says, "In the listing of economies by gross domestic product, the highest ranking Muslim majority country is Turkey, with 64 million inhabitants, in twenty-third place, between Austria and Denmark, with about 5 million each. The next is Indonesia, with 212 million, in twenty-eighth place, following Norway with 4.5 million and followed by Saudi Arabia with 21 million."[11]

In other categories, such as purchasing power, living standards, industrial output, manufacturing output, life expectancy, and ownership of computers, the Islamic countries are far behind.[12] A report on Arab Human Development in 2002, prepared by a committee of Arab intellectuals working with the United Nations, reveals some more interesting facts. Lewis quotes, "The Arab world translates about 330 books annually, one-fifth of the number that Greece translates. The accumulative total of translated books since the Caliph Maa'moun's [*sic*] time [the ninth century] is about 100,000, almost the average that Spain translates in one year."[13]

Lewis goes on to comment on the economic situation, which is no better, stating, "The GDP in all Arab countries combined stood at $531.2 billion in 1999—less than that of a single European country, Spain ($595.5 billion)."[14]

The more astute students of Islam realize that, in the mind of the average Muslim, Islam is much more than just a religion—it is a complete way of life. Because politics, economics, and social actions are fused together, the condition of Islamic dominated societies is telling.

Quoting Lewis again, we learn that "Most [Muslims] would agree that God is concerned with politics, and this belief is confirmed and sustained by the shari'a [sharia], the Holy Law, which deals extensively with the acquisition and exercise of power, the nature of legitimacy and authority, the duties of ruler and subject, in a word, with what we in the West would call constitutional law and political philosophy."[15]

Extreme Islam has its eye on the West with the attitude that the utopian society can be created if Western wealth could be under the control of an Islamic Republic. It fails to look at the possibility, however, that life under Sharia has led to the miserable conditions in which many people in Islamic countries live.

Social Implications of Sharia Law in Central Asia

Much of Central Asia had been predominately Muslim prior to the culmination of the U.S.S.R. and its communist form of government. There was some limited freedom afforded to the Muslims in such countries as Kazakhstan, Uzbekistan, Kyrgyzstan, and Tajikistan.

Prior to the early 1900s, these areas were not radically Islamic as we define them today. With the imposition of atheism, some began to search for their own identity and began to recruit dissidents from all of Central Asia's major ethnic groups. Ahmed Rashid stated: "[They had] little to offer except the deposition of the current regimes and the institution of sharia. . . . Support flows in from across the region, and funding comes from as far away as Saudi Arabia—as well as from the narcotics and weapons trade out of Afghanistan."[16]

The rallying cry from many of the radical groups, some of whom are aligned with *al Qaeda,* seems to be the establishment of Sharia. They do not need or attempt to define the types of reform that they plan nor how they will run the government. They just want to establish Sharia. This was also the case in Afghanistan, where we have already seen the tragic results of that experiment under the Taliban.

Social Implications of Sharia Law in Saudi Arabia

Saudi Arabia is the home of the *Wahabi* movement and is considered one of the strictest Muslim countries. It is here that Sharia law is practiced in its strictest form. Because this society had little outside influence for several centuries, it has stood the test of time. In a report in *Parade* magazine, David Wallechinsky described life in Saudi Arabia:

In Saudi Arabia, one must not criticize the royal family. Trials often are held in secret. Adultery and abandoning Islam are crimes punishable by beheading, and people given the death penalty often are not told their sentence until the execution itself. Lesser crimes are punishable by flogging: Using a cell phone on an airplane earns 20 lashes. Floggings often are given in shopping malls and announced on the public-address system.[17]

And he describes the effects of Sharia on the women of the country:

Saudi women may not drive. If they walk alone in the street, they risk being stopped, beaten or detained as suspected moral offenders. Last March, at a girls' school in Mecca, 15 students died in a fire. Witnesses said the religious police prevented the girls from escaping because they hadn't put on their headdresses and denied male rescuers access because they are not allowed to mix with females.[18]

There are no Christian meetings or churches allowed even among the expatriates. Islam is the only religion allowed to be practiced; thus freedom of religion is an unknown concept. Saudi Arabia is one of the world's most closed societies, both because they do not desire outsiders to influence their people and because few desire to travel to the country for fear of their harsh legal system. Sharia law in this country is one of the best examples of what would probably become universal if a global *ummah* were established.

Social Implications of Sharia Law in Iran

After the revolution in Iran in 1979, the social consequences of an Islamic republic were severe. They included a government constitution that invested final authority in the *fiqh* to the supreme religious-political leader of the state. He is the final interpreter of Islamic law and appoints the Council of Guardians, the heads of the military and judiciary, and the revolutionary guards. He also acts as a check on the president, prime minister, and parliament, and has the right to over-rule each. John Esposito and John Voll report, "Neither criticism of Ayatollah Khomeini nor of the government's ideological foundation was tolerated. . . . Opposition newspapers were banned, and the government used media censorship and its own 'Islamic programming' to promote its beliefs and values."[19]

Esposito continues to show how the revolution changed the state. The Office for the Propagation of Virtue and the Prevention of Sin addressed moral ills of society by banning music and dancing in public. Drugs, prostitution, gambling, alcohol, homosexuality, and pornography were banned. Nightclubs and bars were closed. Prostitution and drug trafficking were made subject to capital punishment. Thousands of teachers were purged, textbooks revised, and coed institutions were transformed into single-sex schools. Islamic associations were formed on campuses and are used to monitor un-Islamic behavior. Women who wore makeup or did not dress modestly or Islamically were punished.[20]

Christiane Bird, in her book *Neither East nor West*, describes that

> every Iranian lives in two worlds—the public and the private. . . . The public is for wearing dark colors, obeying the laws of the Islamic society, and generally presenting a serious and pious face to the world. . . . The private is also for enjoying forbidden music and literature, watching banned videos and TV shows, wearing miniskirts and halter tops, drinking alcohol and doing drugs, and criticizing the Islamic government.[21]

Iran remains the clearest example of what could happen if Islam extremists were to take control of a Western country.

CONCLUSION

Democracy is a form of government best defined as rule by the people. With its doctrine of Sharia, Islam could be best defined as rule by God (theocracy). Is it possible for the two to coexist? There is in Islam itself a debate on this very subject. Muslim states that have signed the United Nations Universal Declaration of Human Rights find themselves ruled by contradictory laws. One law gives citizens the freedom of thought, while the other, Sharia, in its official interpretation based on *ta'a* (obedience), condemns it.

Some argue that not only is it possible for Sharia and democracy to coexist but that it is being practiced in a limited way in the United States today. The only way the two possibly could be brought together, however, is for a more moderate form of Islam to win the debate. History has shown us that the more fundamental forms of Islam have not been ready to accept any form of government other than its own form of theocracy with its own definition of Sharia. Some say that Islam will be mollified in today's global village, but the past twenty years have shown that when Islam takes over a state or country, the institution of Sharia is not far behind. I doubt that democracy and Islam can live and function on a long-term basis without intense conflict.

Sharia not only limits religious and political freedom, making second-class citizens of both non-Muslims and the "people of the Book," but Islamic law also robs societies of freedom of speech, dress, and behavior. Islamic law is clearly designed to advance Islamic religion and stop Christian growth and missions as illustrated by the mandates of capital punishment for those who convert out of Islam.

Sharia law has proven to be both a burden for Muslims and a threat to the rest of the world.

A large mosque filled with worshipers.

chapter seven

The Whole Truth and Nothing but the Truth

The Role of Truth and Fear in Islam

I first met Ali in Frankfurt at a conference for Christian missionaries from around Europe. He was a very impressive man and brought several copies of his new book with him. The book told the hair-raising story of his life as an officer in the Shah's air force in Iran and the persecution that he experienced after becoming a Christian. The stories were vivid and intriguing, showing how Ali had suffered for his newfound faith. I was so impressed with him that I convinced our area director that Ali would be a great person to lead our Muslim awareness group in Europe. The director agreed. So Ali and his new wife of only six months, a talented young woman from Texas, came to work with me in Europe.

Everything went well until Ali had his first opportunity to speak before a church. I was taken aback by his bitterness and harshness toward just about everyone. This continued for about a year. At the end of the year, his wife announced that she was going to divorce Ali.

This turn of events put us into a difficult position because of our board's policy on divorce; thus I had to tell Ali that he had only six more months of employment with us. Several days later I visited Ali and he told me that he had been badly beaten up by some Muslims as he was witnessing to them and that he had hurt his back. Of course, I was sympathetic with his condition. Previously, we had played tennis together. I bemoaned the fact that we could not play tennis for a while. He assured me that he could try but would quit if the pain were too intense. We played for an hour and a half and he did great. We played several more times, but off the tennis court he still complained that his back hurt him greatly.

When the six months were up, Ali left for the States. He soon filed a five-million-dollar lawsuit against the Foreign Mission Board, claiming that we had put him into a dangerous situation without warning him of the dangers. The lawsuit was later thrown out for lack of evidence.

During the time that Ali was working with me, some of my co-workers and I began receiving threatening letters from the Middle East telling us that unless we ceased our work with Muslims, our lives were in danger. They even gave the names and ages of our children and said that they also were in danger. About a year later, we learned that Ali was probably an agent sent to discover what we were doing in our missions work with Muslims.

After this experience, I began to question what Muslims considered truth. I discovered that truth has different meanings for different religions.

Truth in Islam

Is it possible for us to accept Islam as a truthful religion? It is always difficult when a writer accuses a person, especially a world religion, of not telling the truth. We must seek to have a complete understanding of what Islam teaches concerning truth and how it is practiced in the proclamation of their faith.

Islam teaches that there is absolute truth as well as relative truth. Absolute truth never changes despite changes in time and place, while relative truth is dependent on time, people, and conditions. Since both of these types of truth exist in Islam, how does one determine if truth is absolute or relative?

Millions of people all across the globe profess faith in Islam and try to live their daily lives in obedience to its proclaimed truth. Many who seek converts to Islam promote Islam as the one and only true religion and the only valid truth. There is tension in Islam, however, between absolute and relative truth as Muslims seek to make Islam the world's only religion. This inner conflict has been a problem for Muslim peoples throughout history and continues to manifest itself today.

Absolute Truth

Every Muslim will state that truth is a very important section of the foundation of Islam. One author has stated, "The Qur'an has promised that if a person is honest in his search for the truth and is completely willing to surrender and submit to it, God shall Himself guide him to His absolute truth and open His ways for him."[1]

All absolute truth, from the perspective of Islam, is related to God and His existence as the one and only true God. God's essence, names, and works remain true and unchanging throughout time. Other areas of absolute truth are principles of faith that include the concept of divine justice, with its dimensions of unity, predestination, forgiveness, and mercy.

Another area of absolute truth is the divine books; however, the Qur'an is seen as the only divine book that has remained pure and unaltered by man, and therefore, the only divine book of absolute truth. Other books that they see as coming from God such as the *Tawrah*, *Zabur*, and the *Injil* are inferior to the last and greatest revelation of God, the Qur'an; thus, they do not contain absolute truth.

With their high view of Allah, Muslims believe that absolute truth never begins with man but comes only from revelation, that is, revelation from God through a prophet. It is necessary to have religion in order to know absolute truth.[2]

Since Muhammad is believed by Muslims to be the last of God's prophets, his revelations are the source for absolute, universal truth. It is believed that Christians and Jews did not carefully protect the

revelation given to them by God from impurities and human altera-
tions. Therefore, where there are differences in beliefs between the
three monotheistic religions, they claim Islam has the correct belief
and is the source of absolute truth.

Relative Truth

Relative truth, as previously stated, is dependent on time, individuals, or conditions. One Muslim writer states, "Truths showing differences in color, tone and character dependent on time, individuals,
or conditions . . . are relative truths."[3] For instance, the appearance of
color changes when the intensity of light that illuminates it changes.
A person's character may be admired or disdained depending on
the location and time in which his character qualities are displayed.
Most people in most situations admire honest character, for instance.
A family may uphold honesty in their children and urge them to always tell the truth. Yet, if the family were hiding fellow Palestinians
from the Israeli military, they would likely instruct their children to
lie to the Israeli authorities if questioned—and in lying they would
be admired.

So how does a Muslim arrive at truth in such a situation? It is here
that Islam arrives at an understanding not unlike the Christian view
of situational ethics that says that the situations in which people find
themselves determine what is truth.

An example may help to explain the differences in the Islamic
understanding of relative truth. From the perspective of Islam, the
number of relative truths is much greater than the number of absolute truths. Relative truths appear in all areas of life, from the
common concept of relative truth in color and tone, to more controversial areas such as ethics, violence, justice, and legal matters.
Even the interpretation of truth from the Qur'an may be left up to
the reader.

One writer on Islamic truth states, "As long as there is no conflict with the literal meaning of a word and the root of the word is

studied and the rules of the Arabic language are not violated, the understanding of every reader of every verse in the Qur'an can be listened to with respect."[4] From this reasoning, it can be understood how each Muslim has a certain right to interpret the Qur'an as they feel it should be understood. Understanding can change in respect to time; thus, one meaning of the Qur'an can change to another in a different epoch of history, from the vantage point of a different continent, or even from context to context, from reader to reader.

An important theme from the Qur'an is doing good deeds. This is one of the highest virtues of the Islamic faith, encouraged numerous times throughout the Qur'an. However, virtues under certain conditions may not be considered virtuous in others. For instance, one's boss at work may be frank and curt, attributes considered quite appropriate in an office atmosphere. Yet, this same response to young children at home could be considered impatient and unloving.

Al-Ghazzali (1058–1111), one of the greatest Muslim theologians, wrote: "Know that a lie is not wrong in itself. . . . If a lie is the only way to reach a good result, it is allowable. . . . We must lie when truth leads to unpleasant results."[5]

Islam differs greatly in its admonition against or encouragement of violence depending on the situation. Islam professes to be a religion of peace, love, and forgiveness, especially between Muslims. The Qur'an states, "Whoever kills a person, unless it be for manslaughter or for mischief in the land, it is as though he had killed entire humanity. And whoever saves a life, it is as though he had saved lives of all men" (*Surah* 5:32).

Concerning violence in Islamic ethics, one Muslim writes, "Islam basically is a non-violent religion. It does not approve of violence at all."[6] This appears to be a statement of absolute truth, ending the negative statement with an emphatic "at all." However, in the same paragraph of this essay, the author clarifies the "absolute" statement by saying: "But Islam approves of violence (in a highly controlled sense, of course) only to remove zulm, the structures of oppression."[7]

We know from history that Muslims did not hesitate to conquer other peoples using violence; but in these numerous cases it was not the Muslims being oppressed but rather the opposite. The Qur'an itself has many verses that sanction and encourage violence and killing, but such verses are usually within the context of establishing justice for Muslims, and after peaceful men's attempts have resulted in no change. After that, a Muslim appears to have instruction to inflict violence if he or she is feeling oppressed or is being treated unfairly. Therefore, the act of violence is a relative truth in Islam, dependent on the conditions and beliefs of those inflicting violence.

Comparison of Absolute Truth to Relative Truth

One Muslim author gave the following example of the comparison of the two different types of truth. He said that the relationship of absolute truth and relative truth could best be explained by using the illustration of a flashlight beam pointed at a circle painted on a wall. The center of that beam of light is the brightest, while the area around the circle of light is not quite as sharp or clear. However, the area surrounding the circle of light is still illuminated; in fact, the light is being reflected to the circle's circumference. Each ray of light on the circumference of the circle, representing relative truth, is connected back to its source, the center of the beam of light, which symbolizes absolute truth.

The article continues, "What gives the relative truth its particular dimensions and properties, its relevance, is the nature of the receiving point, its own properties, time and conditions."[8] In Islam this would mean that their understanding of God as the ultimate truth is the center; the farther you get away from the center, the weaker the light, but it is all a part of "the light."

In this way, Muslims can take more freedoms in the areas of relative truth and still call a falsehood a truth. As stated previously, Islam sees no problem in showing two different faces when it comes to presenting the truth. With this understanding, it is easy to see how Muslims can say one thing and live another. To them, it is not a lie— just a different perspective.

RELATIVE TRUTH, JUSTICE, AND ISLAMIC LAW

Islam prides itself on the fact that it is a religion of "justice." However, the sphere of justice within a community also has multiple shades of relativism. In its highest form, justice should serve both the individual and the community, but a "disturbance of the peace" can prevent the protection of either. It has been stated, "During such times relative justice, which sacrifices the individual's rights for the sake of the public good, becomes necessary and application of it becomes absolutely mandatory."[9] This might sound acceptable to the Western mind but it also allows the government to strip an individual of his rights for the sake of the "public good." It is this line of reasoning that allows a country like Saudi Arabia to forbid Christians to worship within the country because to do so has the potential of leading good devout Muslims astray and thus damaging the public good.

Often a Muslim will tell a lie instead of telling the truth because of a concern for the community and how he or she understands law and order. Characteristics of Allah and certain principles of faith are proclaimed as absolute truth by Muslims; yet conflicting evidence suggests that Allah's character and principles of faith are more relative than absolute. For example, in Islam the task of obtaining salvation is relative to the person. One Muslim author writes, "'Pious deeds of righteous people are the sins of those near to God.' . . . An act that earns a single merit for one person can earn a million merits for another."[10]

Not only is salvation in Islam extremely relative according to an individual and his personal deeds, but also God himself is shown to be relative and arbitrary toward the salvation of his creation. The Qur'an states, "He punishes whom He will, and pardons whom He pleases, for God has the power over all things" (*Surah* 5:40). Concerning the law given by God to man, Caesar Farah states, "Allah may vary His ordinances at pleasure, prescribing one set of laws for the Jews, another for the Christians, and still another for Muslims."[11]

Christians see God as one who is "the same yesterday, today, and forever" while, in Islam, God is one who changes his mandates and expectations for different people groups of the world. This means that a Muslim who says that Islam is the only real religion may not actually have any assurance of salvation.

Concerning faith in Allah the Qur'an states, "There is no compulsion in religion . . ." (*Surah* 2:256). Muslim leaders will often claim that there is religious freedom in Islam and use the above verse from the Qur'an to support that idea. Many say, "Muslims are absolutely forbidden from forcing their faith on others; this negates the very idea of free will and choice."[12] Yet this idea of religious freedom has been contradicted by Muslims and Islamic governments throughout history and continues to be contradicted today in countries where religions other than Islam are greatly restricted or even forbidden.

How can it be said that one is under no "compulsion" in Islam when essentially no other religious choices or freedoms are given? This is the same concept as when other countries claim to be democratic by offering "people's choice" elections but have only one name on the ballot. This was the case when Saddam Hussein received 100 percent of the votes in the 2002 election in Iraq. Clearly religious freedom is another of the "truths" that is relative in Islam.

WHEN LYING IS PERMITTED IN ISLAM

There are two categories of lies that are not tolerated in Islam. The first category is a lie against Allah. The basis for this is:

> Who can be more wicked than one who inventeth a lie against Allah, or saith, "I have received inspiration," when he hath received none, or (again) who saith, "I can reveal the like of what Allah hath revealed"? If thou couldst but see how the wicked (do fare) in the flood of confusion at death!—The angels stretch forth their hands (saying) "Yield up your souls: this day shall ye receive your reward,—a penalty of shame, for that ye used to tell lies against Allah, and scornfully to reject of His Signs!" (*Surah* 6:93)

The second category of a forbidden lie is one against Muhammad:

> Narrated Al-Mughira: "I heard the Prophet saying, ascribing false things to me is not like ascribing false things to anyone else. Whosoever tells a lie against me intentionally then surely let him occupy his seat in Hell-Fire." (*Surah* 2:378; cf. 1:106–108)[13]

One of the most interesting moral dilemmas for Islam are the cases in which lying is permitted. The traditions tell us that there are instances where deception can be acceptable. Umm Kulthum ("one of the first emigrants who pledge allegiance to Allah's Apostle") said she heard "Allah's Messenger" say, "a liar is not one who tries to bring reconciliation amongst people and speaks good (in order to avert dispute), or he conveys good." Ibn Shihab goes on to say that he had not heard of any exemption granted in any situation when the people spoke a lie with the exception of "three cases: *in battle, for bringing reconciliation amongst persons* and the *narration of the words of the husband to his wife and the narration of the words of a wife to her husband* (in a twisted form in order to bring reconciliation between them)."[14]

This and other areas of written history show us a common Muslim belief is that it is allowable to tell a falsehood on four occasions:

1. To save one's life
2. To effect a peace or reconciliation
3. To persuade a woman
4. On the occasion of a journey or expedition[15]

A fifth could be added to this from other sources:

5. In winning someone to Islam

It could be argued that in each of these cases we are dealing with relative truth and many Muslims will not define this as lying. At least this is the Islamic view of the problem while Christians would see it differently. Christians hold to a much higher understanding of truth. In fact, Jesus himself said that he "is the truth" (John 14:6).

When a Muslim tries to win someone to the Islamic faith, the use of the truth is not always the best way to proceed. If a praiseworthy aim is attainable through the telling of a lie, then this is allowed. There is no more praiseworthy aim than that of bringing someone to an acceptance of Islam.

Many who have carried out business transactions with Muslims have been surprised to see that the deal has been built on deceit. The grounds given for such is that lying is permitted when on a journey, and the journeys during the time of Muhammad were almost always business trips. Therefore, in business, the truth may not always be accepted when the common good is to be achieved. The question comes not in the ethics of lying but in what is the common good. The person telling the lie generally defines the common good.

Often when I have taken part in dialogue sessions with Christians and Muslims, I come away with the distinct feeling that the two sides have never really met on the same plane. Differences of the understanding of truth make it difficult for the two to have a real understanding and a true meeting of the minds.

Understanding Fear in Islam

Many writers on Islam have tried to find one word that will best describe Islam. In my reading I have found different authors using a number of different words such as *justice, sacrifice, submission,* and *community.* It is now apparent to me that the one word that best describes Islam is *fear.* While many will disagree with my evaluation on this subject, there are specific reasons why I have come to this conclusion.

One Morocccan scholar, Fatema Mernissi, used fear as her main theme when writing her book, *Islam and Democracy: Fear of the Modern World.* She bases seven of her ten chapter titles on the different types of fear now faced by the modern Muslim:

- Chapter One: Fear of the Foreign West
- Chapter Two: Fear of the Imam
- Chapter Three: Fear of Democracy
- Chapter Six: Fear of Freedom of Thought
- Chapter Seven: Fear of Individualism
- Chapter Eight: Fear of the Past
- Chapter Nine: Fear of the Present[16]

It needs to be noted that Dr. Mernissi not only concentrates on the fear factor within Islam, but she herself also uses fear as the basis for her arguments in answer to the provocative questions about the possibilities for democracy and human rights in the Islamic world.

The Fear of Allah

Western civilization is built upon the idea of looking forward to the possibilities for mankind. It is dynamic and filled with hope for the future. Islam, on the other hand, is completely Allah-centric and has a tendency to be dominated by an intense fear of Allah. This fear colors how a Muslim sees the past, the present, and the future. A common phrase in Arabic is *insha-Allah* or "as God wills." Another phrase is "so it is written." Muslims are strongly predestinarian and this motivates the life of the individual follower.

The Qur'an stipulates: "O Believers, do not be hasty and forward in Allah and His Messenger's presence but instead fear Allah: for verily, Allah is Hearer and Knower."[17] This verse has two teachings: the first being the respect for Allah's prophet, Muhammad, and the second being the fear of God. Several Muslim writers wrote an article on the signs of fear of Allah. They listed "a number of them":

> The fear of death before repenting; the fear of not living up to one's repentance and breaking one's promise; the fear of not being able to fulfill Allah's obligations; the fear of losing one's softness in the heart and its hardening; the fear of losing consistency; the fear of allowing temptations to

dominate; the fear of Allah making one's self responsible for doing good deeds because of conceit; the fear of becoming arrogant and egotistical due to the abundance of bounties; the fear of being distracted from Allah by other creation; the fear of being led to an evil ending through excessive bounties; the fear of being punished early (i.e., in this world); the fear of being disgraced at the time of death; the fear of being beguiled by the glitter of this world; the fear of Allah revealing one's secret in one's state of oblivion; the fear of being stamped with a bad death at the time of death; the fear of the pangs of death; the fear of the questions of Munkar and Nakeer[18] in the grave; the fear of the punishment of the grave; the fear of the horrors of the horizon (at the time of resurrection); the fear of the awe during the presentation in front of Allah; the fear and shame of being naked (at the time of resurrection); the fear of being questioned about every little thing in life; the fear of the bridge (over Hell) and its sharpness; the fear of the fire, its chains and its torment; the fear of being deprived of Paradise, the Eternal and everlasting kingdom and abode and the fear of being deprived of seeing Allah's tremendous visage.[19]

Fear of Eternal Damnation

Islam is a works religion. That means that the individual must do good works in order to earn their way to heaven. Both the glories of paradise and the agonies of hell are very dominant teachings in Islam. Most Westerners (even those who know very little of the basic teachings of Islam) are aware that a person who is killed in *jihad* has the promise of eternity in paradise and will be ministered to by seventy-two virgins. Although the teaching of an eternal bliss is a dominant theme, there is little that guarantees a person's entry into this paradise outside of dying in a *jihad*. This leaves most average Muslims living in fear of eternal damnation.

Allah has prepared paradise for his devoted friends and hell for his enemies. The explanation of judgment day sounds very similar to that of Christians until Allah brings forth his book of judgment with all the records of people's deeds in them. So it seems that although Allah forgives, he still writes the deeds of a person, good or bad, in a book.

Al-jisr is the bridge that will be laid over hell, over which everyone must pass in order to enter paradise. The disbelievers and those whose bad deeds outweigh their good deeds will then fall into hell. Only the disbelievers, however, will be kept in the consuming fire of hell for eternity. The unbeliever's eye of his heart will then be opened to the "last life" and different periods of visualizing the past for eternity.[20]

Paradise also contains *al-Houdh*—the pool that will appear with cups near to it to quench people's thirst. But those who are allowed to drink will be few.

What then motivates the believer to do good deeds? Is it because of faith that they are moved to goodness? Or is it out of fear of crossing *al-jisr* with too many bad deeds and being driven into hell?

According to the Qur'an, Allah has created man in a form of original character and temperament. In other words, by nature man knows what is good and how to be appreciative, but it is in coming to know true religion that this nature or character is fully developed. The Qur'an commends those whose character of goodness has become strong, and it condemns those whose nature has become dull. It is stated that a Muslim who does good will inherit the life of delight hereafter, but those who do not do good will suffer all kinds of punishment.[21]

K. M. Islam in his book, *The Spectacle of Death*, vividly describes the circumstances of hell that he gleaned from the verses of the holy Qur'an and the *Hadith* of the holy prophet:

> The fire of Hell is 70 degrees hotter than the worldly fire. It has seven levels, and each level has a big entrance. The first level of Hell is reserved for those Muslim sinners and [the second level is for] idolaters who were polytheists, [the third level is for] worshippers of fire, [the fourth level for] atheists, [the

fifth level for] Jews, [the sixth level for] Christians and [the seventh level for] hypocrites respectively. These levels of Hell are known as (1) *Jaheem*, (2) *Jahannam*, (3) *Sa'ir*, (4) *Saqar*, (5) *Nata*, (6) *Haviya*, and (7) *Hutama*. Every one of these extensive levels is replete with incalculable pains, tortures and torments, and multifarious houses. For instance, there is a house *Ghayy*, the severity of its torments is such that the denizens of [the] other six levels pray 400 times daily for salvation from its tortures. . . . There is a pond, *Aab-I-hamim*, with water so hot that the moment a sinner drinks it, his upper lip swells to such an extent that it covers his nose and eyes; the lower, his chest. As this water passes down the throat, his tongue burns; mouth contracts and ultimately this boiling water tears apart the human lungs, stomach and intestines.[22]

The vivid descriptions of hell are long and gruesome. It is understandable why the average Muslim fears that they will not make it over the bridge but rather fall into hell for all eternity.

While it is true that Christianity also has a belief in an eternal hell, the Christian finds security in the words of the Bible that promise that "Everyone who calls on the name of the Lord will be saved" (Romans 10:13). Through a living relationship with Jesus Christ, we have peace, guidance, and an assurance of our eternal salvation. For the Muslim, salvation basically comprises three conditions or beliefs: repentance, faith, and good works. Thus, salvation consists of the declaration of faith, abiding in the five pillars of Islam, and doing good deeds to outweigh the bad ones. However, in Islam it depends on the whim of Allah as to who will find salvation and who will not. Tragically, the average Muslim lives a life of not knowing if Allah will allow them to enter paradise.

Fear of Apostasy

Apostasy is the unbelief of a Muslim who was born into a Muslim family or who has previously publicly confessed faith in Islam.

Apostasy can occur through an overt questioning of the substance of God or the value of the Qur'an, burning the Qur'an out of disrespect, or soiling it, for instance, by turning the pages with fingers that have been licked. It also includes defiling the names of Allah or the prophets, or wearing a belt—a custom assigned to unbelievers. Other acts of unbelief for a Muslim include entering a church, worshiping an idol, or practicing magic. Muslims are considered to have lost their faith when they say that the earth has existed since eternity, thus denying creation by God.

The basis for a charge of apostasy is the determination of two or more witnesses coming forth and giving account of a person's actions. All four founders of the four schools of Islamic law "agree that the apostate whose fall from Islam is beyond doubt—may Allah forbid it—must be killed, and his blood spilled without reservation."[23]

These risks of apostasy produce fear in the life of a Muslim when they come into contact with a non-Muslim. They often see the danger of pressures that might cause them to commit the sin of apostasy. Any Muslim considering conversion from Islam to Christianity, for example, at best can expect to be ostracized by their community and disowned by their family. At worst they can be put to death. The *Hadith* stated that Muhammad demanded the death penalty for anyone who turns his or her back on Islam. The Qur'an states, "Anyone who, after accepting Faith in God, utters unbelief, except under compulsion, his heart remaining in faith—but such as open their breast to unbelief, on them is wrath from God, and theirs will be a dreadful penalty" (*Surah* 16:106).

In Islamic Republics that have adopted Sharia, there is a common fear that enemies will accuse a person of apostasy for personal or financial gain. Several modern-day examples of the results of apostasy are as follows:

1. In Iran, Ruhollah Rowhani, age fifty-two, was executed on July 21, 1998, for converting a Muslim to the Baha'i faith. Others have been sentenced to death in that country for the same reason.[24]

2. In Tehran, Reverend Mehdi Dibaj had converted from Islam to Christianity and was sentenced to death in 1993, forty-five years after his conversion, with charges of apostasy. There was an outcry from the international community and he was released in 1994 after an appeal. He was killed soon thereafter. The same happened to two other pastors in the same year.

3. Cairo University professor Dr. Nasr Abu Zeid and his wife, also a university professor, were forced to separate on the grounds that the husband wrote that Islamic teachings should evolve with the changes in society; he was declared an apostate for such thoughts. Since a Muslim woman must not be married to a heretic, there was an order for divorce. The couple rejected the order and, fearing for their lives, settled in the Netherlands.[25]

The average Muslim is very much aware of these and many other examples. Thus, they live in fear that they might transgress the law and also be condemned to physical pain or death, or even worse, the torments of hell for eternity.

The Fear of the West

Fatema Mernissi sheds some light on this topic by showing us how fundamentally different people from the Middle East view those from the West. She writes:

> *Gharb,* the Arabic word for the West, is also the place of darkness and the incomprehensible, always frightening. *Gharb* is the territory of the strange, the foreign *(gharib).* Everything that we don't understand is frightening. "Foreignness" in Arabic has a very strong spatial connotation, for *gharb* is the place where the sun sets and where darkness awaits. It is in the West that the night snaps up the sun and swallows it. . . . It is there that *gharaba* (strangeness) has taken up its abode.[26]

While visiting in the home of a North African Muslim family living in Brussels, I was taken aback when they asked if all or just some of the Muslims who went to America were killed. I tried to assure them that neither was the case, but I left the family unconvinced. Since Islam sees no separation between the religious and the political, this idea is carried over into their understanding of the Christian West; they cannot differentiate between Western political entities and Christianity.

In many discussions with Muslims, both in the West and in the Middle East, I have come to understand the underlying basis of their concerns:

1. They have been taught to fear the Christian church. Often they will point to historical events such as the Crusades or present events such as the Western world's attitude toward Iraq to prove that Christians have a desire to destroy Muslims.
2. The breakup of families, low morals, and a lack of basic values in Western society all point to a decadent Christian church and a system that should be avoided.
3. They see Christianity as a dying religion in contrast to theirs, which they feel is alive and vibrant.
4. They see a lack of community in the Western social pattern.
5. They see Christians as having no belief system. They cannot understand why Christians do not pray openly five times a day or perform others acts as do Muslims.

Politically, the average Muslim sees the world in only two colors—black and white. They cast the entire West in black, and fail to see any good in it. It is much easier to simply put all aspects of the West into one large basket and then fear the basket because of its size.

Fear of Democracy

Once again we quote Mernissi: "We don't have an Arabic word for democracy; we use the Greek word, *dimuqratiyya*. Two Arabs talking about democracy speak to each other in Greek, all the while remembering that Greek heritage has been forbidden to them on the pretext that it is foreign."[27] It is every bit as difficult to convince Muslims of the value of democracy as it is to convince an American of the value of a dictatorship. Both peoples have grown up within the system and tend to say that their system is the best. One must remember that the ultimate goal of Islam is to set up a worldwide *ummah* or Islamic system that will be headed by only one *caliph*. Since this is the ideal, it would be incorrect to embrace a democratic system.

It is important to note that there are no functioning democracies in the Middle East, although some will argue that there are Muslim countries such as Indonesia and Pakistan that have adopted the democratic system. A closer study, however, will show that, even in these countries, there is a drift to a more theocratic form of government that makes up the Islamic Republic. Muslims who do not live in democratic nations see our form of government as foreign and thus they fear that which comes from outside of Islam.

In the days leading up to the 2003 war on Iraq, some commentators stated that those Muslim countries that opposed the war did so more because of their fear of the creation of an Iraqi democracy in their midst than because of a fear of the Western presence. Most of the surrounding countries did not like Saddam Hussein, but they also did not like democracy.

The Fears of the Immigrant Community

As many Muslims come to the West seeking a better life, they bring with them some of the previously mentioned fears and may accumulate more during the journey. In my position as the coordinator of Baptist missions to Muslims in Europe for the European Baptist Federation, I had the opportunity of visiting many individual Muslims and meeting with numerous Muslim groups. We met to dialogue and find ways that we could render aid. After we gained their confidence, they would share their feelings about living in the West. I have attempted to categorize their fears:

- **Fear concerning the situation in their home countries.** Most Muslims come from countries that are living in periods of political upheaval. Muslims from such places as Libya, Iraq, Algeria, and Lebanon all fear for their families and friends. They continue to keep posted on the latest news. They are constantly concerned with the possibility of a change of government or an assassination. Each of these events could cause a radical change in their personal life.
- **Fear of the new culture.** It is difficult to be an outsider in a strange culture. There is always the possibility that they will be sent out of the country or be forced to move. Some Muslims fear that if one country such as Germany could eliminate 6.5 million Jews, couldn't they do the same to the 5.5 million Muslims living in Western Europe?
- **Fear of Islam.** As Islam grows in strength, radical groups such as the Muslim Brotherhood and *al Qaeda* become more active. The European Muslims also may become radicalized. Coupled together with their fear of apostasy and eternal damnation leaves many in a state of fear of their own religion.
- **Fear from within.** Many Muslims living in Western countries face major identity crises. This is particularly true with the second generation. Are they German or Turk, French or Algerian? They are not sure what their real language is or where they belong. These inner conflicts can turn into fear if no one helps them find their identity.
- **Fear of losing their children.** The second and third generations are growing up in another culture, and parents fear that their children will take on the ways of the world and leave Islam. This is one of the reasons why there is a renewal movement among Muslims living in the West. They want their children to keep the traditions and culture of their background.
- **Fear from 9/11.** Stories abound about how many Muslims have been beaten, persecuted, and killed because of the events of September 11. Even when they are presented with facts that the number of such incidents is minimal, they retain their fear of

possible retaliation. One Muslim girl, who had heard about an attack on a Christian school in Pakistan, during which several children were killed, said to me, "I was afraid it was a Muslim fanatic and now my fears are that Christians will do the same to us."

CONCLUSION

Christianity and Islam are different in many aspects including social philosophies, theology, and culture. In this chapter it becomes apparent that there are also great differences in other areas such as values (truth) and emotions (fear). It is at the last two levels that the differences take on the greatest challenge for those who seek to find a way for both to live side by side. Values form the rock-bottom foundation for a person's character and personality; emotions are where the human being has the least amount of control.

In the search for world dominance, Islam will use truth as they understand it, and this conflicts with the Christian understanding of the term. They will use the emotion of fear as a tool to keep their people within the fences of their faith and to mobilize people against a common enemy. The concepts of truth and fear have proven helpful in the overall Islamic strategy.

chapter **eight**

Power Shortage

*The Power Encounter
Between Islam and Christianity*

World Cup, Davis Cup, Super Bowl—these terms are well known in the contemporary world. There is a craze for sporting events that pit one team against another and even one country against another. Two Central American countries war over a football match. This need for competition, where there is a winner and loser, spills over into the area of religion.

In 1971 an Australian missiologist, Alan Tippet, coined the term "power encounter" to label what he saw as contests between peoples in the South Pacific who were sure of the power of their beliefs, in contrast to the new message of Jesus Christ. Either by design or accident, events took place that pitted one belief against the other. It became clear that the God of Jesus Christ was able to wield more power than their gods. Consequently, many converted to Christianity. Just as it was for the ancient Hebrews, many of today's peoples look to evidences of spiritual power as the clearest way to show the superiority of one faith over another.

Muslims, Jews, and Christians alike recognize the encounters between Moses and Pharaoh (Exodus 5–12). They also honor Elijah for his challenge to the prophets of Baal on Mt. Carmel (1 Kings 18). The ministry of Jesus was filled with power encounters as he took on the

163

forces of Satan and defeated them through healings, miracles, and deliverances. Charles Kraft, one of America's authorities on global power encounters, notes: "Unfortunately, the majority of Christian witness coming from the West has neglected the advocacy of power encounters in the presentation of the Gospel."[1] Muslims, however, have taken this concept and made it an important part of their overall strategy, particularly as an important component of *Da'wah*.

HISTORICAL ENCOUNTERS

Since the beginning of Islam in 622, there have been continuous encounters and conflicts between Islam and Christianity. The power that both sides depended upon was their ability to make war by use of the sword alone. The rapid growth of Islam in the seventh, eighth, and ninth centuries came at the expense of the Christian areas of what is now called North Africa and the Middle East.

With the solidification of the Christian West and the rapid growth of the new religion Islam, the conflicts came to a head in the Crusades, a historical clash of the two ideologies. Battles continued to rage between the two sides for about three hundred years, each side claiming to be both victim and victor. Even now, Muslims will refer back to the atrocities that the crusaders committed on their forefathers as reasons for defending Islam today. Osama bin Laden and others refuse to say that their battle is against the Christians and the Jews but rather use the terms "the crusaders" and "the Zionists." This is a direct reference to the conflicts of the Middle Ages and in some small way connects the power encounters of the Crusades with those in the contemporary period.

After the Crusades ended, there were continuous conflicts between the two civilizations. By the beginning of the Napoleonic era colonization, the world began to see the power of the empires that would become Western Europe. In the two hundred years prior to World War II, the Christian West subdued Islam's political influence.

One *imam* that I spoke with stated, "For many hundreds of years the strategy of Islam has been derailed, but now we are back on track and soon the world will be Muslim." The new independence experienced by Islamic countries brought with it the possibility of new conflicts. These conflicts take on two personalities. One would be actual physical conflict such as that experienced in Lebanon, Afghanistan, and Palestine. The other would be a more subtle form of conflict leading to power encounters between Islam and Christianity on local levels. Both of these are in operation today.

Concerning the more physical conflicts, R. James Woolsey, former director of the Central Intelligence Agency, says, "I have adopted Eliot Cohen's formulation, distinguished professor at Johns Hopkins School for Advanced International Studies, that we are in World War IV, World War III having been the Cold War."[2] He continues by indentifying three enemies of the West in this war: (1) the Islamist Shia, which includes "those who constitute the ruling force in Iran and sponsor and back Hezbollah"; (2) the Baathist parties of Iraq and Syria whom he calls fascists; and (3) the Islamist Sunni, which includes the *Wahabi* movement. The third group entered the war around 1994.[3] These battles will continue as a part of both the *jihad* strategy and power encounters.

About the same time that "World War IV" began, the more missionary-minded Muslims began to study Christian missionary methods and to formalize a strategy that included spiritual power encounters that they felt they could win. The leadership of this movement fell to the Muslim World League, a *Wahabi* organization located in Mecca, because they held both the money and the expertise. They are still active today.

Present-Day Examples of Power Encounters

Dialogue

One branch of Christianity has long urged using dialogue as the primary method of communication between Christianity and Islam. Many still feel that a multitude of problems can be overcome if the two sides can meet and have an honest exchange of philosophies and thoughts.

Over the past forty years, I have had the opportunity to participate in many Muslim-Christian discussions. During this period of time, I have become less enthusiastic about this method.

At a large European Baptist conference held in Germany over the topic of Islam, one of the main speakers had as his title "Dialogue: An Important Tool for Communicating with Muslims." When the speaker stood to speak, I noticed that a small group attending the conference stood and left. I rushed out to ask them why. In strong terms, they said they would not listen to anyone who advocated dialogue with Islam.

Later I realized why they had such strong feelings. Dialogue, by its very definition, is a discussion of two equal parties to share and discuss ideas. The group that left told me that too much is given away in dialogue since we must recognize Islam as an equal party and they must see us as equals, something they seldom will concede.

During many dialogue sessions with Muslims, I was amazed at the hard positions they took. They would be very courteous at the beginning, of course, but when we began to discuss ways of accepting each other, they would not budge on their position.

Often during these discussions, the Christians would bring up the question, "Why does Islam not allow Christians to worship or build churches in Muslim countries?" The question would never be answered. Instead, the Muslims would ask, "Why is it that Christians will misuse the suffering of the poor and needy Muslims by giving them welfare and thus seeking to convert them to Christianity?"

These dialogue conferences would generally end with a standoff but with an expressed desire to meet again. After many such conferences, I became aware that such dialogue was more of a power encounter between the two sides. Islam was not ready to cede anything to the Christians and the more conservative Christians had the same response.

Only liberal Christians and more moderate Muslims still see dialogue as both positive and productive, and they seek an honest exchange with a continued search for common ground. Thus, dialogue continues to be a prevalent, if flawed, method.

Debate

In the last two decades, Islam has begun to replace dialogue with another form of contact, one that fits more with their expressed purposes of victory over the opposition. This is debate. There are two forms. The first is a high-profile debate held with much publicity in a large hall.

The leading proponent of this approach was the popular Muslim cleric Ahmed Deedat from South Africa. This capable man had spent much time learning about Christianity. He knew the different schools of theology and was especially interested in debating any Christian leaders who questioned the validity of the Bible or who held liberal positions on the person of Jesus Christ. He prepared himself well for such meetings with Christian leaders. He chose his opponents carefully, but he was open for challenge from others.

On one occasion, Deedat challenged the American evangelist Rev. Jimmy Swaggart to a public debate. Swaggart was well versed on the Bible but knew little or nothing about Islam and was not aware of Deedat's abilities. At the end of the debate, unbiased persons determined that Swaggart was defeated.

Part of the Muslim strategy was to have the audience openly show their feelings during the debate, intimidating the opposition and supporting their man. At the beginning, rules were laid down that stated that there would be no applause or crowd response until the end. Yet the crowd would boo and hiss when Swaggart made a point and then applaud when Deedat spoke. The longer the debate lasted, the louder the audience's responses were. More than half the crowd were Muslims, giving them the "home-field advantage." The intimidation worked. By the end of the debate, the Muslims could say they had won. Thus, in their own mind at least, they proved the superiority of Islam over Christianity. This is a power encounter in its rawest form.

English-speaking Islamic outlets still carry this on video, and it's available on islamictube.net with the introductory text: "This great debate and the rest of Mr. Ahmed Deedat's American Tour was made possible by the kind patronage and support of our brethren from the United Arab Emirates and the enthusiastic Muslims of the U.S.A.

May Allah reward them all. . . ." They have received a great deal of mileage out of this encounter. Of course, it made matters worse when a short time later Jimmy Swaggart was caught in serious sin, which he had vociferously condemned in others.

On an earlier occasion, Deedat held two debates with a Palestinian Christian, Dr. Anis Shorrosh. The first was held in the Royal Albert Hall in London on December 15, 1985. Although Deedat used similar tactics there, his opponent was not only a Bible scholar but one who understood Islam, having grown up in the Middle East. The results were that, in spite of the intimidation tactics, most observers felt like it was a standoff.

During a second debate, Dr. Shorrosh was winning but the crowd became so noisy and unsettled that they rushed the podium before the debate was over. Security personnel had to sneak Dr. Shorrosh out a side door in order to protect him. One man was stabbed in the uproar. The Muslims again claimed themselves the winner in another power encounter.

In my attempt to buy some tapes of these debates online from a Muslim supplier, I was not surprised to see that the tapes of the debates by Deedat carried a disclaimer saying that those buying the tapes should use them with care in a Western context. The buyer was cautioned by the following warning:

> A word of caution is in order, however. His [Deedat's] militancy and no holds barred approach to Christian apologists, heartening to many a staunch Muslim, also render many of his videos too acrid to be shown to Christians. Those apologetic of Muslims in Western countries would probably have a heart attack watching an Ahmed Deedat video. Nonetheless, there are many masterpieces among his videos too. His debate with Jimmy Swaggart shows Deedat at his best, most generous behavior, simply a gem of an item for Christians to view.[4]

On the contrary, the abuses were so blatant that anyone from the West would be turned off by what happened. Deedat has died, but

I suspect that others will arise and take his place in similar well-publicized meetings.

Local debate is also an effective Muslim strategy. A pastor first receives a letter or a telephone call and is asked to participate in a debate or dialogue. A neutral place is chosen such as a park or an open area. A time is set, and in some cases, an agenda. When the two groups come together, the meeting runs somewhat along the same form as the larger debates. Each has time to give their views with both sides answering. The Muslims will make certain that they have a much larger group than the Christians. They take such meetings seriously, something Christians seldom do. Again taunts and jeers come from the Islamic side. There is little or no attempt by their leaders to quiet them. They become louder and physically move in on the smaller number of Christians. At the end of the meeting, the Christians go home with their tail between their legs and the Muslims mark it up as another victory.

I have seen the local debates used in England and Germany, but as of now, this form does not appear to be used in the United States. I rather expect that this method will be used sometime in the future in North and South America.

There are numerous reports of a new strategy that is gaining favor in the United States with the Muslim community as they encounter Christianity. Muslims monitor newspapers to see when a church is having a special program on Islam. A small delegation from the local mosque will attend. If the program is pro-Islam, then they will remain silent and seek to have fellowship with those attending after the meeting. If the speaker seems to be negative toward their faith, they will either wait until the opportunity for questions or they will demand time to reply to the speaker. Those from the mosque will not address the speaker but rather turn (generally from the front row) and address the crowd. From the time they begin to speak, they will seek to lead and control the meeting, often with success. They have a twofold purpose: to blunt any criticism of Islam, and to use the opportunity to help bring new converts to Islam.

Naturally, some will say that Christians and others will also try to gain the edge in debates, dialogue, and open meetings. What is being done in the name of Islam does not seem out of bounds. The problem is that Westerners show goodwill as a general practice because of America's strong belief in freedom of speech, but they fail to understand that this methodology is not just a diplomatic exercise but an important part of Islam's overall strategy for world dominance. Unlike their Muslim counterparts, many Christians will not see such meetings as power encounters and will fail to take the engagement seriously.

Spiritual Power Encounter

I prefer to reserve the term "power encounter" for confrontation that takes place between two religions such as Islam and Christianity. Spiritual power encounters are inevitable since both see their position as being correct and both are convinced that God and truth are on their side.

Much of Islam is really "folk Islam," which puts a spiritual meaning on important life events such as birth, initiation rites, marriages, funerals, and other life-changing transitions. In their belief system they have many varieties of spirits, such as *garina*, *jinn*, *dews*, *als*, and *pari*; each has a definite influence on the lives of the people. Islam does not separate the spiritual from the political, economic, or academic aspects of life. Many Christians also have a strong belief in spiritual warfare wherein evil spiritual forces are at war with those from God.

These beliefs set the stage for spiritual power encounters that pit the Creator God against Satan. The worldview of both religions allows for such an encounter. Islam, which has not been nearly so influenced by secularism, has a much stronger belief in these unseen forces, and as a result, many of their power encounters are understood as a part of this spiritual warfare. They see Christians (many of whom have long ceased to have a high view of spiritual warfare) as being weak in any encounter where the power of God is expected to intercede. The problem for the West is that the Muslims are probably correct.

Worshipers in Mecca gather around the *Ka'aba* during the hajj.

A new mosque: The architecture of mosques
is now taking on more cultural elements.

A mosque built out of mud in Central Africa.

Mosques are used both for worship and for study of the Qur'an.

Mosques are often in the center of Muslim
cities and relate to all aspects of Muslim life.

Wherever they are, devout Muslims pray fives times a day.

Islamic architecture is very impressive
and often influences the culture of a people.

Women are often in the shadows in Islam. They are seldom
allowed to worship together with the men in a mosque.

Ritual foot washing is required before being allowed to worship in a mosque.

Students learning from the Qur'an in an Islamic school.

In many Islamic cities the market stands are right beside the mosque.

The following are three different forms of encounters between the two faiths:

1. Encounters between religious structures
2. Encounters over theology
3. Spiritual and conversion encounters

Dialogue and debates generally address the first two, but the third is the one that affects the common person. I have had the opportunity of meeting with over one hundred Muslims that have converted from Islam to Christianity. During my discussions, I have tried to understand the reasons for their conversion. I originally thought it would be because of an intellectual conviction of the truths of Christianity or that the person was attracted to the religious structures and traditions of our faith.

I was surprised to discover that in all but a few cases the person who converted had either (1) had a vision of Christ, (2) had a dream where Jesus appeared to them, or (3) heard the voice of God or an angel telling them what to do. At first some of them were reluctant to talk about it for fear that they would not be believed. However, assured that I accept such revelations, they shared their experiences. This could well be the area that the conflict between Islam and Christianity will be fought in the future.

One example of this spiritual encounter occurred in a Muslim section of Kenya. Ralph Bethea, an American Southern Baptist missionary, began work among Muslims in a large city. His love and compassion for the people were apparent to all, and in a short time he gained the friendship and respect of many Muslims in the city.

One day Bethea received a telephone call from the eighty-year-old leader of a mosque who asked if Bethea would "come to our mosque and bless our people in the name of Jesus." At the meeting, the *imam* asked the missionary to pray for his people, and after praying for some in the mosque, a distinguished looking man stood up and brought his eight-year-old daughter to the front, asking Bethea to pray that God would heal her withered legs. The father said that he had heard "there is such power in the name of Jesus."

After the prayer, the condition of the girl remained unchanged. The father thanked the missionary and returned to the back of the mosque. The girl struggled in her father's arms until he put her down and she stood on her legs for the first time in her life.[5]

After this power encounter, many Muslims believed and were converted to Christianity, not because of an intellectual change but because of a real spiritual power encounter.

Intimidation and Terrorism

The question must be asked: Is terrorism the result of a small number of abused persons using whatever means they can to combat what they see as the Great Satan threatening to destroy them, their culture, and their religion, or is it a part of a well-planned strategy?

I contend that when looking at the whole picture one sees that terrorism has its birth in the Qur'an and is being carried out as a part of the means that Islam is using to subject the world to its beliefs. Some of the leading theologians from within Islam seem to agree. Egyptian Dr. Abd Al-Azim Al-Mut'ani, an Al-Azhar University lecturer, wrote:

> Terrorism is a modern term. In Islam, the meaning of terrorism is intimidation, not all intimidation is forbidden by religious law. . . . In the modern age, when [different] kinds of oppression and persecution emerged, some ethnic groups in almost every society were stripped of their rights. When they insisted on their rights, and [when] the despotic regimes rejected them—the oppressed and persecuted found no way to express themselves but by means of [various] kinds of rebellion.[6]

It should be noted that Al-Azhar, associated with Al-Azhar Mosque in Cairo, is considered by most to be the top theological school in all of Islam. Al-Mut'ani continued, "The most recent example of the so-called terrorism are the recent attacks against America. Whatever the interpretations may be, no one disagrees that America is the one who killed and was killed. It is America that killed itself with its distorted policy."[7]

Another man, Dr. Abd Al-Sabour Shahin, from Cairo University, discussed the differences between terrorism and *jihad*:

> The truth is that the way Islam uses the word "terrorism" is honorable, as Allah said: "Make ready for them whatever you can of armed strength and of mounted pickets at the frontier, whereby you may daunt the enemy of Allah and your enemy." The terrorism mentioned in this verse refers to intimidation or threat, not necessarily to damage.[8]

It is clear that both of these scholars see terrorism as a means to intimidate the West.

Webster's New English Dictionary defines *intimidation* as follows:

> (1) To make afraid; to make timid; daunt. (2) To force or deter with threats of violence; cow.[9]

President George W. Bush declared war on terrorism. He continually stated that we are not at war with Islam—but those who really know the Islamic world add, "But Islam is at war with the West." The success of the ongoing war on terrorism is debatable, and one's opinion is directly related to one's political philosophy. Yes, many terrorist cells have been eliminated or badly damaged, but the terrorists have gained a gigantic victory through intimidation. It is no longer possible for an American to go to a football game or fly on a commercial airliner without acknowledging the threat of terrorism. Even the structure of the government changed, with the creation of a Department of Homeland Security to combat terrorism. Intimidation is working very well.

When anyone in the West tries to defame or critique Islam, they unleash tremendous forces that are intended to intimidate. When the British author Salman Rushdie wrote a book that included passages making fun of the prophet Muhammad, Muslims in England took a copy of the book, put it on a stake, and set it on fire. The media covered the story, and soon the Ayatollah Khomeini called for the author to be executed. He did not stop there but added "all those involved in its publication who were aware of its content."

Rushdie was immediately taken into hiding as the debate grew about the condemnation of a Western author using his freedom of speech. While the debate continued, "Translators of *The Satanic Verses* were stabbed and seriously injured in Norway and Italy and, in Japan, murdered. In Turkey, another translator escaped when a fire set in his hotel failed to kill him, but 37 others died in the blaze."[10] Khomeini's supporters succeeded in showing the world that those who would speak out against Islam would bear the consequences.

After the defeat of Saddam Hussein, many began looking forward to a new democratic Iraq, but the Christian church in that country remained under great pressure. In the northern city of Mosul, known now as a *Wahabi* stronghold, local Christians have reported growing harassment of their clergy and church communities. In 2003, "some 15 Christians were wounded . . . when Islamist zealots stoned them coming out of church. . . . Bishops and leading Christian families in the northern city have received letters telling them to convert to Islam, sometimes with accompanying threats, other times offering them cash rewards."[11] By 2008, "hundreds of Christians [were] fleeing Mosul after a string of killings. . . . Flyers had appeared on the streets in Mosul threatening Christians and telling them to leave the city."[12]

Another example concerned the 2002 Miss World Pageant. The organizers wanted to have this widely accepted program located in one of the developing countries and chose to hold it in Muslim-controlled northern Nigeria. A fashion writer from the area, Isioma Daniel, wrote that she felt Muhammad would support such a pageant. Daniel's article was seen as insulting to the prophet Muhammad, and the Information Commissioner of Zamfara, Umar Dangaladima Magaji, endorsed a *fatwa* calling for the Christian woman's death.

The article led to widespread rioting that resulted in more than 215 deaths and the burning of Christian churches. Agence France-Presse reported that Zamfara's deputy governor, Mamuda Aliyu Shinkafi, said in a speech to religious leaders later broadcast on state radio, "Like Salman Rushdie, the blood of Isioma Daniel can be shed."[13]

Intimidation and Christian Missions

Muslims see that many of their own are being influenced to become more tolerant of Christianity or even to convert to that faith. There are few missionaries who have labored for more than ten years in Muslim countries who have not had to attend the funeral of one of their converts or have been involved in hiding a convert so as to protect them from death. The intimidation at this level is certainly great, but there are other methods that they use as well.

Once when I was in Morocco, I was shown a popular magazine displaying photos of many of my friends who were working in North Africa. Their names and, in some cases, their addresses were also given. I was told that the article did not threaten the workers but warned all Muslims to be aware of their devious methods. One colleague from another Muslim country was home on furlough when a magazine from his country did the same thing. This time there were threats against the safety of the missionary and his family.

On May 8, 2003, it was reported that a Jordanian convert to Christianity had been killed by a bomb planted outside the home of a missionary couple in Tripoli, Lebanon. Dutch missionary Gerrit Griffioen realized that there was an intruder in his garden. He called Jamil Ahmad al-Rifai, his next-door neighbor, to come help. They found a two-kilogram bomb in the garden. While Griffioen gave chase, al-Rifai secured the family and then returned to the garden. The bomb detonated when al-Rifai was apparently trying to either diffuse or move it. The blast made the body almost unidentifiable. Griffioen is a widely known and well-respected Christian leader. He and his family have lived in Lebanon for over twenty years.[14]

These intimidation tactics have forced many Western missionary societies to take on a new philosophy of missions. They are going underground. They no longer seek visas using the word *missionary* but rather now have business platforms to gain visas so as to live in their target country. This approach has been somewhat successful in allowing workers to stay in the country, but it has also led to the church becoming silent. The missionaries do all they can to avoid being known as Christians or Christian workers. Thus, they and those they work with have been intimidated into silence.

I spoke with a young Arab man concerning this new method. At one time he had been one of the leaders in the Muslim Brotherhood but had since converted to Christianity. He spent time in jail and even feared for his life because some accused him of apostasy. He told me that the mission societies were very naive in following these practices. First, he said that missionaries did not appreciate the efficiency of the secret services of the countries where they were serving. He said that the governments were well aware of all that was going on with these Westerners. Second, he said that the authorities were happy that they had taken this approach since it had quieted them to the place that the missionaries were no longer a threat to Islam. They could stay if they did nothing. This is another example of the success of intimidation.

As previously stated, physical presence takes on great significance in Islam. This results in every effort to stop the construction of new church buildings or even the use of existing buildings to reach or help Muslims in any way.

I was in a large German city where several members of an evangelical church desired to minister to the large Muslim community nearby. After several months about ten citizens from a predominately Muslim country were coming to a Bible study in a local Baptist church. After they had been meeting for several months, I received a call from the leader of the Baptist church. He informed me that he had received a letter saying that the church building would be burned down if the meetings did not cease at once. The leader told me that they had too much invested in the building so they had no choice but to forbid this group to use the building.

Intimidation was once again successful.

Intimidation and Persecution

Intimidation uses the threat of violence to create fear of what will happen. With persecution, the threat is finalized. Islam likes to picture itself as a persecuted religion. An overview of the history of the Muslim-Christian encounter, however, reveals the reality that it is much more likely that the Christian will be persecuted at the hands of the Muslim.

In his monumental work, *The World Christian Encyclopedia*, David Barrett cites the estimated number of Christian martyrs down through the ages. The numbers are staggering. Barrett reported that from A.D. 33 to A.D. 2000 approximately 69,420,000 men, women, and children were killed because they were Christians. Of that total number, over nine million were martyred by Muslims. Some of the worst situations of mass martyrdom in recent history were Idi Amin's Uganda massacres in 1971, the Sudan holocaust from 1963 to present, and the Rwanda genocide of 1994.[15] One report estimated that approximately 176,000 Christians were martyred from mid 2008 to mid 2009. And that number was expected to rise in ensuing years.[16]

Persecution of Christians by Muslims continues to go unabated. Those suffering the most are the citizens of Muslim countries, Christians who want to live their lives peacefully in their native lands. The most intense persecution of Christians occurs in Egypt, Iran, Afghanistan, and Sudan. In these places, persecution and intimidation are intertwined in such a way that it is often difficult to distinguish between them. Some countries have no Christians left to persecute.

Persecution can be defined as having four levels:

- **Level One:** Persecution (or intimidation) that includes threats that lead to social disenfranchisement of the victim
- **Level Two:** Persecution that leads to material loss and limited possibilities for social advancement
- **Level Three:** Persecution that leads to isolation and separation from family, friends, and culture (prison, for example)
- **Level Four:** Persecution that leads to death and physical injury

There is no level three or four persecution in the West. This is true even among those from Muslim countries living in the West because there are laws against such actions. However, oftentimes the threats of death and injury have been so complete that the actual deed has not been necessary. For example, while a Muslim family will seldom kill a daughter who converts to Christianity, the fear of the possibility will often lead to the desired result of keeping her from following Christ.

Levels one and two are practiced on a regular basis both in Muslim countries and among Muslims in the West. These levels are not only much more prevalent but possibly more effective. In the Islamic culture, the extended family is a support system, providing jobs, training, housing, food, insurance, and so on. When a person disobeys and converts away from Islam, the isolation and threats begin immediately. A person who has grown up with the security of the family network begins to look to the church for such help but usually finds little. In Western society we look to the government to supply those needs. Thus, the new convert is left without a real support foundation. At a high-level conference on Middle East evangelism, one authority stated that approximately 80 percent of all converted Muslims return to Islam, not because of theological considerations but because of cultural needs.

The second level of persecution may be less visible, but it could be considered the most insidious. For those living in Muslim countries, becoming a Christian or blaspheming Islam generally means that the person is condemning himself to a life on the lowest social level. This makes it difficult or impossible to provide for their family. This may play out in various ways:

- A burned-out business
- Children being denied entrance into the better schools
- The unavailability of government-sponsored housing
- Inability to gain an exit or reentry visa
- Transcripts not allowed to be sent outside of the country
- Lack of promotion on the job

In one Muslim country, I met with an anonymous national Christian who had just been released from prison. He had a well-respected position at the main airport. A coworker became jealous of him and reported him as a Christian. In this country they take pride in saying that there are no citizens of their country who are Christians, thus, to punish him would go against this belief. They questioned him and asked if he kept Ramadan the last time. Since he was a Christian, he answered truthfully that he did not. The police then sent him to jail for six months for failure to keep Ramadan. While he was in prison, his family began to suffer financially because they had no money coming in and socially because of the stigma of having a father in prison.

After four months he was very discouraged, but while walking in the prison yard one day, he saw a little section of a newspaper. It was printed in English, and he was one of the few prisoners who knew English. The newspaper came from England, and the small piece he found had a "Today's Devotion" section in it. As he read the Bible verse, he was assured that God had not forgotten him. The Scripture was Romans 8:38–39: "For I am convinced that neither death nor life, neither angels nor demons, neither the present nor the future, nor any powers, neither height nor depth, nor anything else in all creation, will be able to separate us from the love of God that is in Christ Jesus our Lord."

Several days later the man learned that some Christians had heard about his plight and had begun to help the family. After he was released, his director felt that he had been unfairly punished and gave him his pay for the six months and even promoted him.[17] While persecution is an important part of the Islamic strategy, by the grace of God many are able to stand up under the pressures that are brought to bear.

CONCLUSION

The struggle continues between the world's two largest religions. Even if it is an unpleasant thought, it is a fact that power encounters exist between the two into the twenty-first century. The religion promoting such encounters is Islam, but the church is strong and able to defend itself. The battle will continue and even intensify as a part of the present and coming clash of civilizations.

chapter **nine**

Muhammad, the Message, and the Mass Media

Distortions and Manipulation

After the hijacked passenger jets slammed into the World Trade Center and the Pentagon, the authorities tried to determine who was responsible. In a short time it became apparent that radical Islamists associated with Osama bin Laden were behind the planning and execution of these disastrous events. Many Muslims living in America were braced for the expected backlash. To be sure, there were more than one thousand reported acts of violence against Muslims and mosques in the United States, but the media broadly condemned these isolated events, and Americans were told not to judge a world religion on the basis of the actions of just a few radicals.

Most observers expected this to be a black mark against the Islamic faith—one from which it would be difficult to recover. On the contrary, Islam made a giant leap forward. What was not known was that the Islamic strategists had been working for several years in the area of public relations.

Islam did not suffer in America during this period; it actually experienced growth in the six-month time frame after the events of September 11. Mosques all over the United States and Europe were ready with programs to take the bad news and use it to their advantage. In most mosques there were open houses where the public was invited to come and to learn about the "real Islam." *Imam*s were invited to take part in ecumenical worship services—something that had been limited prior to 9/11.

Interest was greatly increased and Americans asked, "Who are these Muslims?" Those in the mosques then said, "Come and visit us and we will show you the true Islam." Those who came were told that Islam was a religion of peace, love, and forgiveness and that there were few real terrorists in their faith. They did such a convincing job that some converted and others became vocal supporters of tolerance for Islam in their communities.

Already during the middle of the twentieth century, Muslim strategists realized that they needed to do a better job of public relations in the West. They began to put into place a strategy designed to change the image of Islam. In the beginning they did not have the experience or the resources to accomplish their goals, but they did lay the foundation for what was later to become an efficient program of lifting the image of their faith.

According to Daniel Pipes, author of the article "How Dare You Defame Islam," the change in Islamic fortunes actually began with the Salman Rushdie affair in January 1989. The Ayatollah Khomeini, the revolutionary ruler of Iran, called upon "all zealous Muslims quickly to execute" not just Salman Rushdie as the author of *The Satanic Verses* but "all those involved in its publication and who were aware of its contents."[1] After Khomeini's pronouncement, the British press splashed the affair in the headlines of their papers. Television made it a major story and everyone was talking about the threat. The story was detrimental to Islam since it portrayed Muslims as having values that are completely different from those in the West.

However, it was this event that seemed to mark the change in both tactics and efficiency of the public relations effort by Muslims. Pipes goes on to state: "During the decade since 1989, many efforts have been undertaken by the forces of Islamism—otherwise known as Muslim fundamentalism—to silence critics. Ranging from outright violence to more sophisticated but no less effective techniques, they have produced impressive results."[2] Between 1989 and 2001 there was a change in reporting of events that involved the Islamic religion. Not only did the press begin to change and write more positive articles about Islam, but they also became quite negative to anyone who went against the political correctness of supporting Islam. One independent journalist living in London, Gwynne Dyer, said in satirical words:

> Rule One: When covering terrorist attacks, do not discuss the political context of the attacks or the terrorists' motives and strategy. . . . Rule Two: All terrorists' actions are part of the same problem. . . . Rule Three: All terrorists are Islamic fanatics. . . . Most of the Western media now know [these rules] by heart.[3]

The point of Dyer's dripping sarcasm is that he felt the Western media did not treat terrorism or Islam fairly. His editorial reads as if it was written by an indignant Muslim journalist expounding the prejudices of Western media against what is, after all, a religion of peace.

ISLAM AND THE MEDIA

Islam is no longer ready to sit back and allow the Western media elite to cover world events unchallenged. Instead, they are taking the initiative in bringing the news to a global audience. Of course, their coverage is biased, but they say that the Western media is also biased—so what's the difference? Al-Jazeera, the Arabic television and press agency known worldwide for upstaging the illustrious CNN with its coverage of the American war in Afghanistan and who suspiciously had exclusive access to Osama bin Laden, has launched an English language TV channel in Europe and is increasing its Washington, D.C., bureau from six to twenty-four staff members. The Western media scene is not just open; it is actively seeking Muslim input.

CNN, not to be outdone in the Muslim world, with its large audience has launched CNN-Arabic in an attempt to reach the vast Muslim television audience worldwide. Following the September 11 events, the British Foreign Office established an Islamic Media Unit to "focus on the Arab media to which it reaches out through personal interaction for an exchange of views."

The Islamic world is now focusing more firmly on spreading Islam through the use of mass media. Dr. Roushdy Shahata, a professor at Halawan University in Egypt, said, "The journalists must always have a good Islamic bias."[4] Being a religious journalist, he can write his subjects from the Islamic point of view. He asserts that the goal of the Islamic media is to broadcast to the entire world.

The main organization that is promoting a better use of the media is the Muslim World League. It has an alliance with several large media organizations. In 2003, they held a conference in Jeddah, Saudi Arabia, concerning ecumenical media. Dr. Abdullah Al-Turki, secretary general of the Muslim World League, emphasized once again the importance of the mass media in the spread of Islam. They made a plan of cooperation between them in order to proclaim Islam and display it in a better light. Al-Turki also insisted that all the mass media cooperate with the *Da'wah* organizations.[5]

There appear to be several components in their unprecedented attempt to communicate their message to the West. These components are:

"We are not . . ."

This is an attempt to change the negative stereotypes of Muslims in the Western world by the emerging Muslim media leaders. For a century the Arab has been seen as a rather dim-witted fellow living in an inhospitable part of the world. When there was the need of comedy relief for a film, the directors could generally do well by inserting an Arab into the script. With the emergence of "political correctness," all minorities benefited from the new unwritten rules concerning stereotypes.

For the Arabs, the use of petrodollars, along with the efforts of some very capable men, gave a new impetus toward escalating this change. Several organizations were formed that had as a part of their purpose statement the influencing of the media. One such organization is the Council on American-Islamic Relations (CAIR), a Washington-based institution founded in 1994. Daniel Pipes has written: "CAIR presents itself to the world as a standard-issue civil-rights organization whose mission is to 'promote interest and understanding among the general public with regard to Islam and Muslims in North America and conduct educational services.'"[6]

CAIR has proven to be a very active organization that has taken part in defending Islam, especially in the media. In its short history it has been involved in various means to intimidate news organizations that portray Islam in an unacceptable light. Among their targets have been writers such as Steven Emerson, Daniel Pipes, and a host of others who dare to take issue with Islam today. One example occurred when President George W. Bush nominated Islamic scholar Daniel Pipes to the board of directors of the United States Institute of Peace.

Charles Krauthammer of the *Washington Post* wrote, "This [nomination] has resulted in a nasty eruption of McCarthyism. Pipes's nomination has been greeted by charges of Islamophobia, bigotry and extremism."[7] Among organizations that have heard from CAIR or felt their criticism are the *National Post, New Republic, Los Angeles Times, Dallas Morning News, Weekly Reader's Current Events* (a children's magazine), and many others too numerous to name.[8] In some cases CAIR will picket the offices of the targeted organization or organize a letter writing campaign. In some undocumented instances, there have been threats addressed to the personnel in the organizations and the facilities where they are located. Whenever there is a terrorist attack or a Muslim is on trial, the news media will have a representative from CAIR or one of the other Muslim organizations defining their faith.

The English-language paper *Gulf News* reported on the Islamic Affairs Department of the government of Dubai—a member of the

United Arab Emirates. The goal of this department, according to its manager, is "to project real Islamic teachings and correct faulty notions. . . . Many non-Muslims and even Muslims maintain devious impressions about the religion. Thus, our task is to correct these faulty understandings."[9] An entire article in the *Washington Post* was devoted to Muslims' efforts to shake off negative stereotypes, chronicling the lives of three American Muslims who work for the U.S. government. All said their jobs help break down stereotypes about Muslims.[10]

The movies and television have proven to be a problem for Islam. In the past, several movie producers have suggested the making of a movie on the life of Muhammad. There was fierce opposition to this because Muslims believe that it is a sin to make an image of their leader. One producer decided to make the movie without an actor playing Muhammad but rather the space the actor would normally occupy would be left free. This also did not meet the approval of the Muslim community.

A few years ago another attempt was made to chronicle the life of Muhammad, "presenting the story of the seventh-century Islamic prophet to an American audience largely unfamiliar with the religion he founded."[11] They decided to go ahead and not show the face of the prophet. They had the film about two-thirds finished when the events of September 11, 2001, took place. They were about to end the project when it was suggested that they make it into a two-hour documentary titled *Muhammad: Legacy of a Prophet.* The documentary told the story of Muhammad together with interviews with scholars and modern-day U.S. Muslims.

The Public Broadcasting Service (PBS) first presented it on December 18, 2002, right before a Christmas show. Rather than just being a film about the prophet, it became a tool for Muslim propaganda. It received raves from the secular press but was considered by many to be a film seeking to win converts to Islam. It is of interest to note that "the film's largest tranche of funding [for PBS] comes from the Corporation for Public Broadcasting, a private, nonprofit corporation created by Congress that in fiscal 2002 received $350 million in taxpayers' funds."[12] The same network aired another documentary

in 1998 on the life of Jesus where the main emphasis was from critical scholars who questioned much of the historicity of Jesus. Islamic
leaders have learned that they need not be afraid of films today but
rather can use them to their advantage.

Muslim strategists did have a setback in the early 1990s when the
film *Not Without My Daughter* was produced. It chronicled the life
of an American woman whose daughter was taken back to Iran, the
homeland of the girl's father. She was not allowed to leave the country; she basically became a slave in a Muslim context where women
have little or no rights. She finally did escape over the mountains
into Turkey. One author notes: "The 1991 film . . . set Muslims back
about ten years in the effort to improve their public image."[13]

Islam has been very successful in the last ten years in redefining
who they are and who they are not. But before the Muslim community can communicate positively to its skeptical Western audience, it must first convince them that Islam is not all bad, and that
the Islamic faith is not the same as Palestinian suicide bombers and
women abusers.

It is amazing to see how big a change there has been in a little over
ten years on how Americans view Islam and Muslims. This was no
accident but rather the result of a well-planned strategy that only
now is really becoming effective. I doubt that there will be many articles, TV productions, movies, or magazine statements that stand
out as negative toward Islam. This is definitely not the case in respect
to Christians and the church.

"We are . . ."

The first element of the Muslim media message, dispelling
negative views of Muslims, often works in partnership with the
second element—projecting positive views of Muslims. As much as
possible, the desire is to show that Muslims, particularly American
Muslims, are decent, hardworking, loving, kind people. In short,
American Muslims are just as American (or just as Western) as any
other ethnic group in the great American melting pot.

This, in fact, was the clear message of a series of public service announcements produced by the Islamic Media Foundation and aired to more than two million viewers across America in November 2002. The series, titled *Your American Muslim Neighbors,* showed American Muslim families in quintessential American activities: attending Little League games, visiting Mount Rushmore, going to worship together (albeit to a mosque), and so on. The images were altogether wholesome, positive, patriotic, and serene.

Shortly after 9/11, the Islamic Media Foundation ran a series of public announcements in keeping with the group's objectives of "letting others know our contributions to the well-being of this society."[14] Adds the *Muslim News,* "Muslim communities across America are on a PR mission to explain what their religion is all about. From political fund-raisers and food drives to open houses at mosques."[15] Once again it is clear to see that their message is that Muslims, far from being bomb-bearing fanatics, are in fact paragons of charity to their American neighbors.

"We believe . . ."

With their atmosphere of multiculturalism, American schools are an excellent place to bring in Islamic propaganda. At the same time that Christians are fighting the ACLU to obtain certain basic rights in the schools, Muslims seem to have an open door to come in and proselytize. As mentioned previously, one textbook used in California schools presented Islam in a very favorable light and suggested that the students might want to dress up like Muslims and experience such activities as the food they eat and how they pray. The students often were asked to take Muslim names and role-play being a follower of Muhammad. If this were done with a Christian context, lawsuits citing separation of church and state would surely follow.

Recently one of the principals of a California school gave me a letter that was addressed to all principals and district superintendents. It was from the Islamic Speakers Bureau. In the letter there were announcements suggesting that the teachers have the students turn on the above mentioned TV film *Muhammad: Legacy of a Prophet* as well as other TV programs showing in their area. They also offered "An Arts and Craft Kit for Presenting Ramadan and Eid During the Winter Holiday Season." In the letter were suggestions that all teachers and administrators attend a staff development training seminar titled "Staff Development Training for Educators and Administrators: Incorporating Islamic Cultural Studies in the Curriculum and Interacting with Muslim Students." They offered to send speakers to the schools to teach classroom courses for grades seven to twelve titled "Orientation on Islam and the Muslim World in the Context of World History and Social Science." Another course for the tenth to twelfth graders was called "Women in Islam." I have included a copy of the letters that made these free offers in appendix B. I was informed that those sending the letters received many requests for speakers.

Five government-employed Muslims interviewed by the *Washington Post* said clearly that they each felt obliged to reach out to non-Muslims and educate people about Islam, especially at the start of Ramadan. Similar to the Christian observation of Christmas or Easter in terms of its universal practice and high importance to the faith's followers, Ramadan is a frequent starting point for Muslims educating non-Muslims about their faith.

WBAY TV, an ABC-affiliated station in the Green Bay, Wisconsin, area, included a brief explanation of Ramadan in a 2002 broadcast about the local Muslim community:

> Muslims from around the Fox Valley gathered to celebrate the beginning of Ramadan. Ramadan will last for one month. It requires Muslims to fast from sunrise to sunset for the next month and to refrain from several vices listed in the Qur'an. . . . Ramadan is time for prayer and fasting. It's also a chance to show the world what Islam is all about.[16]

The *Muslim News* reports: "Many of the nation's approximately 7 million Muslims will use the month of fasting and spiritual renewal . . .

to continue their quest to make inroads into the mainstream."[17] Muslims are making every effort to change the way Americans view Islam.

It's not just during Ramadan that the push for education takes place. The online version of the Saudi Arabian English daily, *Arab News,* has a hyperlink to a long feature on the life of the prophet Muhammad, for the benefit of its English readers who may wish to know more about the Muslim faith. It is likely that there are few, if any, Arab-language newspapers in the West that would include a link to a feature of any length of the Christian view on Jesus Christ.

Following September 11, numerous books by various "experts" appeared on the market purporting to educate their readers on Islam. The *Christian Science Monitor* reviewed one of these, *The Heart of Islam.* Jane Lampman wrote: "In 'The Heart of Islam', a renowned Muslim scholar offers to people 'interested in authentic Islam and its relation to the West' an introduction into the inner dimension of Islamic teachings, as well as its external expressions in law, history, art, and community."[18] Glowing reviews such as this further the educational thrust of the Muslim identity through use of media. In short, the message is clear: "Let us tell you what we really believe." They do, however, report only the side that the Westerners want to hear.

"Come and see . . ."

As Muslims correct and improve their image and educate Westerners about their faith, their next step is to begin to convert others to the faith. M. Yusuf Mohamed, an attorney in the U.S. Labor Department, says there is "a great opportunity forced on us by 9/11. A lot of people have become curious about Islam and want to know more."[19] Anwar Hansan, founder and president of the Maryland-based Howard County Muslim Council, says, "We're trying to reach out to the community now, to remove the fear and ultimately make America a better place."[20]

While this kind of encouragement for outreach may take place Friday after Friday in mosques around the United States, it means little to the wider public until it is published in mainstream media.

What is significant is the way local Muslim leaders are now being interviewed, quoted, and highlighted in print, radio, and television reports. Through Muslim use of media, readers, listeners, and viewers who were already curious about Islam are more exposed to this exotic faith and could become prime candidates for future conversion. One article explained that Imam Mohamad Bashar Arafat of Baltimore "often preaches to fellow Muslims of their responsibility to reach out to other faiths." Arafat tells the worshipers, "It is your duty as a Muslim living in this country, which celebrates democracy, which celebrates religious freedom, to show the beauty and the true meaning of Islam. . . . I think it is the duty of every mosque in America to hold dinners, to hold banquets and invite people."[21]

"Let us tell you . . ."

Overarching each of these other components of the Muslim message is the desire to have an active voice in the mainstream media, that is, to be heard loud and clear in every discussion of issues that relate to faith and in particular to the Islamic world. This is the strategy behind much of the work of the Islamic Media Foundation (IMF), which provides training and resources to help local Muslim leaders become resource people for the mainstream media. The IMF website home page encourages:

> Let's all take advantage of the unique opportunity we have in America, using the broadcast media and the Internet to fulfill our duty of inviting others, to better understand Islam and spread righteousness. First and foremost, we need your du'aa, or supplication, that Allah bless this effort and give it success.
>
> Give from your wealth, knowing that Allah will multiply it for you. And give from your time and advice to make this work fruitful.
>
> May Allah bless us all and reward us with plenty, and give us the strength and ability to spread His word, and share His guidance with all mankind, as it was meant to be.[22]

From its beginnings as a grassroots structure consisting of Muslims interested in media activism, IMF produced *On Sight*, a weekly news magazine program to be used by communities on their local television station. *On Sight* reports on events and issues from a Muslim perspective. IMF has now established the Islamic Broadcasting Network.

Muslim communities around the world are catching this wave. The *Muslim News* says of itself:

- The only independent monthly Muslim newspaper in the UK . . . neither backed by any country nor by any organization or party.
- Subscriptions, advertising and British Muslim businessmen finance The Muslim News.
- The Muslim News reports on what the non-Muslim media does not report.[23]

Another news agency reported that in the United States there was a Muslim television network in the making. Two Arab-Americans, Mo Hassan and Omar Amanat, plan to develop the "first nationwide English-language Muslim television in the United States by the summer of 2004." The founders said that they "hope to help the Muslim community gain acceptance and increased understanding through the forum of media, as Telemundo and Black Entertainment Television have for Hispanics and blacks living in America."[24]

Many other newly created Muslim media groups are being organized in order to propagate the faith. The most successful of the new attempts for Islamic entrance into the world of media was the Arab news network Al-Jezeera, which was launched in 1996 with funding from the government of Qatar. An estimated 150,000 viewers see the channel in the United States.[25]

During the 2003 Iraq war, daily updates about the war were carried around the world. Al-Jazeera was active in its coverage. While the Western media was covering the advance and success of the coalition forces, Al-Jazeera was covering problems and the killing of civilians caused by the troops. Anyone watching the reports from the two perspectives would swear that they were covering two different wars. Al-Jazeera, which was watched by the majority of the citizens of Middle Eastern countries, was able to sway sympathies away from the West. They proved their worth in one short war by replacing CNN as the main news agency watched by Muslims.

There is also the potential that Islamic interests will soon be influencing the mainstream media more. *Newsweek* correspondent Michael Isikoff interviewed Prince Al-Walid bin Talal, the multibillionaire investor who made headlines when he offered $10 million for the 9/11 victims and was turned down by Mayor Rudy Giuliani. During the interview, the prince complained about how the Zionists had "infiltrated" every part of the U.S. government. What infuriated him most was the "Jewish lobby's power over the media."[26]

As Isikoff continued, he noticed on the prince's desk the emblems of many U.S. corporations, portions of which are owned by the prince: AOL Time Warner (his stake: $900 million), NewsCorp ($1 billion), and Disney Corp. ($50 million), not to mention his $10 billion stake in banking giant Citigroup. Isikoff suggested, "But still . . . Surely, prince, given your holdings, you've got a little influence with the American media yourself." "Oh, yes, he told me; he talks to the top executives of these firms all the time. 'I try to tell them not to be biased,' he said."[27]

INFLUENCE THROUGH ECONOMICS

Today's global economic system is both centralized and yet greatly diffused at the same time. Gigantic multinational corporations control an ever-increasing share of wealth and influence but are susceptible to boycotts organized by dissatisfied consumers. In most cases boycotts, some of which are publicized, have little or no effect on the large corporations due in part to their size. If, however, a significant homogenous group does seek to bring pressure, it must be heard.

In the 1970s, 1980s, and even up through today, there have been attempts to have Muslims boycott brands that are sold in Israel. Their purpose was to deny Israel the more commonly used products of the contemporary world. Varying degrees of success were achieved. Some companies' products (soft drinks being one) had to make a decision whether to sell to Israel or to the surrounding Arab states. Those boycotts would ebb and flow depending on a number of issues and were not always related to politics. Businessmen generally found a way around the boycotts so that their own interests were satisfied.

During and after the second Gulf War, businesses and even states were jockeying for use of the world situation for their own benefit. The American public was called upon to order "freedom fries" instead of French fries and to stop buying French perfume, French wine, and French automobiles as a way to show displeasure with France's lack of support for the American position. Citizens in France did much the same by boycotting American goods and even attacking a few American businesses such as McDonald's. One cause of this economic battle has been the growing influence of Islam in France.

The war caused a variety of commercial protests against America. Some of the reported protests include:

- Almost one out of four people in the Asian-Pacific region said they have avoided purchasing American brands. . . .
- German bicycle maker Reise und Mueller has canceled all business deals with American suppliers. . . .
- The Qibla-Cola company, a soft drink maker based in Great Britain that markets to the Muslim community, called for a boycott . . . of "U.S. global brands."
- Consumers in Europe and the Middle East have snapped up 4.5 million bottles of Mecca-Cola, an anti-American soft drink launched in October [2002]. Mecca-Cola—with the motto that translates as "Don't drink stupidly, drink responsibly"—has orders for fourteen million more bottles. The cola is also sold in Middle Eastern neighborhoods and in the USA in Detroit and soon in New Jersey.[28]

The same article reported that "Mecca-Cola founder Tawfik Mathlouthi also plans to open Halal Fried Chicken restaurants, to be called HFC, a jab at the KFC chain. His aim: 'People will stop eating and drinking American goods and using American goods,' he says. 'And that will increase the social problems in the United States and increase joblessness, and Americans will awake from their long sleep and maybe ask the U.S. government to respond.'"[29]

Muslims will continue to attempt to leverage their increasing purchasing power, both to increase their own wealth and, in many cases, to damage American culture.

INFLUENCE THROUGH POLITICS

All minorities in America now feel that even with their small percentage of the total population they can influence public opinion through politics. Recently the announcement was made that the largest minority group in America are the Hispanics, now approximately 13 percent of the population. If the statistics put out by the Muslims, who claim they now have seven million in the United States, are correct, then they would have about 2.8 percent of the population. It should be noted, however, that the real figures are approximately one-half of that estimated by the Muslims. Because of the parity between Democrats and Republicans, this small amount can make a large difference. The more they grow, the more political power they can wield. Many Muslims have claimed that they put George W. Bush into the presidency because they overwhelmingly voted for him in Florida.

Fundamentalists within Islam have learned very well how to use democracy to their own end. The minority Muslim population of Malawi, South Africa, was able to win the election mainly through investing tremendous amounts of funds into the electoral process. In both Algeria and Turkey, fundamentalists have come close to succeeding. In other countries, Islamic candidates have been thwarted not because they did not have the votes but because of fear of what would happen if they did take over the government politically.

Islamic involvement in the political process is much more advanced in Europe than in the United States. In England there is now a shadow government that has been created by the Muslims to act on their own issues but also to be prepared if the opportunity ever comes to take over the government. In Belgium, an Islamic delegation arrived in the country to hold a meeting with the government, and in effect the whole of Europe since Brussels is fondly called the heart of Europe. Dr. Al-Turki of the Muslim World League said, "The European parliaments are a very good way to reach within the countries." He also noted that there are many Muslims in the Belgium parliament who are making good progress in the proclamation of Islam. Because of the good relationship between the Muslims in the Belgium government and the country, the Muslim World League was able to do the following on their trip:

1. They received permission to have a prayer room in the Brussels airport.
2. They received permission to build a new Islamic cemetery.
3. They got some laws changed so that the Muslims can practice their religious commitments.[30]

In Holland there are seven Islamic parliamentarians, many of them members of Dutch political parties. Dr. Marzouk, the president of the Islamic University in Holland, said, "The Muslims in this country must be ready to govern Holland because of the increasing numbers of Muslims and the decreasing numbers of the original people of Holland."[31]

A successful part of their mega-plan is to bring both educators and politicians to the Islamic faith. Here are some examples of their successes.

1. Alexander Kronemer is involved with American foreign affairs. He has a master's degree in comparative religions from Harvard University. He has also worked in the Middle East. He married an American Muslim woman and became a Muslim himself. He was the producer of the recently released film on the life of Muhammad.

2. Dr. Kasper Ibrahim Shahin became a Muslim on June 10, 2002. He is a scientist, economist, and the professor of technology at a state institution in the United States. He is also the president of this institution and is very well known by former presidents George H. W. Bush and Ronald Reagan. He became a Muslim as a result of the influence of his Islamic friends. It was stated that "he too wants to bring Islam to other scientists and prominent people in America by the use of mass media, but first he wants to bring his family into Islam."

3. Dr. Murad Hofmann, the former German ambassador to Algeria, "found Islam as the logical religion and one that was very close to the human mind. He found that Christianity is a faded religion. He is using all of his influence to spread Islam in Germany and around the Globe."

4. Jonathan Birt, the son of a former director-general of the BBC became a Muslim and married a Muslim woman and changed his name to Yahya. It was reported that his goal is to spread Islam in the United Kingdom and help his family embrace Islam.[32]

These are just a few of the names of prominent converts as reported in the *Middle East Newspaper.* Islam sees the need to concentrate on the main policy makers. One of the many rumors surrounding the death of Princess Diana was that she was killed by the secret service because she was considering marrying a Muslim. The rumor was probably false, but concern about the possibility of Muslim royalty was real.

CONCLUSION

In the seventh century, Muhammad learned much from the Christians and Jesus concerning the belief in one God. So now Islam is learning much from them again, but this time in the realm of public relations. Radio, television, the Internet, and print media are now full of the battle for the minds and souls of the present generation.

Encouraged by recent successes and well financed by oil dollars, Islam has come out of the dark ages.

To say Islam is close to surpassing the West in public relations would be a gross overstatement. But it is also foolish and incorrect to dismiss their efforts in this arena. Only time will determine if their efforts will be successful enough to make great gains in influencing the thinking of the average Westerner.

chapter ten

What in the World Is Allah Doing?

An Overview of the Present-Day Expansion of Islam

One friend from Europe, who was a practicing Muslim, spoke with me after making the *hajj* into Mecca. He told me that there was a large sign on the road just outside the Holy City that stated, "Islam now has over One Billion Adherents." Islam is without question the largest non-Christian religion in the world. The exact numbers are hard to come by, but one highly respected demographer, Patrick Johnstone,[1] gave the following figures for Muslims and Christians at the turn of this last century:

Religion	Population Percentage	Adherents	Annual Growth
Christian	32.54%	1.973 billion	1.43%
Muslim	21.09%	1.279 billion	2.17%

He goes on to add that only the religions that have a growth rate of over 1.39 percent are increasing faster than the world's population. Many will question these numbers, but they appear to be the most accurate ones available. Muslims often say that they are the fastest growing religion in the world, and Johnstone seems to support this claim; although if evangelical Christianity is separated out of the larger Christian church body, then their growth rate would be larger than that of Islam. Johnstone claims that the growth rate of evangelicals in the world is 4.7 percent and that of the Pentecostals is 4.5 percent.[2]

Today Islam is spreading by both peaceful and militant means. There needs to be a distinction made between conversion and forced submission, the first depending on *Da'wah* and the second being related more to *jihad*. Also, it should be noted that the greatest increase in Islam, particularly in the West, is coming not by conversion but rather by migration and large family size. These arguments must be put aside because the focus of our discussion needs to be on the Islamic strategy for the future. It will not be feasible to take an in-depth look at all the countries of the world to see what Islam is doing, but rather we shall look at the major areas of the world and, in some cases, concentrate on some of the key countries where Islam is either growing or using innovative means for expansion.

THE MIDDLE EAST

To be sure, Islam dominates the Middle East, but this is not sufficient for those who seek a more radical Islam. There are undercurrents of dissatisfaction that run deep in countries that have not put Sharia in place or who have failed to declare that they are Islamic Republics. Countries that fall into this more moderate category are Egypt, Jordan, Lebanon, Kuwait, and Iraq.

Prior to the second Gulf War, Iraq was ruled by the Baath party and thus did not have an extreme Islamic government. In chapter 1, it was stated that the second step of Ayatollah Khomeini's plan for world dominance was encouraging the creation of Islamic Republics in the surrounding Muslim countries whether by revolution, war, or negotiation. The Iran-Iraq war of the 1980s ended in a deadlock, thus Khomeini's plans were blocked. However, the success of the coalition forces in defeating Saddam Hussein gave the Shiites new hope.

Soon after the end of the war it was reported, "Beating their chests and chanting praises to Allah, tens of thousands of Shiites flooded the southern city of Basra on Saturday to welcome home their exiled leader [Ayatollah Mohammed Baqir al-Hakim] whose brand of hard-line Islam could play a decisive role in shaping the religious and social face of the new Iraq."[3]

Later in the article, al-Hakim was quoted as saying, "Sharia has to lead this country."[4] The battle for Iraq continues between those who support a Western form of democracy in a Middle Eastern country and those who desire an Islamic Republic.

The sad history of contemporary Lebanon writes another chapter in the attempt of Islam to have complete dominance over all of the Middle East. The war left the country and its beautiful capital city, Beirut, in ruins. Pierre Francis, a Christian leader in Lebanon, wrote his Th.D. dissertation on the causes and effects of the war. He wrote, "Lebanon has been an area of continued struggle between the power of Islam and that of Christianity. According to results, and not necessarily motives, the Civil War in Lebanon of 1975 to 1992 constituted a contemporary link in the chain of the Muslim conquest from the perspective of Islam."[5] In his dissertation, Francis's main theme is that the cause of war was Islam's attempt to replace the Christian-led country with an Islamic Republic, thus removing the only Christian state in the area. They almost succeeded.

The number of Christians in the Middle East continues to decrease due mostly to immigration. They feel that they have a brighter future in the West.

AFRICA

Possibly no part of the world shows more clearly the violent side of Islam than Africa. The continent has experienced bitter warfare in

Algeria, terrorist attacks in Kenya, genocide in the Sudan, massacres of Christians and the burning of their churches in northern Nigeria, just to name a few. Johnstone's statistics for this continent[6] are as follows:

Religion	Population Percentage	Adherents	Annual Growth
Christianity	48.37%	379.4 million	2.83%
Islam	41.32%	324.1 million	2.53%

Both major religions continue to make rapid advancements at the expense of native tribal religions, but neither of them is outdistancing the other at this time.

In Africa, the late Muammar Gaddafi, former president of Libya and a known Muslim fundamentalist, actively attempted to influence the Organization of African Unity (OAU), which had been declining and, for all practical purposes, was dead. President Gaddafi then called for the creation of a new pan-African organization. He took the lead in the formation of an alternate to the OAU. Many saw that Gaddafi was anticipating being the new head of that organization.

The Muslim North is very active in trying to place their people in influential positions of leadership for future expansion. For the sake of clarity the continent should be seen as having two parts: the first being what is often called North Africa, which is predominately Muslim, and the other is all of Africa south of the Sahara, which is more Christian.

North Africa

Islam retains a strong hold on this area, but it continues to try to convert the remnant of Christians living in the countries that extend from Morocco to the Sudan.

The first country we will look at is Egypt, which is approximately 13 percent Christian, most of whom belong to the Coptic Orthodox church that traces its beginnings back to the conversion of the Ethiopian eunuch in Acts 8. There are also pockets of Roman Catholics, Presbyterians, and Baptists, to name a few.

This very populous country was the birthplace of the Muslim Brotherhood, one of the first of the modern fundamentalist movements. This extreme form of Islam has had a history of exploiting economic problems to mount a series of attacks against Christians, tourists, and any others who block them from achieving their aims. Christians, particularly in the southern part of the country, have suffered much from economic and physical persecution.

Once when I was in a large town in the south, an older Christian Egyptian woman came to me in tears and wanted me to help her find her granddaughter. I was told that the thirteen-year-old had been kidnapped by Muslims and would be held hostage until she converted to Islam. Later I was informed that this was a common practice in that part of the country. Another Christian told me that his pharmacy had just been burned down for the second time, and he had been warned either to convert to Islam or leave.

Among other activities practiced by Egyptian fundamentalists are:

1. Demanding that all non-Muslims be considered *dhimmi* thus losing most political rights
2. Imposing dress and behavior codes on all
3. The incitement of various forms of discrimination against Christians
4. Takeover of professional organizations, such as the bar and medical associations
5. Destabilizing the country so as to take over the country and declare an Islamic Republic
6. Persecute and even assassinate secular critics
7. Construct new mosques but forbid new churches from being started or church buildings from being repaired or built

Further to the west in Algeria, economic failures and an attempt at democracy after the War of Liberation in 1962 led to a situation where it appeared that the Islamic Political Party would take control of the government, but the results were annulled by the government unleashing a civil war, which has caused over one hundred thousand deaths. Many of the Christians, who constitute less than 1 percent of the population, were also killed. Once again political instability was used as an excuse to persecute the Christian minority.

The ravages of war have had an unusual result in Algeria; today there is more growth of the Christian church there than any other country of North Africa. All of the countries of North Africa have seen some limited growth, but the efficiency of the Muslim persecution and the Islamic-leaning governments have slowed this growth.

Sudan is possibly one of the saddest examples of the abuse of Islam in their road toward world domination. In 1983 it was declared to be an Islamic Republic. This decision included the institution of a form of Sharia in the country that applied to both Muslims and non-Muslims alike. Since about one-fourth of the country was Christian, this caused hardships on this minority.

The constitution offers some religious liberty, but reality has shown that there has been, and still is, a brutal attempt to convert Christians to Islam. There have been countless examples: the bulldozing of churches, persecutions of individuals, denial of human rights, death by starvation, and the destruction of Christian institutions such as hospitals and schools.

Over one million have been killed in the predominately Christian southern provinces. Sudan remains the most gruesome example in the world today of *jihad* being practiced in order to further Islam.

Sub-Saharan Africa

Sub-Saharan Africa is an entity of its own and is separated from the predominately Muslim North Africa by a large desert region. According to Patrick Johnstone, the number of Muslims in this area by mid-2001 was 7.14 million.[7] In this part of the world the countries with the largest Muslim population are Mozambique, Malawi, Madagascar, and South Africa.

The growth of Islam in this area came from two historical movements. The first was the expansion by trade down the East African coast on to Mozambique from A.D. 750 to 1500. The second was the migration from 1500 to the present into the coastal areas of Western Africa, Central Africa, Sudan, Ethiopia, and Uganda. This includes South Africa in the eighteenth and nineteenth centuries.

Several years ago during a dialogue meeting with some Muslim leaders in Europe, one of them told me their strategy for this area. It was quite simple and has proven to be successful. He said the plan called on Islam to make a march to the south. It would start in the northern part of the continent and move south, trying to win black African countries one at a time. If they came across a country or an area that was difficult and would require more time, then they would just jump that area and continue to the south.

He stated to me that Kenya was one that had proven to be harder than expected. Nigeria is an excellent example of this strategy at work in that the north is Islamic while the south is strongly Christian. They continue to move to the south, burning churches and causing problems with those who resist.

As already stated, Muslims are building a new mosque every mile close to the main highway that leads to the south as a visual expression of their march southward.[8]

Every type of strategy spoken about previously in this book has been and is being utilized in Africa. Muslims see education as an important step toward their goal. One Christian missionary who was speaking about Rwanda stated that one in four of the college professors at the National University are Muslim, although 90 percent of the students are non-Muslim. About a dozen Egyptian and Pakistani professors are working at the university at no cost to the country. The government of Saudi Arabia is paying their salary.[9]

Oil dollars are readily available for the Islamic work in southern Africa. A good example of how the use of strong finances has been successful is the example of Malawi, the country of David

Livingstone. Christianity has a long and illustrious history here. Today a little over three-fourths of the 9,670,000 citizens are Christian. Islam only has approximately 15 percent. In one of the recent democratic elections, one of the candidates for president was a Muslim. Large amounts of money came in from foreign sources and Bakili Muluzi, a Muslim, won the election.

A 1998 report titled "Religious Freedom in the Majority Islamic Countries" stated, "Numerous signs point to a growing Islamic influence in the country. Many Muslim students have obtained scholarships to study in Saudi Arabia and other Islamic countries, the number of mosques has grown enormously, following a precise expansion strategy."[10]

Some predict little growth of Islam despite the political pressures, but others see that Islam has been revitalized by Muluzi's election.

The key to conquering southern Africa is the Republic of South Africa. It is the jewel of the region because of its strong economy and governmental structure. Prior to the radical changes brought on in South Africa because of the collapse of apartheid, it was generally viewed as a Western nation and thus considered in the Christian camp. Now it is considered a neutral state, and some of the countries of the Middle East feel that it could be tilted toward their culture, religion, and way of life.

By the mid-1990s over 81 percent of the population considered themselves Christian. This compared to the eight hundred thousand or 2.4 percent who declared themselves Muslim. Most of the latter came from Southeast Asia and were centered on the coast. Once again the strategists in Mecca could read the political changes in the country, and they began to make plans to exert a disproportionate amount of pressure for their mission cause. As the newly predominately black government began to take action, few noticed that there were inroads made by the Islamists.

South African theologian Martinus Pretorius, now the professor of systematic theology at the Evangelical Theological Faculty in Leuven, Belgium, stated, "Even though in South Africa [Muslims] have only about 2 percent of the population, they constitute 20 percent of the cabinet. Two portfolios they occupy are the Ministry of Justice and the Ministry of Radio and Television. During the Apartheid period they were very busy laying a foundation for *Da'wah* among the blacks. Now they are reaping a degree of success."[11]

In conclusion, it is apparent that the battle for the hearts and minds of sub-Saharan populations will be active in the future. Those who follow Jesus Christ would be well advised that they cannot put this part of the world on the back burner but rather should become involved in the activities of this volatile region.

ASIA

Asia is extremely large both in land mass and in population. It has a surface area of 23.5 percent of the world's land, when you include Russia east of the Ural Mountains. Approximately 61 percent of the world's population lives in this area.[12]

Asia is the only continent where Christianity is not the largest religion. Islam points to Asia proudly and claims that it is on this continent that they have had their most successful *Da'wah* experience. The number of Muslims is over 900 million and still growing. The Muslim country with the largest population is Indonesia with over 171 million. Justin Long, in an evaluation of the growth of Islam, stated:

> Islam's growth . . . shows no sign of tapering off. Though it, like Christianity, got off to a slow start, it has now claimed more than 25% of Asia, and could well approach 30% by 2050. The contest between Islam and Christianity now faced in Africa will shortly be seen in Asia as well, as Islam grows as a majority in many Asian nations, and a substantial minority in others (including China).[13]

In many parts of Asia, Islam crept in quietly at the beginning but now has decided to take a more aggressive approach. They are faced with some huge problems, one being the diversification of Islam due to the many deep, preexisting religious beliefs and practices, resulting in different expressions of faith than those practiced and expressed in the Middle East. John L. Esposito wrote in his book *Islam in Asia:*

> The expansion of Islam in Asia produced a variety and diversity of Islamically informed societies. All Muslims shared a common faith, a confession of their belief in the one God and in his Book and the teaching of his Prophet. However, Islam encountered peoples of vastly different historical backgrounds, languages, ethnic/tribal identities, loyalties, customs, and cultures. In a very real sense an Arab Islam was transformed into Persian, South Asian, and Southeast Asian Islam through the process of assimilation and synthesis. Despite the common core of belief and practice epitomized by the Five Pillars of Islam, Muslim societies differed in the extent and manner to which religion manifested itself in public life—politics, law, and society.[14]

As a result, the growth of Islam in Asia has been and continues to be manifested in a variety of ways. All methods seem to be used in this strategic part of the world including *jihad* and *Da'wah*. Because Asia is where most of the world's Muslims live, it is an especially appropriate place to examine the growth of Islam.

The size of the area is such that we shall divide it into four subareas: South Asia, Southeast Asia, East Asia, and the Pacific Region. Even with this breakdown, the complexity of the area has many overlapping movements and ideologies within Islam.

South Asia

Another term for South Asia could be "The Indian Subcontinent"; this area would include the countries of Pakistan, India, Afghanistan, and Bangladesh. In this part of the world, Islam has an important impact on political stability. These four countries have an approximate total of 282 million followers of Islam. The percentages of the population range from 99 percent in Afghanistan to 12 percent in India.

Pakistan with over ninety-one million has been described as the "only state explicitly established in the name of Islam."[15] It was established because of political and religious strife in India in order to provide a state where Islam could be expressed both politically and socially. Despite this, however, the role of Islam in the country remains unclear until now.

Up until recently Pakistan's Muslims, like other Muslims in the region, tend to follow a school of Islam that is less conservative, and hence the support for strongly and overtly religious parties has been minimal. Satu Limaye argues that because Islam was spread primarily through the preaching of Muslim *Sufi* saints and since the *Sufi* teachings contrast with the more conservative teachings in the Middle East, the former Hindu converts are less conservative.[16]

Today there is an ever-increasing influential fundamentalist movement. Acts of terrorism such as the murder of the journalist Daniel Pearl and the bombing of Christian schools and churches demonstrate that radicalism is alive today. There is a battle within Islam itself in the region. Both the moderates and the fundamentalists are seeking to control the future of the Islamic movement.

Because the subcontinent is heavily Muslim, much of the growth of Islam in this part of the world is due mainly to large families. Intense dislike and conflict between Hindus and Muslims have threatened war in the area but have not led to mass conversion to Islam. At one time, some of the leaders of the "Dalits"—Oppressed or Untouchables, the lower castes of India—were suggesting that it was foolish for them to remain Hindus since they were so ill-treated. Suggestions were made that this caste would in total convert to another religion such as Christianity, Buddhism, or Islam. One of their key leaders, Ram Raj, has said that he and other leaders "have been investigating the Muslim and Buddhist religions, as well as Christianity. Muslim and Buddhist leaders have assured them that they would do whatever was needed to bring the 300 million outcast Hindus into their camp."[17]

When they met with Christian leaders, they were told that the Christians could not help them because they would not be able to handle the repercussions from the Indian government.[18] Ram Raj said that he was "keenly disappointed to hear this as Christianity had been his first choice."[19] Because of the lasting conflicts and also because of the bitter history, the leaders of the outcasts excluded Islam as a possibility. No final move to either of the other two religions has taken place.

The situation in India is rather different since Muslims comprise only 12 percent of the total population, but their impact on the stability of the country is significant. This minority status puts Muslims in another situation. Shahabuddin and Wright, in writing on India, stated:

> The role of Islam, and therefore of Muslims, in public life both potentially and actually differs fundamentally in countries with only a minority of Muslims in their populations from those with Muslim majorities. Extremists on both sides, Muslim and non-Muslim, may think that the minority situation can be changed into a majority one by religious conversion, higher birthrates, or immigration, but the chances of this reversal happening in India are highly unlikely.[20]

Hindu-Muslim violence continues today with little change. As tensions rise at the regional level between India and Pakistan especially over Kashmir, Islam seems to have lost its focus. At the international level, this area continues to gain attention. The war against the Taliban in Afghanistan, the nuclear arms of India and Pakistan, and political unrest all add to the newsworthiness of South Asia. The Muslims have increased their connections with the Middle East and with international Islamic movements, thus showing that there are strong undercurrents that continue to support the expansion of Islam in South Asia. Their strong presence throughout the region cannot be ignored.

Although centuries ago Islam was probably brought to South Asia through peaceful means, it seems as if Islam continues to grow today in the region through conflict and conquest as well as large families.

Southeast Asia

Most historians date the entry of Islam into Southeast Asia around the thirteenth century. Islam was introduced to the region primarily through Gujarati traders from the Indian subcontinent and the preaching of *Sufi* sages. The region is composed of a string of islands along a route connecting India and China. It includes as its major countries Indonesia and Malaysia.

Many of the Muslim communities of South and Southeast Asia remain discrete and separate, both in the ideal norms they profess and in the day-to-day practices they pursue.

An example is Indonesia where approximately 87 percent of the population is Muslim. Johnstone and Mandryk have made three distinctions within that 87 percent. They write that approximately 30 percent are "high identity, high practice"; approximately 35 percent are "high identity, low practice"; and approximately 35 percent are "low identity, low practice."[21]

Although Indonesia has resisted becoming an Islamic Republic, it still remains a strongly Islamic country. According to Limaye,

> Islam has never played a central role in [Indonesia's] politics. Nevertheless, there has been persistent tension between those advocates of a more prominent and formal role for Islam in the country, and those who resist making Islam an organized political actor. . . . A central point about the Islam in Indonesia is that it is not monolithic.[22]

It is Indonesia that only recently became the hotbed for radical Islam. When al Qaeda was forced out of Afghanistan, this country with its strong fundamentalist movement was considered the heir apparent especially for the Pacific region. They have had a history of attacking Christians and other non-Muslims in rather brutal fashion.

Reports continue to flow that tell of forced conversions and atrocities against those who refuse to come to Islam. I have had the opportunity of working for some time in Indonesia, and am kept well informed of what is happening in that country. Because the country is composed of thousands of islands, the central government cannot and truly does not want to exert control over the Islamic extremists. The war against Christians goes on unabated.

Through my contacts, I receive constant updates of events. The number and depth of the atrocities are such that it would take another book just to describe. Here are just a couple of the statements written to me from the area:

> In the early hours of Sunday morning (August 4, 2002), as the seaside village of Matako, 32 km east of Poso, slept peacefully, *jihad* terrorists struck terror into this Christian community. The attack began at 3:30 A.M. with cries of— Allahu Akbar! Allahu Akbar! . . . six homes of the church's members were burned down. . . . The Presbyterian Church was also attacked and damaged. . . . Five members of the church were shot.[23]

> On Monday, July 22, 2002, at 11 A.M., in the Mayoa rice-fields, near the city of Pendolo, 36 km south of Tentena, three Christians from the village of Mayoa were working in their rice-field and clove plantation when they were attacked by a group of armed *jihad* warriors when they were shot near the Koropanghk group irrigation unit.[24]

There are literally thousands of examples where radical Muslims have attacked Christians, burned down their churches, and intimidated the believers. This continues today.

Today in Malaysia, approximately 55 percent of the population is Muslim. In several of the states the leaders have declared themselves an Islamic Republic and said that their form of law would be Sharia. There has not been support from the central government nor the police for such action thus the proclamations have not been enforced. The number of attacks against non-Muslims has not nearly reached the intensity of Indonesia.

Concerning Malaysia, Caesar Farah writes, "Islam is so solidly identified with the Malay culture that *masuk melayu* (lit. 'to become Malay') is the designation for becoming a Muslim. . . . Islam is still a significant and integral factor in Malay culture as reflected in their world view, in their literature, and oral traditions."[25] The Islamic resurgence is leading to political uncertainty in the country and the radicals seem to be growing.

In conclusion, Islam is deeply imbedded in Southeast Asia. The battle now is between the fundamentalists and the moderates as to who will control the fate of the governments. In only the last few years, those advocating Sharia and Islamic Republics have been winning converts to their side. The Christians and the non-Muslims have been on the sidelines with the radicals attacking them and attempting to force them out by means of *jihad.* There seems to be little interest in the more quiet and subtle tactics used in *Da'wah* in the West.

East Asia

The dominant country is this area is China where, according to Farah:

> [Islam entered China] in 651, second year of Yonghui of the T'ang Dynasty. . . . Shortly thereafter, Arab and Persian Muslim merchants began to arrive by sea and by land. . . . The extent of contacts can be judged by the fact that Chinese annals record thirty-seven formal missions from Muslim rulers to China by the launch of the ninth century.[26]

During these early penetrations, the people known as the Hui emerged, and they were the most responsive to the message of Islam. They have been the primary propagators of Islam throughout China. They represent an interesting mix of Chinese, Middle Eastern, and

Central Asian cultural, religious, and historical traditions. Today, it is the Hui that are the most dominant of the ten Muslim minority groups recognized by the Communist government.

The Hui Muslims have a significant presence throughout China, while the other Muslim minorities are primarily concentrated in the northwestern part of China. At the present time the major Islamic influence is coming in through the Islamic countries of Central Asia. Three of the central problems faced by the Muslims of China are (1) cultural assimilation into the country, (2) continued pressure from the Communist state, and (3) factionalism among their believers.

Islam must face the problem of having more freedom than prior to 1990 but still functioning under definite restrains. Limaye reports that "there are now more mosques open in China than there were prior to 1949, and Muslims travel freely on the Hajj to Mecca, as well as engaging in cross-border trade with co-religionists in Central Asia, the Middle East, and increasingly, southeast Asia."[27]

The division among the different factions has much to do with their interaction with the various branches of Islam now present in the world. The new freedom does afford them the opportunity to practice *Da'wah* among the citizens of their own country. *Jihad* is not an option.

Pacific Region

Many historians date the entry of Islam into the Philippines around the fourteenth century, two centuries prior to the arrival of the Spanish colonizers. Farah notes that "in the sixteenth century the islands of the Philippines were in advanced stage of Islamization when King Phillip of Spain . . . gave the orders to his admirals 'to conquer the lands and convert the people [to Catholicism].'"[28] However, Muslims in the southern islands were able to resist the attacks. With the arrival of the Spanish, the northern islands of Luzon and the Visayas were converted to Christianity while the southern islands of Mindanao and Sulu were Muslim converts.[29]

Known as the Moros, Filipino Muslims comprise approximately 5 percent of the entire population of the Philippines and are centered in the southern islands close to Indonesia. In 1983, an Islamic *Da'wah* Council of the Philippines was organized for the purpose of bringing all Muslim organizations under one umbrella. Some very high-profile terrorist attacks as well as kidnapping of Westerners have given an international face to the Muslim rebellion. The political and social instability in the region has not been a source of any significant growth in the area. *Jihad* is practiced thus putting the lives and property of Christians in danger in the south.

EUROPE

Of all the continents of the world, Europe is probably the number-one target by the Muslim strategists who are seeking world dominance—Eastern Europe, because of the fall of Communism and the vacuum left in the spirits of people; Western Europe, because they perceive it as being decadent, they feel that it will collapse from the inside, leaving its population desperately seeking for an answer to life's questions to which they feel that they have the answers.

The two areas, East and West, were separated for about eighty years by the Iron Curtain and only now are seeking new means to come together. Because of this historical separation at least for most of this generation, I shall also separate Europe into two parts to help in our understanding of how Islam hopes to take over this continent.

Eastern Europe

Demographers generally separate the former Soviet Union into two parts; the area east of the Ural Mountains are placed in Asia and generally referred to as Central Asia, while the area west of the Urals is in Europe. For our purposes of looking at the advance of Islam, we will include the Asian part in with Eastern Europe.

The dominant religion of most of this area is Christian but with a strong Islamic presence. In broad terms it can be said that the indigenous peoples of countries such as Kazakhstan, Kyrgyzstan, and Uzbekistan are Muslims, while the Russians and their related people groups are Christians. Both the ethnic and the religious separation have caused problems in the past, and a strong sense of nationalism in some of the states since the fall of the wall has intensified this conflict. Nationalism and anti-Russian sentiment have given rise to those calling for a nationalism that is defined by both race and the Islamic religion.

Because of the strong religious persecution under Communism, all religions had only a nominal presence. Islam had suffered as many were willing to obey the laws of the land and to cease to be active Muslims. After the collapse of Communism, many of the Muslim countries to the south of the Soviet Union saw their opportunity to do *Da'wah* in the north. Turkey, Iran, and Saudi Arabia began to flood these areas with both *daa'is* (missionaries) and funds. With the fall of the atheistic government, the breakup of the U.S.S.R., and the hefty influence from the south, there was a revival of Islam in Central Asia.

It is not only Islam that is being propagated but a militant Islam with many different organizations vying for the hearts and heads of the people. Such groups have exacerbated the problem that the governments have in Central Asia as the extreme form of Islam, propagated by Osama bin Laden and others, continues to have a growing influence. When Russia invaded Afghanistan, the resistance used the concept of *jihad* to fight against their enemies from the north. After the defeat of the Soviets in Afghanistan, the Muslims continued to use the same tactics in attempting to drive the Russians (and thus Christians) out of former U.S.S.R. states.

In his book *Jihad: The Rise of Militant Islam in Central Asia*, Ahmed Rashid describes a number of radical movements now growing in Central Asia. One of the most popular, widespread underground movements in Uzbekistan, Kyrgyzstan, and Tajikistan is the Hizb ut-Tahrir. Rashid states: "The HT has a vision of uniting Central Asia, Xinjiang Province in China, and eventually the entire ummah (Islamic world community) under a khilafat (caliph-ate). . . ."[30] He goes on to say: "HT leaders believe that Central Asia has reached what they call 'a boiling point' and is ripe for take-over."[31] The point at hand is that they see world conditions as such that Central Asia can become the center of the reestablishment of the unified Islam.

In countries such as the Balkans and others to the west, Islam has had a long history of conflict. Bulgaria and Bosnia have strong communities of Muslims. They hope to use these communities as beachheads that can lead to the conversion of that area. In the Bosnian war, much physical support in the way of arms and financing came in from the Islamic countries. The same is true in Chechnya. The main effort for advancement in these areas could be called a combination of *jihad* and *Da'wah* depending on the circumstances. It should be noted that there have not been many converts to Islam in this area recently.

Western Europe

Western Europe has been flooded with Muslims who have come from almost all the Muslim countries. Who are they and where did they come from? Here is an overview. They are:

- **Guest workers.** These are generally to be found in Germany, Austria, and Switzerland. At first they were blue-collar workers that came to fill the menial and poorly paid positions in these countries. There was a great need for such workers since there was radical economic growth in these countries. It was the intention of both the host and the guest that they would return home. Many came to earn funds that could then be used to buy land or a house in the home country. With time, the men brought their families with them, and they began to set down roots.
- **Immigrants.** These differ from the guest workers in that their original intent was to live in the new country. The majority of

Muslims in England and France fall into this category. They had certain rights, since they lived in areas that were colonized by the host country. Often these immigrants find it hard to accept that they are anything but a citizen of the European country where they find themselves. In most cases the immigrants came to the West as a family unit.

- **Refugees.** As wars and famines hit areas in Asia, Africa, and the Middle East, many refugees are created and a small number of them find their way to Europe. They can be single persons or complete family groups. Their stay is often considered as temporary, but with time they become more established.
- **Students.** Numerous young people come to Europe for a period of up to seven years in order to study at one of the European universities. They often are very bright people who plan to return to their homes and often become leaders in their countries.
- **Businesspeople.** With the economic strength of the Middle East countries, many businesspeople have bought second homes in Europe and spend a great amount of time there.
- **Tourists.** Again, due to the favorable economic strength of the Middle East countries, many Muslims have made Europe their vacation and shopping choice. They will often spend extended periods of time in Europe.
- **European Muslims.** There is a small but growing group of indigenous Europeans who have converted to the Muslim faith and are active in the practice of their faith.

Beginning in the 1970s and 1980s, the Islamic communities of Europe began to find their own identity and even realized that they had an obligation to their religion to try to encourage other Muslims to live their faith in the foreign land. This then led them to see that it was possible for them to perform *Da'wah* with the Europeans, thus Islam became much more dynamic and some would say more radical. All the methods of *Da'wah* described in the previous chapters are now being used in Western Europe with some success.

I estimate that the number of European Christians who convert to Islam is roughly the same as the number of Muslims living in Europe who convert to Christianity. The Muslim growth is mostly through an increase of immigration and the fact that they have a tendency to have large families. Some of their success is in the area of public relations. It is here that they spend many resources.

THE AMERICAS

South America and the Caribbean

The Arab immigrants who have moved into this area over the last two hundred years practice Islam in Latin America. They come from three different sources: the Indo-Pakistani immigrants, the descendants of East Indian indentured laborers, and African-American converts to Islam in the West Indies. Latin America seems to be one of the target areas for conversion. In all the countries, Muslims are building magnificent mosques that are financed mostly by the oil-rich Muslim countries.

While making a trip to Carracas, Venezuela, I was shown a beautiful large mosque across from the Hilton Hotel. I was told that it was one of the largest in South America and also housed a training center. Another example is the new mega-mosque in Buenos Aires, Argentina. It has a fifty-meter high white ceramic dome. The project began in 1995 and had a construction cost of $15 million, paid by King Fahd of Saudi Arabia. The land was donated by the Argentinean government.[32] They have translated and published a large number of their books into both Spanish and Portuguese. One of the organizations that is active in the region is the fundamentalist Jamat-e-Islami. They are having some success in converting the native Latinos to their faith as well as the black South Americans.

The total number of Muslims in the area is quite small when compared to Christians. Johnstone states that 91.65 percent of the population are Christians while only 0.34 percent are Muslims. They number roughly 1.4 million.[33] There are some indications that Islam is targeting Hispanics in the United States with the hopes that it will affect the southern part of the continent in the future.

North America

Much of what has been written has looked at the plans now being used in North America. The total numbers range from Johnstone's 4.6 million to the Muslims' estimate of over 7.0 million. At this point a word of caution should be given. Muslims do not always have accurate statistics and they often will greatly exaggerate their numbers. This does not take away from them or their growth, but it does warn us not to take all the figures about size too seriously.

In America it is mostly African-Americans who are converting to orthodox Islam, and not just to the Nation of Islam. There are some Anglos and some Hispanics, but these numbers are few. In studying the strategy, one would have to say that the area where Muslims are committing most of their resources in the West include Western Europe and North America. Once again their main emphasis is to do the work by an expanded use of *Da'wah*.

Areas of success, apart from their work with the minorities, could be said to be the building of mosques, student work, work with prisoners, and the effective public relations endeavors that have changed how people in Canada and the United States perceive Islam.

Conclusion

Islam continues its march forward as does Christianity. However, it is a sad commentary that in countries where Islam rules, Christians struggle to stay alive. Conversion to Christianity in lands ruled by Islam can mean more than prison—it can be a death sentence. In the West, Muslims are free to proselytize and grow and they are taking advantage of Western religious tolerance in order to expand their base for world dominance.

After the attacks on the World Trade Center on September 11,

2001, many were quoted as saying, "The world will never again be the same." There was no catastrophic change in the world's demography, but rather the change was more of perception. Suddenly, news concerning conflicts involving Muslims now landed on the front pages of newspapers instead of being buried on the back pages.

The changes between Islam and the West are hard to understand or map out for the future. However, as one begins to study this encounter, it becomes apparent that Huntington's "Clash of Civilizations" and Woosley's "World War IV" are now realities. Islam is now on the march in many parts of the world. It has its strategy and battle plans in place, but Muslims still have many weaknesses that they seem unwilling to acknowledge. It seems that the non-Islamic world is not ready to lie down and surrender.

What in the world is Islam doing? Although they are doing much, their real successes come into question.

Poverty of the people in the shadow of a mosque in a Middle Eastern city.

chapter eleven

Measuring Success One Country at a Time

Will Islam Really Take Over the World?

How Islam Plans to Change the World—the title of this book seems to make the assumption that Islam will be successful, but this is very much in question. Of course, the ultimate aim of Islam is complete world dominance, and many Muslims feel that it is inevitable.

As noted earlier, Islam is the world's fastest growing major religion, and Muslims are having some success in most regions of the globe. They have tremendous financial resources and momentum on their side. But is it realistic to say that they can and will conquer the world in the future?

Let's look at the facts and try to determine if they can accomplish this monumental task. I have identified twelve successes and twelve failures.

TWELVE SUCCESSES

No religion can carry the title of the world's fastest growing major religion without doing some things right. In trying to evaluate what Islam is doing right, it will help to bring together all the activities and strategies that have led them to where they are today—a growing faith. Following is a list of their successes.

1. They have been successful in having a global strategy. Islam is the only major world religion with a mega-strategy. The only other one that I am aware of is the Mormon church, but rather than being a major world religion, they fall more into the category of a sect. Even the evangelical and Pentecostal branches, both of which have a higher growth rate than Islam, do not have a solid mega-strategy in place. A mega-strategy means that all the resources of an organization are in place and working together for a common goal. Because Islam does not compartmentalize life into different and often conflicting areas, it has an opportunity of utilizing its followers to promote their faith. An example concerns their diplomats who are active in various countries in the building of mosques and in the proclamation of Islam. In the Christian world, the Christians among the diplomats might go to church but do little to really promote missions. In Islam's strategy they have tried to combine all the different facets of life into one for the purpose of a global witness.

2. They have been successful in using international trade as a tool for growth. In the history of the expansion of Islam, trade played an important part in the extension of the faith of Muhammad. On the other hand, history shows that the large trading companies, formed by the colonizing powers, were more often against the missions rather than helpful. Today international businesses with bases in the Christian West are of very little help in the promotion of the Christian faith. However, Muslim businessmen are actively promoting their faith and are helping to build mosques all over the world. The average Muslim businessman sees a responsibility to promote the growth of Islam.

3. They have been successful in using their students to do *Da'wah*. Generally the students going to study overseas and

especially in the West are focused upon the task of influencing others to their faith. Not all students are actively engaged in the promotion of their faith, but student work and work in schools remain a high priority, receiving both finances and encouragement.

4. They have been successful in reaching the blacks of the world, both in Africa and in the West, especially in North America. They have played the race card very effectively and have led many to believe that Christianity is really racist while Islam is for all races. The success of their African strategy is to make people believe that Islam is the only religion that accepts a person for who they really are. They use such things as the slave trade of the past to discredit Christians, without making mention that history has shown that blacks were the leaders in this trade.

5. They have been successful in portraying their theology to Westerners in terms that can be accepted by them. They effectively use terms such as love, grace, forgiveness, fellowship, and compassion to try to communicate Islam. These terms are not dominant in Arabic; the concepts have been used to refer to Islam when in reality this is not the case. Most people in America and Europe see Islam as comparable to Christianity in content because of Muslims' carefully planned strategy of communicating their faith in the West.

6. They have been successful in the use of the large amounts of petrodollars that have been made available to them by the Gulf States including Saudi Arabia. This is probably the single most important success that they have. The readiness to use these resources has made the task much easier in many of the other areas.

7. They have been successful in the prisons in the West. As already mentioned, they win mostly young minority inmates to their faith. They give converts a new name and identity as well as taking care of their families until they are released. They also help in getting the person started again in society. Also to

be noted is that these converted persons are often good recruits for the more radical forms of Islam, which advocate terrorism and intimidation.

8. They have been successful in the use of intimidation. Through terrorism and other means, they have been able to bring fear into the lives of many in the world. It remains to be seen if this fear leads to growth, but in some cases the intimidation has led some weaker Christians to accept Islam instead of fighting. This is true in countries where Islam has a large majority and the Christians and others are weak. Examples include Egypt and Indonesia.

9. They have been successful in the use of force. *Jihad* in some parts of the world has been helpful in adding to the growth. Possibly the best example of that is Sudan. As Islam becomes the dominant religion in some areas of the world, more *jihad* activities can be expected to bring growth to the area conquered.

10. They have been successful in changing the image of Islam. This is especially true in North America and Western Europe. The picture of the slow-minded Arab on a camel is no longer shown, but it has now been replaced with the image of a dedicated Muslim who takes his or her religion very seriously. They have upgraded their literature and are effectively using mass media. Their greatest failure in this area has been with the Israeli-Palestinian conflict where they have come up as losers because of the more effective Jewish control of the issues in the media.

11. They have been successful in the construction of numerous mosques in the world, many of them large and beautiful. There is no question that their physical presence in so many different countries has given Muslims much to boast about. It is not only the size and beauty of the buildings that is impressive but also the numbers and locations in so many countries of the world.

12. They have been successful in the portrayal of both the simplic-

ity and the piety of their religion. The five pillars are known all over the world and form an easily understandable basis for their religion. Most see them as being genuinely religious, which is a large plus factor for them. This simplicity of faith has been a great asset for their growth in the urban areas around the globe.

TWELVE FAILURES

1. Islam is not growing as rapidly as it claims. It is generally believed that Muslims have a tendency to exaggerate their growth, and since Islamic countries do not keep the same type of records that are kept in the West, it becomes very difficult to verify the growth rate. The number of persons who change to Islam because of a real conversion is small. Most of the growth comes from either a forced conversion or from Muslims having large families.

2. They have failed to contextualize Islam into the more dominant world cultures. To become a Muslim means that the women must take on a semblance of the same type of dress as in the Middle East. Simply said, to become a Muslim often means a rejection of one's cultural norms, values, and background and the taking on of a foreign way of life. This will continue to be a hindrance for seeing large numbers in other cultures convert to Islam.

3. They have failed to convince the world that they are a peaceful religion. The continued use of *jihad* and terrorism has helped growth in some areas but also worked against them and their rather effective public relations strategy. Every new attack and atrocity is a constant reminder that there is an inseparable tie between Islam and conflict. Many have been turned off from this religion because of the facts that are now available to all in the global environment. It seems that they have conflicts with most of the major religions of the world thus making their chances of success in some parts of the world less probable.

4. They have failed to convince practicing Christians that Islam is better than Christianity. Because Islam is a post-Christian faith, many of their leaders proclaim that it is superior and even use texts from both the Bible and the Qur'an to show that Jesus was expecting the coming of Muhammad to make his revelation to the world perfect. This teaching simply has not been accepted, thus putting into doubt that there will ever be a mass turning from the faith of Jesus Christ to that of Muhammad.

5. They have failed to stop Christian missions. They see Christian missions as their number one enemy. At this time the Christian church continues to grow in Islam's backyard. I doubt that the number worldwide who convert from Christianity to Islam is equivalent to the number who convert from Islam to Christianity. The exit through Islam's back door is much bigger than they want to or will admit.

6. They have failed to fill the many mosques that they have built. In many parts of the world the mosques stand empty. They expect and hope that soon they will be filled with people from the areas around the mosques, but only time will tell if this will happen. Just the building of a mosque does not always mean a change of faith by those who live close to it.

7. They have failed to make people believe their threats. Over the last twenty years many voices have come out of Islam declaring *jihad* against a country or a people, or they have spoken of their destruction for not obeying Allah. Like the boy who cried "Wolf," many of these threats go unrealized to the point that they are not taken as seriously as before. This has had a tendency to discredit their religion.

8. They have failed to form a Muslim country with a democracy that could appeal to the modern-day person. They continue to lag in this area, and thus those who might convert must think twice about what a Western Islamic country would really look like. The creation of an Islamic Republic in Iran has had the effect that many from that country have become disillusioned with Islam and are looking to leave.

9. They have failed to provide an education system that will prepare their young people for life in the modern world. So much of their education is rote memory of the Qur'an; thus they fail to encourage the creative process in children. This leads to a lack of advancement as well as to a lack of improvement of the average Muslim's standard of living.

10. They have failed to relieve the fear that is so deeply ingrained in their faith. New believers begin to experience this and they soon become disappointed in their new belief, but fear stops them from expressing their doubt. Essentially, their fears feed upon their fears.

11. They have failed to give assurances to their followers for the future. They have not developed a strong theology for the future outside of a worldwide *ummah* and they certainly have not provided a personal assurance of a victorious life with God after death.

12. They have not been able to completely dispel the stereotype of the Muslims being people who live in the desert in the Middle East. Because of their monoculturalism, this image continues despite strong attempts to change how they are perceived.

In observing the facts, I believe that Islam will have constant growth in the future but mostly among those people groups that already adhere to Islam. Westerners perceive that Islam is growing because Muslims now live next door, but the actual growth will be "biological," because of large families, not because of conversions.

If Christian missions were not present in the world today and were not as dynamic as they are today, then the growth of Islam would be much greater. Christianity remains the number one buffer against Islam, a fact readily recognized by those who seek a worldwide *ummah*. Christianity and Islam will remain the two largest religions, both seeing converts from the other and both seeking to win the world to their belief. Both will have approximately the same growth that is a little better than the world's growth rate.

The main hindrance to both of the religions will be secularism with its many different facets. A few other world faiths will show some growth—but none are in a position to challenge the two leading ones at this time.

Looking into the Future

Some historians say that history is cyclical, that it continues to repeat itself, while others say that it is liner, or that repetition is not necessary and thus difficult to predict. What does the future hold for the two great religions? Will there be a clash of these two cultures that will result in a war?

Huntington writes: "A global war involving the core states of the world's major civilizations is highly improbable but not impossible. Such a war . . . could come about from the escalation of a fault line war between groups from different civilizations, most likely involving Muslims on one side and non-Muslims on the other."[1] There are other possibilities.

Three key questions must be asked:

1. Is a decline of the West and Christianity, as has happened in all other advanced societies, inevitable?
2. Is Islam destined to realize its dreams of a worldwide *ummah*?
3. Is it possible for Islam and Christianity to live together with a real appreciation of the other's religion and culture?

The inclination of most Westerners, quite naturally, is to answer the first two questions with a strong "no" and the last one with a weak "maybe." Those from the Middle East would answer differently. They would say a strong "yes" to the first two and a reluctant "maybe" to the third. The answers would come from a hopeful allegiance to their own history and values, and not particularly from the facts.

Both Islam and Christianity have a strong eschatology (view of the end times) that comes from their worldview. Both turn to their holy books to substantiate their view.

Views of the End Times

Islam

Once while visiting the Great Mosque in Damascus, my guide pointed to one of the tall, graceful minarets, "the minaret of Jesus." Muslim tradition says that on the summit of this minaret, Jesus will descend, not in judgment but to kill the Antichrist and the people of Gog and Magog, as well as to proclaim Islam as the true religion. The world's improvement will be during the reign of Jesus, who will live for about forty years on earth. He will die while waiting for the Day of Judgment.

Islam does believe in a great judgment day, a time when all will be judged for the kind of life they have led. But prior to this, the world will continue to improve until the day comes when the whole earth will live under the banner of Islam and all its peoples will live under Sharia law. After this has occurred, the judgment day will come. Even during the dark ages of Islam, this hope of conquering the world was kept alive in the hearts of the *imams*. They have a tendency to look at all world events as leading up to their takeover of the world. Their somewhat illogical actions must be understood in light of this theology. Many could not see why a man like Saddam Hussein would continue to stand up against the West even when all logic pointed to a defeat of Iraq. He kept feeling that Allah was going to intervene and give him victory. When the tragic accident of the Columbia spaceship occurred, Saddam, who was facing an attack from the United States, published a statement declaring that Columbia's destruction was the "'beginning of Allah's punishment' upon the USA and its Mideast Zionist ally. The statement noted that the Israeli astronaut killed in the shuttle breakup, Ilan Ramon, had participated in the 1981 Israeli Air Force destruction of Iraq's nuclear reactor near the town of Osirak."[2]

Islam feels that the West will ultimately fail from within. They point to a number of reasons for this belief. Huntington gave five reasons why he sees the West in danger. Islam would point to the same deficiencies. They are:

1. Increases in antisocial behavior, such as crime, drug use, and violence generally
2. Family decay, including increased rates of divorce, illegitimacy, teenage pregnancy, and single-parent families
3. At least in the United States, a decline in "social capital," that is, membership in voluntary associations and the interpersonal trust associated with such membership
4. General weakening of the "work ethic" and rise of a cult of personal indulgence
5. Decreasing commitment to learning and intellectual activity, manifested in the United States in lower levels of scholastic achievement[3]

Huntington goes on to say, "The future health of the West and its influence on other societies depends in considerable measure on its success in coping with these trends, which, of course, gives rise to the assertion of moral superiority by Muslims and Asians."[4]

Most Muslims with whom I have spoken feel that the last great power that must be overcome before the world rule of Islam can begin is the United States; thus, the term that is used all over the Islamic world to describe the United States is "The Great Satan." For them the devil will use this bastion as his last holdout before Islam will be successful. With a philosophy like this, there seems little hope that Islam will ever come to a place of compromise with the West.

Christianity

The Christian view of the last days is both simple and complicated. Simple, in that most Christians feel that the world will continue until Jesus Christ returns and that there will then be a day of judgment. At that time those who have disobeyed God will be separated from him and cast into hell, while those who have accepted Jesus Christ will reign with him for eternity. It is, however, far more complicated in that there are large varieties of belief regarding what will take place before the Day of Judgment comes.

A basic concept is that there will be a thousand-year reign of Jesus Christ before the final judgment. This is based on Revelation 20. There are three differing ideas as to when and how this thousand-year period will take place. Some say it will be before Christ returns (postmillennialism); some say after his coming (premillennialism); and some say there will be no literal thousand-year reign (amillennialism).

The postmillennialist view would be most comparable to the Muslim view, in that this view says that the world will get better and better (and more Christian) until man has developed a near-perfect world and Jesus can simply come and set up his kingdom. This would mean that the church would conquer all evils (including Islam) until the end. This was a very popular concept in the 1920s and the 1930s. Many said that man had conquered alcohol (with Prohibition), war (with the League of Nations), and other evils. Hitler even used this belief as a theological basis of his formulation of his thousand-year *Reich* (Kingdom). After the rise of fascism in Germany and Italy and World War II, postmillennialism became very unpopular and few in the church today see this as a real possibility.

Both the amillennialists and the premillennialists would see a somewhat darker side of the future. They take literally the words of Jesus in Matthew 24 when he said that before he returned:

> You will hear of wars and rumors of wars. . . . Nation will rise against nation, and kingdom against kingdom. There will be famines and earthquakes in various places. . . . There you will be handed over to be persecuted and put to death, and you will be hated by all nations because of me. . . . Many false prophets will appear and deceive many people. (Matthew 24:6–11)

Those holding to this view are not surprised by the persecutions and problems coming from the revival of Islam. They state that this has been predicted and the words of Jesus are now coming true. They see Muhammad as one of the false prophets mentioned by Jesus.

The premillennialists have a tendency to look at every world event and see a biblical fulfillment of prophecy. The war with Iraq (Babylon), the creation of the State of Israel, and its Muslim opposition all point to the return of Jesus Christ. They have a tendency to point to different systems, religions, and persons as the Antichrist.

One interesting theory that is gaining some allegiance by the more radical premillennialists is that there will be a joining together of the Roman Catholic Church (whom they pointed to as the Antichrist before the rise of Islam) and Islam. For them the rallying point will be Mary; they believe it is no coincidence that Mary is revered as the Lady of Fatima (where she appeared to some peasant children), which is the name of the wife of Ali (the fourth caliph). Proponents believe that both Islam and Roman Catholicism will accept Mary, join together, and thus become the Antichrist who will attempt to take the world away from God. It would be safe to say that very few accept this theory as credible.

Most Christians do not attempt to predict what will happen between Islam and Christianity. They are concerned that Islam is growing but are still satisfied with the prominent position that they enjoy living in the West. Some see an immediate and dangerous challenge to their way of life by Islam and are concerned for the future.

SCENARIOS FOR THE FUTURE

In the emerging world of multiculturalism, mass immigration, and changing worldviews, we must attempt to predict what will be the logical consequences of the events of today.

History has shown us that life on earth is, if nothing else, unpredictable; thus, one who tries to make a prediction is often playing the fool. What is now being predicted is done in light of the conflict of the two great religions. It does not take into account the other civilizations such as China, who will play an ever-increasingly important role in world affairs. Theology and eschatology will be brought to bear. Also, missiology will help in looking at growth and decline of religions in the world this century. Here are five possible scenarios for the future:

1. There will be a rise in influence of the moderate branches of both Islam and Christianity. As this happens, there will be better conclusive dialogue between the leaders of the two faiths. Both sides will see that they must find a way to coexist and will create a framework whereby this will be possible. Intense competition that leads to physical conflict will decrease to an extent that both will find strength from each other. The fact that both share a common heritage and a common belief in the one God will be the base from which this cooperation can begin. They would realize that they must share the stage with other ideologies such as secularism, Buddhism, Hinduism, etc. Both would continue to do their missions and *Da'wah,* but within agreed upon limits and bounds. Civilization would benefit immensely from such a solution. This would be the best possible alternative to the present conflict. My problem with this possibility is that at the present time the moderates not only are ceasing to grow in influence in their respective faiths, but are losing adherents.

2. The Islamists will be correct. Islam will continue to gain adherents through both *Da'wah* and *jihad.* There will be minor wars of liberation together with persecutions of non-Muslims in such a way that the "Path of Muhammad" will increase in both size and power. One by one, countries will become Islamic Republics. The first big step toward this end would be the capitulation of Israel. This would then be followed by either the conversion or ousting of all non-Muslims from the Middle East and other areas controlled by Islam. Of the Western powers, Europe would convert to Islam first with the United States being the last great stumbling block before Islam. America would fall because of the excellent propaganda from Muslims combined with the moral decay of a failed Christian society.

3. The apparent status quo between the two religions will continue. Islam will continue on its course for world dominance, reverting to ways that have led to its resurgence. There will be a continuance of persecution and attempts at *jihad*. The rest of the world will not continue to tolerate such action and there will be an ever-increasing division of the world into two or more major camps. Two of these civilizations will constantly wage war against each other. These wars would be wars of words combined with economic war, propaganda war, and actual physical conflict. The phrase the "Clash of Civilizations" would become reality and relations between the two would deteriorate. The results of such conflicts would depend upon a number of factors, which includes not only the inner strength of each society but also their military might. In the near future the Western civilization would have the upper hand.

4. As Islam and Christianity continue to have conflict with each other, one of the other world-class civilizations such as China will gain such strength that it becomes the dominant force in bringing in a "Brave New World" society. Because of the drained strength of the two great religions, they will have little or no stamina to defend themselves.

5. Islam will continue to grow and will become more brutal in its attempts to conquer the world. There will be a rise of terrorism in all parts of the non-Muslim world since they have discovered how effective this can be. The nations of the world will be subjected to suicide bombings. A number of wars such as those against Iraq and Afghanistan will take place but will be ineffective since Islam has learned to fight not from a position of military strength but from the shadowy back alleys of urban societies. Christians especially will be marked for death and persecution. Islam will never completely take over the world but will have successes and there will be some growth. In this scenario, the world would face a long period of instability.

What are my impressions? After spending much time trying to understand the two civilizations that are the theme of this book, and in studying the eschatology of both religions as well as looking at the political realities of the complex world in which we live, I have developed some ideas as to what will happen.

I see somewhat of a status quo developing with neither making much gain at the expense of the other. Islam will have the upper hand in some parts of the world such as sub-Saharan Africa and Central Europe. There will also be a growing Islam in Western Europe, not by converting the ethnic Europeans but by an increase in immigration and large families. Blacks in America will continue to come to Islam for a short period of time, but there will be a revival among the Christian blacks that will slow the growth of Islam.

I tend to accept the last of my five scenarios. There will be continued conflict between the two civilizations. It will lead to many losing their lives through conflict and persecution. Ultimately there will be one large conflict before Jesus Christ does return, not to proclaim the merits of Muhammad but to establish his kingdom. The ultimate victor in this process will be Jesus Christ, not Christians.

In trying to predict the future, I am reminded of watching *Apollo 13* on video. Some children were present and during the movie it looked as if the spacecraft would be lost and all in it killed. One of the children was greatly concerned and began to cry. I said, "Don't worry; everything will be all right."

The somewhat emotional child said, "How do you know?"

"I already know how the movie is going to end," I replied.

Christians who are concerned about the present situation as well as the future only need to go to the Bible to see that God has already told us what the real ending will be. We shall be victorious in Jesus Christ, the only true King of Kings and Lord of Lords (Revelation 19:16).

As I mentioned in the preface, the real antidote for the problems before us is clear. Let's become much more active in living out our Christian faith and proclaiming the truth as found in Jesus Christ.

Together, let's dedicate ourselves anew to these all-important tasks.

As Islam seeks to dominate the landscape, the height of the minarets is important in the construction of new mosques.

chapter **twelve**

What Can We Do About It?

Reacting and Helping

The success of the first edition of this work gave me opportunity to give both lectures and interviews in many countries on Islam's strategy to take over the world. Usually, after the lecture there was time for questions. Many of the questions followed this line: "You have shown us that Islam presents a real threat to the Western world and that we need to be concerned about what is taking place, but what can we do about it?" The question is fair and needs to be taken at face value. How does the average non-Muslim living in a Western context approach the problem? Many do not want to sit on their hands and watch but rather want to be active in finding a solution.

As we answer this question, let's first look at tactics used by the Muslim community. Islam has been very successful at intimidation, especially in Europe and the United States. When you speak against Islam, Muslims find ways to put you into the spotlight and call you a bigot. The politically correct crowd is always ready to cast stones at those who try to identify the problems. Westerners are not good at using intimidation as a tool to get their way.

Often Muslims will spread lies about what Christians and Jews believe. Once I was in the home of a North African family in Brussels, Belgium, and the lady of the home said, "I have been told that Christians in the United States eat Muslim children." She was simply repeating what she had been told. Lies can be both damaging and very effective.

Another tool used by Islam today is to spread hate. As far as Islam is concerned, there are only two types of people in the world—those of the House of Islam (*dal-al-Islam*) and those of the House of War (*dal-al-harb*). Muslims are often told to only associate with those of the House of Islam. It is implied that they should hate and fear the others.

A fourth tool is to reconstruct history. Many times in speaking with Muslims about Christianity I am asked about the Crusades. They see this as a time when angry Christians killed and raped innocent Muslims. Few really know the facts of this period of history. When the Crusades are studied, it is apparent that both Muslims and Christians committed atrocities.

Often Muslims will react in a negative way toward Christians. This, however, cannot be our response. There are no real advantages in taking a negative stance toward either Muslims in general or Islam as a religion. The solution is not to take the low road but to use Christian principles of honesty and fairness in combating Islam. This is always the best way.

How Then to Proceed?

During a discussion with a Muslim *imam* in Germany, the topic came around as to who is the greatest enemy of our two faiths. Of course we both mentioned secularism, but the *imam* made a fascinating statement. He said that "prior to 1990 the greatest enemy of Islam was Communism, but now the greatest enemy of Islam is Christian missions." This was just one man speaking but in other readings it is apparent that many agree with him. A dominant teaching in Islamic schools is that the West is decadent, that most Western women are immoral, and that the West will soon disintegrate because of its lack of a practiced value system. Muslims believe that Sharia law is the only solution to this decadent way of life. But here come Christians who do have a strong set of morals, who do live lives as described in the Bible, and who do teach others to follow the traditional Judeo-Christian values. Islam has as a major part of its strategy the filling of the moral vacuum with their brand of morality, but nowhere in that strategy is a system that offers a better and more complete value system. It is no wonder they fear Christians who are active in living and promoting their Christian faith.

In attempting to give an answer on how to proceed, two possible solutions will be offered. One is passive and the other is active.

A PASSIVE SOLUTION

The passive solution is to simply live out our lives as Jews or Christians and allow the Judeo-Christian system of values to be our guiding light. The influence that secularism has on society today is overwhelming. More and more people get their values from the likes of Oprah, rather than from the Bible. Even many self-professed Christians do not recognize the secular agenda, and Scripture is being covertly undermined. Especially in Western Europe the numbers attending a church or a synagogue are decreasing every year. In Germany the loss of membership of the Lutheran church is alarming. They project they will lose about one half of their members in the next thirty years. The same is true in the Anglican church in Great Britain. As stated elsewhere in this book, a large number of British citizens who converted from Christianity to Islam identified the main reason: Christians did not seem to take their faith seriously. Muslims are often shocked to know that Christians pray. They see their people pray openly but Christians only pray in the church or at home.

Now Islam is faced with a dynamic movement of evangelical and charismatic Christians who really live their faith. They attend church and live after the dictates of the Bible. The challenge of Islam should be a wake-up call to all in the Western world. We need to revisit our faith and begin to take it seriously, or we could be in danger of losing it. It is interesting to note that Islam claims to be the fastest growing religion in the world. Though they are growing quickly, both evangelical and charismatic Christians have a faster growth rate than that of Islam, even when Muslim growth due to high birthrates is considered. The growth rate of all three groups is as follows[1]:

Muslims, 1.82%
Evangelicals, 2.06%
Charismatics, 2.42%

Passive solutions are being practiced in many parts of the world, albeit with little results. The advantage is that people are becoming aware of the problem and are ready to become involved. This solution is open to all who have Jewish or Christian backgrounds. A revival of interest in faith would blunt the sharp edge of the sword of Islam.

An Active Solution

Once when speaking in a large German church about the growth of Islam, I was approached after the lecture by a young German college student. She related to me how she had met an exchange student from Saudi Arabia who was in one of her classes. Once after class they began to talk about religion. She thought he might be interested in exploring the truths of Christianity and she began to share her faith with the young Muslim. He showed real interest. They made an appointment to speak further the next week. The next time he was joined by two more of his fellow countrymen who put pressure on her to convert to Islam. Muslims are active in their witness for their faith. This should be true for Christians also. An active way of stopping the growth of Islam is for Christians to become more vocal in proclaiming their own faith.

For many Christians such an aggressive approach of telling others about their faith is daunting. In our modern world where political correctness is the rule of the day, witnessing to Muslims appears to be taboo. Religion must be kept to one's self. There are several reasons for this:

1. Universalism and inclusivism suggest that if a person believes strongly in the faith that has been revealed to them, then they are going to heaven and there is no need for them to come to the Christian God or to accept Jesus Christ as Savior. Several years ago at the yearly conference of the Lutheran Church in Germany, one of the main speakers stated that there is no longer a need to send out missionaries to the peoples of the world, since, as he said, "We now know that there is salvation in all religions of the world."

2. Religion is viewed as personal and therefore should be kept to one's self. Attempts to try to change another's religion are considered in bad taste.

3. There is real danger in witnessing to a Muslim. This danger is twofold. First, there is danger for the person doing the witnessing. Real persecution is a possibility for the witnessing Christian. Recently a Christian family from the Middle East living in the United States was killed by persons of their home country who pretended to be converted. Other cases include Koreans being killed in Afghanistan, Germans in Turkey, and Americans in Madagascar. The list could go on and on. In each case, the only crime that the Christians were guilty of was witnessing to Muslims. But there is also a real danger for the Muslims themselves. If they appear to be interested in the life-changing message or if they do convert, then they face potential ostracism, beatings, or death at the hands of other Muslims.

4. The last reason is simple. Life is just easier if we let the Muslims go their own way while we go ours. This seems to be the attitude of most in the West today. It is a rather fatalistic way of thinking, especially in light of the rapid growth of Islam today. In Germany they call this *Vogelstrauss Politick*, "Ostrich Politics." If we ignore the threat maybe it will go away so let's just stick our heads in the sand.

These reasons are compelling but they do go against the teachings of Jesus, who said, "Therefore go and make disciples of all nations, baptizing them in the name of the Father and of the Son and of the Holy Spirit, and teaching them to obey everything I have commanded you" (Matthew 28:19–20). With the threat of a growing antagonistic religion that seeks to destroy the Christian faith, however, it is necessary for us to turn the tables and make every effort to win Muslims to the belief that Jesus is the Messiah. The phrase "all nations" in Matthew 28:19 (*panta ta ethna*) does not allow the Bible-believing follower of Jesus Christ to just ignore one-sixth of the world's population.

In the past, the only way to be a witness to a Muslim was to go across the ocean, but most people in the West today know of a Muslim family who lives in their neighborhood. It is imperative that we be witnesses to those who are followers of Muhammad. So how can we do it?

Four Suggestions

Several years ago a world-class expert on Islam, who teaches at a well-known seminary in the United States, wrote me and others who were interested in evangelizing Muslims. He had been given a grant to study the best ways to bring Muslims to Christianity. He wanted as much input as he could get. I sent him the four basic ideas I had developed. After about two years I received an article with his recommendations. He had four points—four points that were surprisingly similar to mine. There are hundreds of books and articles written on the subject, but the actual practice of sharing one's faith is rather simple. Here are the four points I have developed over years of being active in this work.

Method One: Bridge Building

Dr. Donald McGavran, a world famous missiologist, in his groundbreaking book *The Bridges of God*, wrote: "God has bridges to faith built in all philosophies and religions. These are philosophical, theological, or practical aids that can become the starting points for leading a person to the ultimate end of belief and baptism."[2]

A good example of this approach is seen in the experience of Don Richardson who went as a missionary to the Sawi tribe in Netherlands, New Guinea. The account of Richardson's experiences were published in the best-selling book, *Peace Child*. He took his family to this primitive tribe to witness for Christ. After Richardson learned how to communicate with this rather aggressive people, he told them the story of Jesus, emphasizing his last days on earth and the resurrection. After the story was finished the tribesmen saw Judas as the hero of the story—the highest character trait in the belief system of this tribe was deception. Judas was the arch-deceiver. As Richardson tried to reach them with the idea of love he failed. This was not in their mind-set.

The culture was very war-like. After another war with a neighboring tribe the missionary told the people that if they did not stop their fighting then he was going to go home. They had become accustomed to the medicines and iron tools that he brought, so they decided to seek a peace treaty with the other tribe. On the day the treaty was to be formalized, the missionary observed how they did this. The fighting men from one tribe lined up facing the men from the other tribe. In the middle, two young ladies, one from each tribe, stood back to back with their legs spread apart, and one of the men took the newest born child and passed it through the legs of the two women. They then claimed that this child was the peace-child; as long as this child lived there would be peace between the two tribes.

In that ceremony, the missionary saw the God-given bridge to faith. He explained to the people that there was a war between mankind and God. The only way to find real peace was for there to be a child that came from both man and God. This child was Jesus Christ, and if the tribe wanted real peace they would need to accept Jesus as the peace-child. Success followed.

This is only one example of how a bridge can be found. Some think that the fact that the name of Jesus is found twenty-five times in the Qur'an could be a bridge. Generally speaking, Muslims do accept that Jesus lived and was a prophet, but the Qur'an denies that he was crucified and that he rose from the grave. This bridge has not been as successful as first hoped. Others believe that Mary is highly respected by Muslims and see this as a possible bridge. Many authors have suggested numerous other bridges.

If someone really wants to discover the bridge that he or she can best use then time needs to be put into the study of Islam. One must read the Qur'an and spend much time reading the history of Islam as well as the Hadith. One needs to understand this religion in depth in order to build workable bridges to bring Muslims to Jesus Christ.

Method Two: Putting the Christian Faith into a Muslim Context

The purpose of contextualization is to avoid making people change cultures in order to become a Christian. Dr. McGavran stated in one of his classes that the major reason most people do not change religions has nothing to do with theology but rather is because of culture. Particularly in Islam, religion and culture are totally mixed. Islam is a way of life that prescribes living habits, economics, family life, politics, and so on. Thus for a Muslim to become a Christian implies a rejection, not just of one's religion, but of one's entire culture.

Contextualization is a means to make it easier for one to become a Christian by allowing the individual to keep any cultural forms that do not contradict the Christian message.

When I was living in Austria, I traveled to Augsburg, Germany, to preach in an English-language church. There, I met a young man from Pakistan who had converted to Christianity. He related to me how unhappy he was in the church. There were few young people and he said he needed more fellowship. At the time I was leading a very active youth ministry in Salzburg, so I invited him to come live with me in Austria. I told him that we had youth meetings on Wednesday night, Friday night, Saturday night, and Sunday night, and he could go to church on Sunday mornings. He came to Salzburg, and we got him a job, an apartment, and a car. For a while he seemed happy, but after two months, he began to complain. I felt that we had done all we needed to do, but he still was unhappy. "Why?" I asked. His answer was new to me. "Brother," he answered, "when you invited me to come to Salzburg, I thought I would become a part of your family. You would be my guru and I would follow you around most of the time I was not working." I began to realize the signficance of the fact that he was coming from another culture and I was treating him like I would treat a European. When young Muslims come to Christianity, it often means that they are leaving their culture behind. The Muslim family provides most comforts in life, including such things as health insurance, unemployment insurance, financial help, fellowship, even marriage counseling. In European culture, this does not exist. To rip a person out of their culture and expect them to thrive is not always realistic.

In a conference in 1993, many of the top experts on Islam from around the world agreed that probably 80 percent of Muslims that convert to Christianity convert back to Islam because they cannot function in the new culture. It should be noted, however, that recently when this was studied it was discovered that a much higher percentage of converts now remain in the Christian faith. Much has to do with the fact that Christians are now much more culturally sensitive.

In October 1998, "John Travis" (a pseudonym) developed a tool for understanding contextualization in the Muslim context, which he explains in "The C1 to C6 Spectrum: A Practical Tool for Defining Six Types of 'Christ-Centered Communities' (C) Found in the Muslim Context." He uses two terms that need defining: *Insider* refers to language and forms used by the target culture (Muslim) while *Outsider* refers to the Western-Christian forms and language. He lists the six distinctive characteristics of each community.

C1: Traditional Church Using Outsider Language
C2: Traditional Church Using Insider Language
C3: Contextualized Christ-Centered Communities Using Insider Language and Religiously Neutral Insider Cultural Forms
C4: Contextualized Christ-Centered Communities Using Insider Language and Biblically Permissible Cultural and Islamic Forms

C5: Christ-Centered Communities of "Messianic Muslims" Who
     Have Accepted Jesus as Lord and Savior
C6: Small Christ-Centered Communities of Secret/Underground
     Believers[3]

The best way to understand this categorization is that the higher
the number, the more the language and cultural forms of Islam are
used in both worship and communicating Christ. Two examples
are: (1) Can we use the name Allah to describe the Christian God?
There is a great debate in Christian theological circles concerning
this problem. At the C6 level this is always accepted. (2) Another is
the use of the word *mosque* for *church*. Also, should the believers
wear Western clothes or traditional Islamic clothes? Many new
churches are being started in Muslim countries using the various
level of contextualization. Sometimes it is hard to see any Christian
influence in the C6 models, but they still accept Jesus Christ as Savior.

In response to what is happening, some Muslim countries have
enacted laws making it a crime for any non-Muslim to use the name
of Allah to refer to their God. There is a new movement going on in
Christian circles called the "Insider Movement." Those who support
this direction advocate the more radical C5 and C6 levels while more
mainstream Christians only go as far as C4.

For the person desiring to be a witness to Muslims by using contextualization, they need to give much time and thought into how best
to bridge the cultural divide in order to make the gospel acceptable.

A good example of an attempt to see if contextualization works
was an experiment I made in 1998. I was the consultant for Church
Growth for Europe and the Middle East, thus having contact in both
areas of the world. In Israel, the Baptists owned a lovely retreat center
in the middle of the country. In trying to get Christians from different cultures together to share their faith they held a yearly conference with four different groups of Christian leaders attending:

1. Baptist Pastors from Russia
2. Baptist Pastors from Germany

3. Messianic Jews from Israel
4. Converted Muslims from the Middle East

In the beginning, it was apparent that it would be hard for these four groups to agree on most things. The best way to bring unity was to emphasize the lordship of Jesus Christ. During this conference it was decided to hold a "Christian Mosque Service." The leader knew a young missionary who had done much research in the area of contextualization. He was invited to come to the Baptist Village and hold a contextualized worship service.

The service was interesting. It began with him in his Arabic garb standing on the roof and giving the call to prayer. Instead of the normal Islamic statement, he recited part of the gospel of Luke in Arabic. Before anyone could go into the service they needed to take off their shoes and wash their feet, ears, and nose. The auditorium was divided; the women were behind a curtain and the men were in the front. Each person had a defined space where they sat on the floor. Everything was done as it would be in a mosque except the message was of Jesus Christ and not of Muhammad. Those in attendance would stand, kneel, bend, bow, and do all the other activities that would be expected of a Muslim in one of their worship services.

Afterward I interviewed each of the groups to discover their reactions. The results were interesting. The Russian pastors stated that there was only one way to worship God and all other ways were evil. The German pastors were happy and said that they wanted their churches back home to also experiment with these forms. The Jewish believers said they had a bad feeling during the services because they felt they were compromising with the enemy. The reflection from the converted Muslims was the most interesting. They all agreed with one answer: "Brother, we have been saved by Jesus Christ and now you are trying to put us back into the forms that we have been saved from. We reject this method."

One published method of witnessing to Muslims, "The Camel Method," gained a degree of success using these ideas. The name comes from the story that Muslims love to tell that says God has one hundred names but people only know ninety-nine of them. Only the camel knows the hundredth name of God. This is why it appears that he has a smile on his face. The Camel Method begins by stating that the Christian also knows the hundredth name of God: Jesus. Many other cultural forms are also used in this method.

Contextualization is still in the formative stage. Many see it as the way of the future, while others see it as an unhealthy compromise of the faith. Each person must make their own decision. In Southeast Asia this method has enjoyed great success.

Method Three: Spiritual Intervention

From speaking with more than three hundred Muslims who have converted to Christianity and have remained in the faith, I know that many have had a special visitation from God that has helped them to become Christians. Approximately 95 percent of those had a vision or a dream of Jesus or heard his voice, which played an important part in their conversion. It seems that the Holy Spirit is working in the lives of those who are seeking him. Given that some Christian theologians today believe that signs, wonders, and miracles were only for the time period prior to the birth of the New Testament church and are not valid today, it's important to restudy this early church phenomenon in today's contemporary society. It does not seem to be a problem for those who have had such an experience. They believe it is real. Someone has said that the person who has had an experience is never at the mercy of the one who has an argument. In the last several decades, there has been an explosion of growth of the church in Muslim areas, and in most cases, signs, wonders, and miracles have played a significant role. It appears that God is working in a new and exciting way in the lives of many Muslims.

It is a fact that most people living in the secularized West have a problem with signs, wonders, and miracles. In 1982 Paul Hiebert published an article in *Missiology* called "The Flaw of the Excluded Middle." In this article, Hiebert points out that most Western

Christians tend to live without the awareness of the "middle" world of supernatural beings and activity, which is part of everyday life in most non-Western cultures.[4]

For Hiebert the two extremes are (1) those who see a demon behind every bush and (2) those who totally deny the existence of a spirit world. A good place to be is in the middle of the two extremes. *A Christian who rejects the possibility of divine intervention in the conversion process should not get too involved in the process of bringing Muslims to Christ since so many are experiencing divine intervention.* True, there are other ways to witness to Muslims, but one should never discount divine intervention.

In the early church, the disciples were called by Jesus and he "gave them authority to drive out evil spirits and to heal every disease and sickness" (Matthew 10:1). Of course the next question is: If this is true why is it that all Christians today do not have this power? One real possibility is that God reserves this unusual strength for situations where only he can work. This was true in the early church when most structures in the society were against the new church, and it is true today when witnessing to Muslims since they have much to overcome in becoming Christians. It has been said that martyrdom gives life to the church. This seems to be true in most cases, but not with Islam simply because Muslim persecution is so complete and aggressive that it has proven very effective in stopping the church.

The cases of Muslims having some form of a divine intervention are too numerous to ignore. Throughout history there have been reports of such happenings in individual cases but since the turn of the century the numbers have increased considerably. Here are some of the visions and dreams that I can personally attest to. They are not hearsay or urban legends but real cases with real people.

The Voice of God

A businessman from one of the North African countries was a well respected leader in his city as well as a devoted Muslim. He had some encounters with Christians and was aware of their message of salvation in Christ but decided to remain a follower of Islam. In fact, he even made the decision to go on a pilgrimage to Mecca, a *hajji*. One of the required activities for completing the *hajji* was that he had to walk seven times round the *Ka'aba*, the large draped building that contained the holy black stone. All who participate wear a similar white garment, ensuring that no one is better clothed than the others. He reported that while he was going around the *Ka'aba* and praying, he heard a voice saying, "Jesus Christ is the Lord." At the time he wondered if it was the voice of God or a Christian who was willing to risk death by being a witness in Mecca. As he contemplated this, he got to the other side and heard the voice again. He was so convinced that it was God who was speaking to him that when he returned to his home he converted to Christianity. Today he lives as a secret follower of Jesus in his country.

Family Honor

At a meeting in North Africa, one young Muslim from the Middle East gave his testimony. He related how his father came to him and reported that his sister had announced that she had become a Christian. Since he was the oldest son, it was his duty to kill his sister. He did not want to, but he knew that the honor of the family was at stake. He decided to kill her on a certain night. He purchased a large knife, and while she was asleep he went to her room and was ready to thrust the knife into her body. He just could not bring himself to do the final deed. It seemed to him that some power was staying his hand. He went back to his room and fell asleep. He then had a vision where Jesus told him that his sister had found the right path and he too should give his life to Jesus Christ. That night he also became a Christian. Later that week, both he and his sister fled the home and went into hiding rather than face certain death. Both today are practicing believers.

The Iranian Doctor

A medical doctor and his family had been attending a Christian church because he was interested in the teachings of Jesus Christ and he wanted to look into becoming a Christian. During a sermon, the pastor related how a person had been enveloped by the Holy Spirit. The description was that the person was standing in a desert place and a cloud came over him and suddenly he knew the real truth of Jesus Christ. After the sermon, the doctor came to the pastor and said that during the week he had almost exactly the same dream. When the cloud came over him he knew at once that it could not be from man because a voice pointed him to Jesus Christ. The man is a practicing Christian today.

In undertaking the responsibility of evangelizing Muslims, the Christian should expect that there will be divine intervention, even spiritual warfare, in the encounter between Islam and Christianity. It is important to remember that "the one who is in you is greater than the one who is in the world" (1 John 4:4).

When well-known missiologist Dr. Donald McGavran was close to death, he was visited by his close friend, Dr. Art Glasser. During that last conversation, McGavran, whose mind was sharp to the very end, asked Glasser, "Art, what part of the Great Commission has the church of today failed to understand?" Glasser first considered the word "go." But he concluded that this could not be the weakness because the church is sending out a large number of missionaries. The next phrase of "make disciples" came to his mind and he remembered the growth of the church worldwide. Then he thought about the word "baptizing." But again the church is baptizing more than ever before. Lastly, he thought about the word "teach." He thought about the large number of Bible schools, universities, and courses now available.

Glasser replied that he was not sure what part of the Great Commission the church had ignored. McGavran then replied, "Art, that part of the Great Commission that the church has ignored is when Jesus said, 'All authority has been given to me.' Art, do you realize that the church has forgotten that Jesus has all authority in heaven and earth? The church today has access to this authority."

As the West tries to find answers to the growth of Islam today, Christians must remember that they are not in a place of inferiority to the rapidly growing faith of Islam, but rather it is the Christians who really have this great authority, given by Jesus Christ to his church. It is no wonder that Islam seems to present a wall of indifference to us. God has now entered into the scene. Dreams, visions, and voices are now commonplace and more Muslims are coming to faith in Christ today than at any time in the last century and possibly in all of history. The prayer of the church must be that Jesus will break down the strongholds of Islam and open the minds of our Muslim neighbors to the truth of Jesus Christ.

Method Four: "But the Greatest of These Is Love"

The words of Paul in 1 Corinthians 13, "But the greatest of these is love," may sound simplistic. All Christians know that love is an important building stone in the life of both the church and its disciples, but can it actually become a witnessing tool? The "love encounter," as some have named it, has become germane to the evangelistic process. The strength of love in Christian theology and the absence of it in Islam have given our faith an edge over Islam. Muslims are taught how to argue theological points and how to find fallacies in the Christian faith, but when they come up against love, they seem to be in an uncomfortable position. Though they can use the word *love* they cannot fully understand its implications as Christians do. Someone who is looking for a way to help Muslims can simply practice love as outlined in the Bible. Possibly the best way to reach Muslims is through love.

The Love of Allah in the Qur'an

Shortly after the events of September 11, most mosques in the San Francisco area held open houses. Their signs stated such things as,

"Come and Learn the Truth about Islam" or "Islam is not a Terrorist Religion." They wanted to try to blunt the negative criticism that appeared in America after the downing of the World Trade Center. It was interesting to learn that they were using a form of literary contextualization. They were using Christian terms to describe their faith. Islam was described as a religion of "love, forgiveness, peace, and compassion." Is Islam really a religion of love in a way that is equal with Christianity? I think not.

As previously stated, in the Qur'an there are ninety-nine names of Allah revealed to man. One of these names is *al-wudud*, "the loving." This name is attributed to Allah two different times in the Qur'an; *Surah* 11:90 says, "merciful and loving is my Lord," and *Surah* 85:14 states, "He is oft-forgiving, full of loving-kindness."[5] In both of these references, Allah's love is linked with his mercy and forgiveness. This love is in reference to the Muslim's faith and works. Dennis Grill, author of "Love and Affection" in the *Encyclopedia of the Qur'an* says, "The name *al-wadud* gives the clear expression to the reciprocity of love between God and humans."[6] Gerhard Bowering, who wrote "God and His Attributes" in the same encyclopedia, points out, however, that this name which qualifies God to be "loving" has an unsettling counterpoint in a Qur'anic verse depicting divine love answered by human love: "He loves them and they love Him."[7] It is necessary to examine the word "love" as it appears in the Qur'an.

Ahabba is the verb used most frequently in the Qur'an to express the idea of love. It is used sixty-four times, and another common verb, *hubb*, is used nine times. These verbs are used in the Qur'an to express love between humans, individuals loving earthly pleasures, as well as Allah's love. Let us focus mostly on the verbs as they are used to express Allah's love for mankind. In the Qur'an concordance, the most repeated phrase is "God loves the good-doers." This phrase is found in *Surah* 2:195, 3:134, 3:148, 5:13, and 5:93. The next most common phrases are "Allah loves the god-fearing" (3:76, 9:4, and 9:7) and "Allah loves the just" (5:42, 49:9, and 60:8), each found three times in the text. Most of the other verses pertaining to the love of Allah are in a similar conditional format.

Other verses put a condition on Allah's love:

Allah loves those who repent (2:222).

Allah loves those who cleanse themselves (9:108).

Allah loves those who put their trust in him (3:159).

It is apparent that Allah loves those who obey him, but what of those who do not? The Qur'an has a number of verses that state who Allah does not love:

- the corrupter
- the shouter of evil words
- the aggressor
- any guilty ingrate
- evildoers
- the proud and boastful
- the guilty traitor

When we examine these verses related to Allah's love, we get a good picture of what and who he loves and does not love. His love is conditionally based upon the actions and deeds of his followers, depending on if they are good or bad.

The Love of God in the Bible

The central theme of the Bible is love. In 1 John 4:8, we find the ultimate description of God—"God is Love."

In the Old Testament, "love" as shown by God to an individual or to Israel is explicitly mentioned more than twenty-five times, and is a constant theme that is seen throughout Israelite history. Similar to Allah, God is said to love righteous persons (Psalm 146:8) and righteousness and justice (Psalms 33:5; 37:28), but he also demonstrates a different kind of love that is unique to Yahweh. This love is unconditional. In the midst of Israel's rebellion and disobedience, God still loves his chosen people. He states, "I have loved you with an everlasting love" (Jeremiah 31:3).

The Hebrew word *hesed* is found in the Old Testament about 250 times. There is no English equivalent, but it is often translated as "steadfast love," "loving kindness," or just "love," and is used in reference to God's covenant with his people. God's forgiveness in the Old Testament is closely related to this *hesed* as well. He repeatedly forgives Israel because of his steadfast love for his people. James Windrow Sweetman, author of *Islam and Christian Theology*, says that the "ideas expressed by the words *hen* and *hesed* result in a conception of God which infinitely surpasses that found in the Qur'an."[8]

In the New Testament there are four words used to mean *love*. The most important for this discussion is *agape*. This word or derivatives from it occur 341 times in the Bible. It is often defined as "unconditional love" or love that is given without requiring anything in return. According to the *Baker Encyclopedia of the Bible*, "*Agape* means to love the undeserving despite disappointment and rejection."[9] This is a totally different type of love than the one found in the Qur'an. Jesus told many parables which explicitly defined this type of love: The Prodigal Son, The Lost Sheep, and The Lost Coin, among others. Scholar Peggy Starkey writes that each parable "demonstrates God's love of outcasts and sinners and describes God as good, gracious, merciful and loving."[10]

The climax of God's love is demonstrated in his Son Jesus Christ. Ephesians 2:4–5 states, "But because of his great love for us, God, who is rich in mercy, made us alive with Christ even when we were dead in transgressions—it is by grace you have been saved." Even while we were in sin, God loved us and sent his one and only Son to die in our place. First John 4:9 beautifully describes the love of God demonstrated to the world by sending Jesus Christ. John writes that "this is how God showed his love among us: He sent his one and only Son into the world that we might live through him." Jesus Christ is the ultimate expression of God's love for us. Sadly, this saving aspect of the works of Jesus is completely missing in Islam. The Muslims see Jesus as both a good man and a prophet, but they miss the ultimate truth in Christianity—the love of God. Muslims deny this love by their insistence that Jesus did not die on the cross. His death on the cross is the main teaching of the Bible in respect to God's love for us.

Using Love in Witnessing

Now we come to the core of this discord: How can we use love in attempting to bring a Muslim to faith in Jesus Christ? Thus far we have discovered that fear is a dominant factor in the lives of most Muslims. The Qur'an adds to this fear by portraying God as one who loves only the deserving, thus man must work hard to receive Allah's love. The Bible, however, portrays God as one who loves people unconditionally. To please him we must come to him by faith. No matter what we do, he will still love us. But showing this love is much more difficult than it might seem. Muslims are taught to fear Christians, especially those who are witnesses. One woman in Belgium said she was taught, "they will steal our souls and send them to Hell for eternity."

The "love encounter" is the theme of many books on missions. The teachings in the Bible are so clear that we must seek such an encounter to be obedient to God. In respect to this encounter, David Hesselgrave writes:

> As in the case of prayer, love is often related to special strategies such as incarnational ministry, missionary identification, the servant role, winning a hearing, bridging, and bonding. But love, like prayer, should characterize *all* missionary encounters with the world. It should not be distinct from any of them.[11]

Another writer J. I. Bavink addressed this topic and speaks about the "truth encounter":

Meeting-in-love includes the recognition of myself in the other person, a sympathetic feeling of his guilt and a sincere desire in Christ to do with this man what Christ has done with me. . . . I cannot really look another person in the eye without being reminded of the darkness out of which Christ has called me.[12]

Possibly the best teaching that can be given to those who want to try this method can be observed in a short television commercial. In the United States there was a TV ad that begins with a scene of one side of a basketball court. Then in slow motion Michael Jordan, one of the greatest basketball players in history, is seen making two gigantic steps toward the basket, and with strength and accuracy, he slams the ball through the basket. The next words on the screen are "*Just Do It.*" This very simple lesson possibly says all that needs to be said. Christians should just love the Muslims with whom they come into contact.

One help can be found in ministry evangelism. The basis of this method is to find a felt need and then to meet it. All people have felt needs. Seldom do they wear signs telling others what it is, but with both prayer and observation, these needs can be determined. Once they have been discovered, then ways must be found to meet these needs. Here it is important to remember that love demands that we meet these needs not just to bring the Muslim into our faith but to genuinely help them without asking anything in return.

In the case of Muslims, Christians must understand that they live in fear of their neighbors and especially of Christians. Sometimes just a smile, a helping hand, or looking after their children when the parents must be gone are ways to begin a friendship. It is not always necessary to begin to use the Bible to convert them. First a foundation of love must be built. When the time is right, they will ask why the Christian is helping so much. This provides believers a chance to explain the love that God has given to them in Christ Jesus. There is a tendency by most in the West to shun Muslims. The heavy black dress of the women and the standoffishness of the men often give us an excuse to remain aloof.

Another good way to begin dialogue with Muslims is to ask them about their religion. We as Christians have been taught that talking about religion is off limits in a polite discussion. This is not true for a Muslim. They enjoy discussing their religion and often wonder why we seldom speak about our beliefs. They sometimes feel that we are ashamed of our Lord. We should not begin by telling them they are sinners, but begin by asking them about Islam. If we listen, we can learn much about their faith. If we continue to learn from them, the time will come when they ask about our beliefs. At this point, we can just give them a general description of what we believe. We should not at this time feel that we must win them to Christ. They too just want to learn. The message of Christ will begin to penetrate their hearts, but it could take many years before they understand enough to take the crucial step into a saving relationship with Christ.

Many have pointed out that people from Islamic countries are often great hosts. As good relationships are built, invitations will be forthcoming to visit in their homes and the guests will get a royal reception. Many from the West who have been so graciously received see this as love, but often there is in the Middle Eastern culture a demand that this hospitality be returned. Because of this cultural tradition, Westerners could also invite Muslims into their homes, so as to build up better relationships, but we still should not mistake their hospitality for love.

As previously stated, many Muslims who have converted to Christianity return to Islam. One reason is that they are initially impressed by the love shown by Christians and their church, however after they commit to being a Christian, leaving their culture and support system, and coming to the church, they find that they are closed out of a continued close relationship to the inner lives of both the Christian church and their Muslim families. They are told to come to church and read their Bible, but we stop showing them the same love as before they accepted Christ. They are taken aback by this change. If we are to use love to bring a person from Islam into faith into Christ, then this love must continue. It is here that many will be forced to count the cost of witnessing to a Muslim. It is practically the equivalent of an adoption. They have a great need to be a part of the family of God.

Conclusion

Both Islam and Christianity are missionary religions. Both are in a battle to bring others into their religion. At this time evangelical and charismatic Christianity are growing faster than Islam, but Islamists argue otherwise.

Christians should always be guided by the command of Jesus "to make disciples of all nations." This very command means that we have been given the task of being witnesses to Muslims wherever they can be found. Today they are in every city and every town in the West. Our duty before God is to find them and to share with them the wonderful love of Jesus Christ. This rather simple method is one that all in the Western world can participate in if they are concerned about the growth of Islam today.

New mosque in a rural area in Southeast Asia.

appendix **a**

Quotes from Middle Eastern Sources (2002)

In an attempt to better understand the current thinking on *Da'wah* and the strategy on the part of both Muslim scholars and the Islamic media, I asked one of my doctoral students to do research in sources written in Arabic and readily available in the Middle East. This student now lives in Germany but was born and grew up in one of the core countries of the Middle East. He spent several months studying numerous sources, the main one being the *Middle East Newspaper*. He did the translations from Arabic into English since he is fluent in both languages.

The endnotes are somewhat different than those generally used in the West, but one can still determine both the validity and the source of the statements. The purpose of this addition to the book is to help the reader see that much of what has been written thus far is not fictitious. There is definitely a prevailing attitude in the Middle East that both sets Islam against the West and seeks to further the growth of Islam in the world.

Appendix A is divided as follows:

1. Connecting Islamic Religious *(Da'wah)* Institutions with Aid Organizations and Other Institutions
2. The Use of Dialogue in *Da'wah*
3. The Ecumenicalization of Islam
4. Political Ambitions and How They Help *Da'wah*
5. The Constitution of the Islamic Infrastructure
6. The Institutionalization of *Da'wah* in the Western Context (Para-Mosque)

1. CONNECTING ISLAMIC RELIGIOUS (*DA'WAH*) INSTITUTIONS WITH AID ORGANIZATIONS AND OTHER INSTITUTIONS

The cooperation between the Islamic organization (*Da'wah*) and other Islamic institutions is very important to fulfill one goal: the proclamation of Islam as soon as possible. Through this cooperation, the organizations are saving time and efforts in the establishment of an Islamic nation (*ummah*) and law (Sharia).

Connecting Works with Aid Work Organizations

Shaik Aqil Alaqil, the chairman of the Mecca relief institutions Al Haramain and Al Shariefain, confirmed that all *Da'wah* works and relief work in the West have overcome all of the problems incurred since September 11. According to Shaik Aqil, the work of these organizations, besides the relief work, also includes *Da'wah* to Islam. In this newspaper article, it also stresses that the first goal of this organization is *Da'wah* bringing non-Muslims to Islam. This organization has thirty-one branches inside Saudi Arabia and twenty-two other branches all over the rest of the world, including the United States. One of the goals of the organization is to help prisoners by providing them different ways to experience Islam. Sometimes the organization will pay the small amount required to purchase the release of these prisoners. They have also established Qur'an teaching circles, and they build prayer rooms. The organization has also built approximately one hundred mosques around the world and has held conferences in which Islamic beliefs were taught. This organization paid 1.3 million riyal ($400,000) in their support of Qur'an teaching circles. They have paid approximately 1.0 million riyal ($250,000) in their support of helping prisoners.[1]

Concerning the Relief World Islamic Organization (located in Kuwait), the chairman stresses that they are involved with six thousand charity projects around the globe. One of the main thrusts of these charity projects centers on the proclamation of Islam. Other projects include building mosques, schools, universities, hospitals, clinics, orphanages, and other educational institutions. In just a six-month period, they have spent the equivalent of millions of U.S. dollars in the carrying out of these projects. Some of the members of this organization are leaders in the *Da'wah* field. The president stresses that all Islamic organizations should coordinate with each other. These organizations deal with the Islamic Institution for Education, Science, and Culture.[2]

Along with the relief projects, the Abdulaziz bin Baz Charity Foundation (ABCF) is helping the Islamic *Da'wah* organizations in the proclamation of Islam to the Muslim minority in the West as well as the non-Muslim majority. Recently this organization produced a film called *True Islam,* which introduces the religion to the world. It was produced in English and French and will be broadcast by the biggest broadcasting companies in the Western world (United States, Europe, and Australia). One of the goals is to have this film translated into all of the vital languages around the globe.

The primary subjects of the film are:

- The Islamic role in building the world culture through history
- The normality and mediation of Islam
- The importance of dialogue between Islamic nations and other nations and religions
- The role of Islam in giving mankind freedom through Allah
- Islamic roles within scientific research
- The Islamic role in establishing Western culture

The primary goals of the film are:

- The proclamation of Islam to the world
- Displaying Islamic teachings and principles
- Explaining Islamic beliefs
- Encouraging non-Muslims to embrace the religion[3]

Recently, the ministry of Islamic affairs held a conference in Jeddah, Saudi Arabia, concerning the Islamic organizations under the religious administration and their spheres of influence. All Islamic organizations present confirmed that the most important relief work they can give to the non-Muslim world is presenting Islam . . . the acceptable religion before Allah (*Surah* 3:19).[4]

Da'wah Through the Mass Media, Governmental Institutions, and Organizations

The Islamic world is now focusing more firmly on spreading Islam through the use of mass media and governmental organizations. One of the primary ways this occurs is through the Islamic relief organizations. Dr. Roushdy Shahata, a professor at Helwan University in Egypt, said, "The journalists must always have a good Islamic bias. Also, being a religious journalist, he can write his subjects from the Islamic point of view." He assures that the goal of the Islamic media is to broadcast to the entire world.[5]

There are many cases of cooperation between Islamic institutions and media organizations. Recently, the Islamic Institution for Education, Science, and Culture met with an Islamic online organization. The purpose was to set up conferences, educational meetings, and Islamic studies for access on the Internet. This will give a better view for Islam in the West via the Internet. They also dealt with the translation and publishing of Islamic science and cultural books.[6]

Dr. Fahad al Tajash, the chairman of a Saudi company for research and publishing, confirmed that the cooperation between his institution and the Muslim World League was regarded as a major step in helping the Islamic nation and in spreading Islam. He also emphasized the importance of such cooperation between all Islamic organizations around the globe. This would help the spread of Islam and also help it to be seen in a better way.[7]

The relationship between the Muslim World League and a newspaper in the Middle East is considered the most significant of the reported organizational alliances. In 2001, they held a conference together in Jeddah, Saudi Arabia, concerning ecumenical media. Dr. Al-Turki emphasized once again the importance of the mass media in the spread of Islam. They made a plan of cooperation between them in order to proclaim Islam and display it in a better light. Al-Turki also said that all of the mass media must cooperate with the *Da'wah* organizations.[8]

2. THE USE OF DIALOGUE IN *Da'wah*

Dialogue is one of the main strategies in the proclamation of Islam to the Western world. After the discovery that the religion could not be spread in the West through the use of war, they started employing another strategy . . . living in the Western countries and gradually spreading Islam and establishing the Islamic nation. Therefore, the Islamic organizations are now having some type of dialogue with the entire world.

Thoughts About Dialogue from an Islamic Perspective

When dialoguing about Islam in the West, members of an Islamic organization will refrain from making references to the Islam of Medina. This includes all of the scriptures that deal with killing all of the non-Muslims and treating them badly. The scriptures also say that the only acceptable religion is Islam and that the whole earth must become an Islamic nation. Instead, the dialogue revolves around the Islam of Mecca. This is when Muhammad was a weak man and didn't have many followers. He would show love and mercy, saying that his new religion is a peaceful one that respects all other nations and religions. The Islam of Medina is known as the bloody side of Islam, and the Islam of Mecca is known as the good side of Islam. Furthermore, Allah has promised to all Muslims that he will establish them on earth if they believe and do righteous deeds (*Surah* 24:52).[9]

Dr. Yusuf al-Qaradawi, one of the more famous Islamic scholars, confirmed that Allah has allowed the Islamic religion to spread into the whole world through the use of wars. But because they are no longer able to do this, they must use another way to proclaim Islam. We can see from this statement that Allah had legislated the war against anyone who is not Muslim and anyone who stands against Islam. But they do not say this during any dialogues with Western officials.[10]

Along the same lines as Dr. al-Qaradawi, Dr. Al-Turki, the secretary general of the Muslim World League, said, "We must learn many things from the battle of Bader (a war that was led by Muhammad during the second year of establishing Islam in Ramadan against the non-Muslim in Mecca during their way to the north of Mecca to do business)." In this battle, many men were killed from both sides. Yet we see Dr. Al-Turki referencing it as something that we must learn many things from.[11] In addition to these, we also have one of the most famous Islamic priests (Sheik Ibin Athemin) confirming that there is only one party before Allah, which is Hezeb Allah (God's Party), which basically means that the only religion acceptable to God is Islam.[12] Ibin Baz is also quoted as saying that the only people who are close to the heart of God are Muslims.[13]

The Islamic nation would still condone the spread of Islam through the use of warfare. They are not able to do this because of the Western abilities in warfare and sometimes must even avoid the subject in their history.

Islamic Dialogue (with the Western Government)

The Islamic organizations in the West always display the Islam of Mecca during their dialogues so that the Western world may only see the peaceful side of the religion. The side that loves Allah and other nations and respects their decisions to choose the religion that they want. The side that proclaims that Islam is against any kind of terrorism, especially the kind that is to proclaim Islam. During the last meetings of the Muslim World League, Dr. Al-Turki confirmed that Islam is against any kind of terrorist activity and that Islam is a tolerant religion.[14]

Generally, all of the Islamic organizations and their leaders emphasize that Islam is against terrorism and does not distinguish itself among other religions that are not Muslim. Dr. Abed Al aziz Bin Authman Al Tuaigy (the president of the Islamic Institution for Education, Science, and Culture) said that Islam is a tolerant religion that loves all mankind.[15]

Dialogue with the Professors and the Educational Institutions

Having dialogues with professors and educational institutions is very important because it is through them that access will be gained into the government, thus beginning the change of Western legislation. This will allow the Islamic minority to practice their beliefs and proclaim Islam. During a meeting for the Islamic intellectuals in the Muslim world, they emphasized the importance of all professors having training and exposure to the true Islamic beliefs, so they can display those beliefs during global conferences.[16]

Another approach in reaching the Western intellectuals is through the scientific study of the Qur'an. The Muslim scientists purposefully seek out Western scientists for this very reason. Dr. Al-Turki said, "It is very important to reach the academics in the west, to visit the colleges which have orientation studies, and to dialogue with their professors in order to display the good side of Islam." He said this before his visit to a college in Scotland.[17]

Dr. Al-Turki and a large Islamic delegation visited Germany on June 17, 2002. The aim of the visit was to have a meeting with the scholars and politicians in Germany and then in the whole of Europe, and finally in the United States. During the visits, the delegation explained the Islamic teachings about war and terrorism.[18] After finishing the visit to Germany, the delegation went on to the United Kingdom for the same purpose.[19]

As we can see, the most important Islamic organization in the Islamic world is the Muslim World League, which is supported by Saudi Arabia. This league contains sixty Islamic organizations gathered from the entire Islamic world and plays a very vital role in the displaying of Islam to the Western world, especially within the governments and educational institutions.[20]

Dialogue Through Conferences, Global Meetings, and Exhibitions

During a humanity conference, the participants emphasized the importance of dialogue with the West and Christians, and the necessity of presenting the good principles of Islam to the Western masses and their governments.[21]

An Islamic delegation participated in Earth Summit 2002 in Johannesburg. Dr. Al-Turki and many Islamic leaders accompanied them. This conference was considered the largest one in the world. The aims of the Islamic delegation were:

1. To show the importance of Islamic toleration with (and within) other nations
2. To help other nations get rid of their problems by the application of Islamic solutions (offered by Allah through the Qur'an) to Earth-related problems
3. And mainly, to proclaim Islam to the whole world[22]

During an exhibition, Yussif Islam—a British *daa'i* (who embraced Islam years ago and wants to proclaim it through his exhibition in London)—confirmed that the main goal is doing and proclaiming Islam to non-Muslims. One of the participants was the Islamic British photographer Abed.[23]

Sometimes the Islamic minority has held their exhibitions in Christian churches. One such event happened in Amsterdam, Holland. One of the visitors was the queen of Holland, and she said that it is time to learn many things from the Islamic culture and people should get used to seeing a Muslim woman in parliament.[24]

3. THE ECUMENICALIZATION OF ISLAM

The ecumenicalization of Islam, or the Islamic law, is also one of the Muslim World League's strategies to proclaim Islam to the world. The organizations are using this approach because of the danger of the worldly ecumenical focus to the stability of the Islamic nation in the West and also in the Islamic countries. This is why the whole of the Islamic organizations are holding meetings and conferences to deal with this new wave of ecumenical focus.

Recently, most of the Islamic organizations met in Mecca to submit their suggestions about how to deal with this. The mass media perspective simply confirmed that the journalists must have religious training and know basic Islamic teachings. Dr. Al-Turki said that it is very important for journalists to know the major principles of Islam so that they can give the Islamic solutions to the world problems. He also called for cooperation between all Islamic organizations with the mass media in the Arab world and in the West. He also said that the Islamic organizations are preparing to have an Islamic mass media institution.[25]

Dr. Gaffer Edrissi, the president of the Islamic American University, said, "I'm not against the ecumenical movement. . . . I see it will insure that Islam is a global religion and its prophet Muhammad is a prophet for the entire world. Through the ecumenical movement, the world will be like a small village and this village doesn't need more than one prophet, which is Muhammad. Furthermore, the Islamic legislations are very flexible and we can apply them in any time and in any place."[26]

King Fahd, the king of Saudi Arabia, said, "We must get benefit from the ecumenical movement because it is still in the beginning and we must Islamize it as soon as possible to help the Islamic nation."[27]

4. Political Ambitions and How They Help Da'wah

Political and Administrative Activities

An ambition of Islamic organizations is to have a representative in the American Congress, in the European parliament, and in a scientific society or institution that has good relationships with prominent people. Dr. Al-Turki stresses, "We must reach the scholars and the politicians in the West because their governments depend on their decisions within research."[28]

The executive director of the Council on American-Islamic Relations (CAIR), Nihad Awad, said, "The Muslim minorities are working hard to be a powerful instrument during the next presidential election in the United States." He added that there are one hundred thousand Muslim voters from seven big states. Furthermore, the Muslims have finished establishing an educational and religious infrastructure in North America, so now it is time to establish an Islamic political infrastructure.

CAIR is working hard to train Muslim leaders to be politicians. Only in this role can Muslims ensure a strong future in North America and Canada. After what happened on September 11, 2001, this strategy became more than a hobby; it became a must for Muslims.[29]

Paul Findley, a member of the Middle East committee in Congress, confirmed that Muslims are now in very sensitive and important positions in America. They are making their presence known within public political decisions as well. They helped George H. W. Bush get elected by contributing sixty thousand votes to the critical state of Florida. With this on their side, they are pushing Islamic organizations to cooperate with any future presidential candidates.[30]

An article on an Islamic website pointed out that there are many Islamic students who want to get involved with politics. Islamic institutions and organizations are training them to be powerful elements in the support of Islam in the future politics of the West.

This article also pointed out that Muslim men getting married to non-Muslim women will increase the number of votes for an Islamic political candidate because of their tendency to vote along with their husbands.[31]

Recall the discussion in chapter 9 under "Influence Through Politics"—notably the words of Dr. Al-Turki: "The European parliaments are a very good way to reach within the countries."[32]

Islamize the Politicians: The Shortcut to Reaching the Western Governments

Sometimes the strategies of dialogue, the Internet, and sending delegations are not enough. So some have been implementing another method for the past fifty years. It is to simply Islamize the governor, prominent people, and politicians of the West. Through these individuals, Islam can be shown in a good light to the general populace.

Again, the discussion in chapter 9 under "Influence Through Politics" addressed this issue and offered several specific examples. Recall particularly the words of Dr. Marzouk: "The Muslims in this country must be ready to govern Holland because of the increasing numbers of Muslims and the decreasing numbers of the original people of Holland."[33]

5. The Constitution of the Islamic Infrastructure

In order to guarantee a good future of the Islamic nation in the West, it is important to have an Islamic infrastructure that will have the ability to take care of the Islamic people in every aspect of life. They are going to need the proper religious training in order to keep the Islamic nation strong all over the globe. It is useless if they have mosques that teach only a few individual people without having an educational infrastructure that can reach the whole Islamic generation. Educational institutions can implant Islamic beliefs in a better way than can mosques.

The Constitution of Islamic Educational Infrastructure
and Religious Infrastructure

Many Islamic organizations in the West have helped their people
by building them schools and Islamic institutions, thus giving them
a higher profile in the society. The students of Al-Azhar University,
Cairo, are presently studying how to plant new Islamic colleges in
the United States and Europe that will teach Islamic law and how to
make *Da'wah* among non-Muslims, while also learning the Arabic
language.[34]

According to Dr. Al-Turki, the Saudi Arabian government has established thousands of mosques and Islamic educational institutions
and schools around the globe in order to proclaim the Islamic religion to the non-Muslim West.[35]

It is easy to see the role of Saudi Arabia in the spreading of Islam.
In the United Kingdom, London and Edinburgh are the centers for
Islamic activity. Islamic books (approx. 92,000) concerning the Islamic *Da'wah* have been given to these locations for distribution. Almost 500 copies of the Qur'an and about 34,100 collections of other
books have also been distributed. This type of activity is apparently
normal according to the Islamic leaders of these areas.[36] The establishment of a European Islamic university is a primary goal of the
Muslim World League. It will teach religion, law, medicine, engi-
neering, and so on.[37]

Right now it is difficult to establish an Islamic infrastructure of
education in America. But there are enough mosques. However,
there is a school in New Jersey that is Islamic and has seven hundred
students. There are plans to build two similar schools in the near
future.[38]

Dr. Ali Qara Daghi, President of the Belief Section of the Islamic
University in Qatar and a member of the European Council for Islamic Research says, "The educational infrastructure should continue to be a focus even after the religious infrastructure is in place."[39]

In the August 10, 2002, edition of the *Economist,* a special report
on Muslim activity in Western Europe was featured. It focused on

whether there were some things about Islam that make it impossible for it to integrate into liberal Western societies. The conclusion was that there is nothing in Islam that makes integration impossible but that there are several obstacles that must be overcome. One obstacle concerns the prayer leaders of the mosques and their involvement with the community. They apparently are ignorant about the countries in which they are placed. Forward thinking *imams* said that if Europe is to be served appropriately, then *imams* must be trained in Europe rather than in the Middle East, Pakistan, or North Africa. This leads to the suggestion of European states establishing and funding these schools in order to counter this problem.[40]

Establishing a Global Islamic Infrastructure for the Islamic Mass Media

The need for an Islamic mass media is increasing day by day, especially after what happened in New York and Washington, D.C., on September 11, 2001. Obviously, it isn't enough to only have local Islamic mass media in Islamic countries when their felt need is to show the good side of Islam across the world. In order to make this happen, they must establish a global infrastructure of mass media that will have the ability and the capacity to display the Islamic point of view to the Western world within a short period of time.

Recently, a Saudi businessman revealed that an Islamic satellite for the West will soon be built. All of the Islamic *Da'wah* materials will be in English and French, and soon they will produce programming in all vital languages of the world. The aim of this channel will be to proclaim true Islam to the West and to help the Islamic world financially by encouraging the Western investors to do business with Islamic countries.[41] Egypt has also developed a satellite channel, which proclaims Islam to the Muslim world as well as to the Western world. It provides a defense for the Islamic religion.[42]

Saaid Tantawee, Al-Azhar high priest, said, "The Islamic nation must have this kind of mass media to help our people live in the Western countries and (for the) spreading of Islam without any kind of problems from the western nations."[43] The Islamic Institution for Education, Science, and Culture said that it "will adopt this project to help the Islamic nations . . . to be a powerful instrument in the future."[44]

The Islamic channels currently broadcasting their programs to the West are the:

1. Islamic Channel, sponsored by Saudi businessman Shaui Saleh Kamel
2. Andaloos Channel from Spain
3. Al Manar Islamic Channel from Lebanon, sponsored by *Hazeb Allah* (God's Party)
4. *Al Rahman* Channel (the Mercy One Channel) from Indonesia
5. Islamic City Channel in the United States, which reaches 2.5 million Muslim viewers
6. MTV Channel from the United Kingdom (selected programming)[45]

There is a possibility that Muslims will soon rent a Western channel to broadcast Islamic programs every Sunday morning. There are Islamic channels in Arabic nations.[46] And there is an Egyptian sponsored channel in Germany that also has programs in the Middle East and North Africa.[47]

6. The Institutionalization of Daʾwah in the Western Context (Para-Mosque)

A para-mosque is any spiritual ministry whose organization is not under the authority of a local Muslim congregation or body.[48] Or a para-mosque is an organization that was formed as an alternative to those established in previous centuries.[49] The Federation of Islamic Associations, for instance, founded by the Cedar Rapids Muslim Community in 1952, has gone out of its way for the advancement of the religious, cultural, and social aspects of all Muslims on the American continent. It is working toward Muslims becoming strong through their Islamic heritage, the interpretation of Islamic teachings, and the setting forth of Islam's lofty principles, which it shares together with other religions whose adherents live among the non-Muslims of America. This federation has been a powerful agent in the spreading of the Islamic culture to the widest possible boundaries among America.[50]

Another example is the Council of Muslim Communities of Canada, established in 1972. The objectives of this agency are:

1. To present the Islamic way of life as defined by the Qur'an and *Sunna*
2. To strengthen bonds of brotherhood among Muslim communities and individual Muslims
3. To promote mutual appreciation and friendly relations between Muslims and non-Muslims
4. To stimulate Islamic thinking and action in the North American setting
5. To coordinate activities of member communities and communicate with the entire Muslim world[51]

The Islamic Information Center of America

Musa Qutub is from Jerusalem and was educated in the Quaker community. He established the Islamic Information Center of America in 1983 with John Merenkov, an American doctor. The center has three objectives:

1. To deliver the message of Islam
2. To inform non-Muslims about Islam
3. To aid U.S. Muslims in delivering the message to others[52]

These goals are fulfilled by contacting people, giving lectures, conducting seminars, publishing writings, handing out literature, and utilizing the mass media.

The Muslim Student Association and Islamic Society of North America

The Muslim Student Association and Islamic Society of North America started in 1963 with seventy-five students at the Urbana campus in Illinois. It sought to improve students' knowledge of Islam, to perpetuate the Islamic spirit, explain Islam to Americans, and promote the restoration of Islam in students' home countries. They have a magazine called *Al Ittihad* (which is the Muslim's equivalent of *Christianity Today*). One of their brochures states that "the most important task is da'wah among non-Muslims, as the campus is where the most curious, the most inquisitive, and the most open-minded audience for Islam [is]."[53]

Rabitat al-Alam al-Islami (The Muslim World League)

The Muslim World League was founded by the Saudi government in 1962. It is a low-church organization dedicated to *Da'wah* in those countries where Islam is a minority religion. It assists Islamic centers, youth camps, and summer schools. It provides teachers and *imam*s, and develops prison ministry, fellowships, and grants. It produces television and radio programs as well as a Muslim newspaper. Muhammed Ali al-Harakan felt that the World League was to "perform the obligation to jihad, to propagate Allah's religion."[54]

There are many more Muslim organizations in the United States, including:

- The Association of Muslim Scientists and Engineers
- The Islamic Medical Association
- Islamic Societies of Georgia and Virginia
- Islamic Circle of North America (located in Canada)
- The Ahmadiyya (nonorthodox organization)[55]

appendix **b**

Islamic Speakers Bureau

In December 2002, many principals and other education supervisors in California received an offer from the Islamic Speakers Bureau to provide speakers and courses for public schools. Their argument was that many Muslim students were experiencing or might experience "discrimination or harassment," thus they wanted access to the classrooms as steps to reduce the level of intimidation.

A random checking of schools shows that some administrators have accepted these offers for purposes of "multicultural understanding."

The following are copies of one set of letters that was received by a school administrator in the San Francisco area.

Islamic Speakers Bureau
(408) 296-7312 or (888) 296-7312

December 2002

Dear Curriculum & Multicultural Supervisors and In-service Training Managers, Greetings of Peace!

Islamic Speakers Bureau (ISB) is a program of Islamic Networks Group (ING), a nonprofit organization that supplements existing education about Islam and Muslims in the context of World History and Social Studies in middle and high school classrooms. As we enter our eleventh year of operation, the ISB delivers over 1200 presentations a year.

Muslim students of various racial and ethnic backgrounds make up an increasing percentage of the school population. There are approximately 250,000 Muslims in the Bay Area, with over 20,000 Muslim students in public schools.

In the aftermath of the tragic events of September 11th and the threat of war with Iraq and possibly other Muslim populated nations, Muslim students, more than ever are the targets of prejudice, harassment, and even hate incidents. Even if Muslim students do not experience such obvious discrimination or harassment, it is excruciating to hear the constant negative discussions of Muslims and even Islam in the news, the classroom, and among students. Muslim students may often be experiencing real trauma that they are unable to discuss with their peers or teachers, for fear of humiliation. Parents are often unaware or helpless to alleviate the situation.

An understanding teacher, counselor, or administrator can make an enormous difference in a student's life and school experience. We suggest the following training seminars and presentations in the classroom as steps to reduce the level of discrimination or harassment:

STAFF DEVELOPMENT TRAINING:

Title: "Staff Development Training for Educators and Administrators: Incorporating Islamic Cultural Studies in the Curriculum and Interacting with Muslim Students"

Intended audience: All Educators and Administrators

Subject matter:
- Common Stereotypes
- Sources of Stereotypes
- Overview of Islamic Culture
- Incorporating Islamic Culture Studies in the Curriculum, Grades K–12th: Tools and Resources
- Understanding Muslim Religious Practices
- Tips for Interacting with Muslim Students

Training Period:
1.5–2.0 hours

Training format:
Interactive, where questions can be asked throughout.

Handouts:
- Booklet titled, "An Educator's Guide to Islamic Religious Practices," published by CAIR
- Booklet titled, "Discover Islam, The Reader," published by Transcom International
- "Catalogue for Teachers & Librarians, Grades K–12th," published by Islamic Speakers Bureau

Fees:
Negotiable, based on available district funding. Willing to provide it at no cost if funding is not available.

Equipment needed:
Overhead projector & screen, or laptop, LCD projector and screen

PRESENTATION IN THE CLASSROOM FOR GRADES 7TH–12TH:

Title: "Orientation on Islam and the Muslim World in the Context of World History and Social Science"

Intended audience: Students, Grades 7th–12th who are studying a subject relating to Islam or the Muslim World. (Note: California's Social Studies Content Standards include a unit on Islam in seventh grade, and units on other parts of the world including the Muslim world in ninth, tenth, and twelfth grades.)

Subject matter:
• Terminology
• Islamic History
• World Population of Muslims
• Islam versus Culture
• Islam in America
• Beliefs and Practices of Muslims
• Islamic Holidays

Presentation period:
40–90 minutes, depending on teacher's request

Presentation format:
Interactive, allowing questions to be asked in the course of the presentation.
   Presentation also includes visual aids and display of cultural symbols and ethnic clothing.

PRESENTATION IN THE CLASSROOM FOR GRADES 10TH–12TH:

Title: "Women in Islam"

Intended audience: Students, Grades 10th–12th who are

studying a subject relating to Islam or the Muslim World, with particular emphasis on women's studies.

Subject matter:
- Stereotypes
- Sources of stereotypes
- Women's conditions in pre-Islam Arabia
- Identity based on Qur'an & Sunnah
- Women's spiritual nature
- Relationship with men in the public sphere
- Relationship with men in the domestic sphere
- Muslim female role models
- Important women in early Islam
- Muslim women today
- Muslim women tomorrow

Presentation period:
20–90 minutes, depending on teacher's request

Presentation format:
Interactive, allowing questions to be asked in the course of the presentation.

Presentation also includes visual aids and a display of cultural symbols and ethnic clothing.

About Our Speakers:

- ISB speakers adhere to the First Amendment Center's "A Teacher's Guide to Religion in the Public Schools," which we also apply to all public facilities. For more information on the guidelines, visit http://www.freedomforum.org.
- ISB speakers are also certified after a rigorous process of training, testing, and observation in a live setting by veteran trainers, who have a combined training experience of 50 years or more.

- ISB is also a founder and active member of NNASB (National Network of Affiliated Speakers Bureaus), whose charter can be found at http://www.ing.org/about/page.asp?num=11

TEACHER'S KIT FOR PRESENTING RAMADAN AND EID, GRADES K–6TH:

Especially important in the winter holiday season, this kit was designed for public schools teachers and Muslim parents to provide tools for incorporating Ramadan and Eid holidays in schools arts and crafts programs.

Kit includes two books as follows:

Book 1:
Islamic Speakers Bureau School Series
Presenting Ramadan and Eid in Elementary School Grades K–6
Kit for Parents and Teachers, 4th Edition
Islamic Networks, Inc. 2001, 127 pgs.

Table of Contents:
Part One: Introduction
Part Two: Presenting Ramadan and Eid in Grades K–6 (actual presentation scripts)
Part Three: Teaching Materials for Grades 4–6
Part Four: Coloring Activities
Part Five: Art Projects
Part Six: Lunar Activities
Part Seven: Supplemental Activities

Book 2:
Ramadan Activities
Teacher Created Materials, Inc. 2000, 16 pgs.

Table of Contents:
Islam: A Brief Overview
Ramadan—The Month of Fasting
Comprehension Questions
Ramadan Word Search
Ramadan Activity Calendar
Make Your Own Tasbih (Muslim prayer beads)
"An Ordinary Day" Instructions
"An Ordinary Day" Game board
Write Your Name in Arabic
An "A-Mazing" Trip to the Mosque
Muslim World Matching
Extension Activities and Resources
Answer Key

Kit's order form is enclosed with this letter.

Also attached is a Calendar of Important Islamic Holy Days

For further information, please do not hesitate to call our office at 408-296-7312. You may also schedule a speaker through our website at http://www.ing.org.

Sincerely,

Maha ElGenaidi & Ameena Jandali
Hosai Mojaddidi
ISB Co-Founders
ISB Scheduler

Islamic Speakers Bureau
(408) 296-7312 or (888) 296-7312

Announcements
Visit our website at
http://www.ing.org/speakers/subpage.asp?num=l &pagenum=l

For Islamic Resources for Research Topics Relating to Islam &
the Muslim World.

**Tune in to KQED, Television Channel 9 for the following
programs:**

- **Wednesday, December 18th at 9:00 p.m.** for the national
  broadcast premiere of **Muhammad: Legacy of a Prophet.**
  This special tells the story of the 7th-century prophet who
  changed world history in 23 years and continues to shape
  the lives of more than 1.2 billion people. This lively, thorough and honest portrait of the man and the prophet takes
  viewers to ancient Arabian sites where Muhammad's story
  unfolded and into the homes, mosques and workplaces of
  some of America's approximately seven million Muslims to
  discover the many ways in which they follow Muhammad's
  example. With some of the world's leading scholars on Islam providing historical context and critical perspective,
  viewers learn not only who Muhammad was, but also what
  most American Muslims believe Islam teaches and how
  their beliefs are increasingly shaping society. Actor Andre
  Braugher narrates.

- **Wednesday, December 18th at 11:00 p.m. for Muslims
  in Appalachia.** A documentary exploring the hidden life
  of Muslims living in the heart of the Bible Belt. Interviews
  with local Muslims along with comments by Yvonne Haddad of Georgetown University and others combine with

scenic footage of the Appalachian Mountains in all seasons to provide the viewer with a portrait of Islam's presence, contributions, and tensions with modern Appalachian life. The program explores the ways in which minority status affects individual faith and community life. By filmmaker Steve M. Martin.

- **Thursday, December 19th at 9:00 p.m.** for a special rebroadcast of **FRONTLINE: Muslims**, produced by Independent Production Fund. The events of September 11 left many Americans questioning how such atrocities could be perpetrated in the name of religion: specifically, the religion of Islam. Yet even as United States opinion polls reflect a collective sense of mistrust toward a religion few Americans know much about, Islam continues to be the fastest growing religion in the United States today. What is Islam? What do Muslims believe in? And how does their faith shape their lives, their identities, and their political ideologies? *Frontline* explores these and other questions in this special report that examines the fundamental tenets of Islam and the causes behind its current worldwide resurgence. Through interviews with dozens of ordinary Muslims from such diverse countries as Iran, Malaysia, Turkey, and the United States, *Frontline* illuminates the perspectives, conflicts and tensions that are shaping today's Muslim world.

Outline of a large mosque by night.

A Brotherhood of Conquest

A Look at the Muslim Brotherhood Today

My first personal contact with the Muslim Brotherhood took place in Port Said, Egypt, in the early 1980s. I was invited by the Baptist Union of Egypt to be the main speaker at their yearly weeklong conference. During this period of time, I was working as the Consultant for Evangelism and Church Growth for the Middle East and North Africa. My topic was "How can churches in Egypt grow?" When coming to the first meeting held in a mid-sized church building, I was amazed to find several well-armed soldiers standing at the front of the building. Since I had never experienced this before, I asked if they were afraid of us and they replied, "No, but we are afraid of those in the area who want to kill you." These were not comforting words, but it was good to know that they were standing guard to protect us.

With me at the conference were two younger missionaries who were assigned to Egypt. At that time, only the Southern Baptists had missionaries who were approved to receive Egyptian visas and work openly as missionaries. This came about after an agreement between then U.S. president, Jimmy Carter, and the president of Egypt, Anwar Sadat. Because of their friendship, Sadat allowed three Baptist missionaries to live and work in Egypt. Both of my colleagues were young and rather dark complected. They had bushy black beards and I had a rather short graying beard. Midway through the week, I noticed that my two young fellow missionaries had clean-shaven faces. The beards were gone. My curiosity was aroused and I asked them the reasons for this act. They replied that the leadership of the Baptists in Egypt told them that the only persons who had beards in their country were members of the Muslim Brotherhood and that it was a sign of their loyalty to that organization, thus it was strongly recommended that they remove the beards. Upon hearing this, I inquired whether or not I too should shave. They replied that they had spoken with the leaders about my beard and were told that there was an exception to the rule: Old men could wear beards.

After that, it seemed as if a majority of the men that I met on that trip had the indicative black beards. If what we were told was true, then there were certainly many members of the Brotherhood active in Egypt at that time. Only later did I realize that my observation was correct. The Brotherhood was certainly strong in Egypt.

Because of this experience, my interest in this organization grew. During my studies in the next years, I discovered that there was no really simple way of understanding the Muslim Brotherhood (MB; also known as the Muslim Brothers). The organization has been very successful and has expanded rapidly into other countries.

The Scope of the Muslim Brotherhood

The organization started in 1928 in Egypt, and it was there that they experienced their most rapid growth and exerted their greatest influence. For this reason, some see the MB as only an Egyptian phenomenon. During the high-profile revolution in the spring of 2011, most press reports mentioned the danger of the MB taking over the country, so that even those who knew nothing about the MB began to associate them solely with Egypt. Some reports claimed that the MB was a political party, while others stated that it was more of a welfare organization that did excellent work within the country.

Many were unclear about who the MB really were, but one thing was clear: they were deeply imbedded in Egypt.

Others have identified the larger, global reach of the MB, pointing out that extensions of the MB are found in most nations of Africa, Europe, and the Middle East, and that they are even active in the United States. The MB has spun a web of many sister organizations that were influenced by the MB or directly started by members of the MB but that operate under different names. One problem faced in understanding the scope of the MB is that the different branches have sought to create an identity apart from that in Egypt. Many are prone to announce that they are the same as the MB, only that they are indigenous in another country.

Erroneously, there is a tendency in Europe and the United States to understand all Muslim groups expressing anti-Western sentiment to be homogeneous. Many, especially in the Western world, when speaking about radical Islam and terrorism, will use the term "Muslim Brotherhood" in a generic sense. Those who accept this idea see all violence and terrorism against the West as being a part of the MB. This usage is incorrect since there are many other organizations indigenous to the Islamic world that have no organizational connection to the MB. *Al Qaeda* and the Muslim Brotherhood, for instance, are often used interchangeably, but *al Qaeda* members do not consider themselves related to the MB.

The MB *does* exist in a global world and is represented in many counties, but should be used only to refer to the specific organization by that name. The most comprehensive definition that I found was the Wikipedia article:

> The Society of the Muslim Brothers . . . is an Islamic transnational movement and the largest political opposition organization in many Arab states. The group is the world's oldest and largest Islamic political group, and the "world's most influential Islamic movement." The Brotherhood has as its slogan "Islam is the Solution."[1]

Origins in Egypt

Around the early part of the twentieth century, new political and religious movements took root. It was during this time that Marx wrote his *Communist Manifesto*, and this period also saw the rise of Hitler in Germany and Mussolini in Italy. Also, sometimes overlooked by Western scholars, this time frame also gave rise to a number of modern Islamic movements. These movements were often in direct response to the challenge of European colonization of the Middle East and North Africa. On one side, these movements were revival movements within Islam, but they also had a political element.

An Egyptian intellectual by the name of Hassan al-Banna (1906–1949) founded the Muslim Brotherhood in the city of Ismalia in March 1928. With six others, he laid the foundation for what was to become very significant within Islam in the twenty-first century. Al-Banna was a pious Muslim who was well educated in Cairo, where he learned about the dangers of Western relativism. He also was introduced to a number of Islamic reformation movements going on at that time. Al-Banna called for a return to the original Islam, which included the adoption of Sharia law. In fact, the credo from the very beginning gave an outline of the founder's ideology: "Allah is our objective. The Prophet is our leader. Qur'an is our law. Jihad is our way. Dying in the way of Allah is our highest hope."[2]

Early on, the movement was apolitical and concentrated more on the use of Sharia to bring about the ideal Islamic state. Its leaders were active in all areas of Egyptian life because they felt Islam had failed to remember some of the basics laid out by Muhammad, such as concern for the poor and needy. After about ten years, the leadership changed direction because they felt that to accomplish their goals they needed also to enter into the world of politics. It was apparent that the MB and the secular government were on a collision course. Al-Banna himself was twice elected to parliament but was forced to resign to avoid bloodshed between the government and his followers.

While al-Banna was the Supreme Guide of the movement, the most influential spiritual leader was Sayyid Qutb (1906–1966), an Egyptian who became a leading ideologue of Muslim fundamentalism. He was born in Upper Egypt and also studied in Cairo. While working there, he was given the opportunity of studying in the United States from 1948 until 1950. This experience of a close encounter with Western morals turned him against the West. He developed a strong anti-American bias because of his experiences in America; thus, this country became his main target. During his stay, he was shocked by the almost total lack of good moral behavior as he saw it. This, combined with what he felt was an unhealthy support of Israel, radically formed his theological and ethical ideology. Bernard Lewis states that "this threat [the degeneracy and debauchery of the American way of life] . . . became a regular part of the vocabulary and ideology of Islamic fundamentalists,"[3] and led to the term "The Great Satan," now often used in demonstrations in Iran and other Muslim countries.

Later History

During the 1930s, Hitler's young men wore brown shirts, while Mussolini's fascist followers wore black shirts. At the same time, the Egyptian MB youth were encouraged to wear green shirts. Because of their anti-Jewish and anti-English sentiment, the MB developed close ties with the German government during the 1930s and these relationships remained intact up to the end of World War II. Two books, Hitler's *Mein Kampf* and the anti-Semitic text *The Protocols of the Elders of Zion,* were printed and widely distributed in the Middle East, extending the hostility against the Jews and Western societies. During this period of time, the movement grew. Wikipedia reports the following: "By 1936, it had 800 members, then this number increased greatly to up to 200,000 by 1938. By 1948, the Brotherhood had about half a million members. Robin Hallett says: 'By the late 1940s the Brotherhood was reckoned to have as many as 2 million members.'"[4]

By the end of World War II, it was apparent that the MB was a force to be reckoned with. They were deeply embedded in the life of the Egyptian people, both in rural and in urban areas especially among the poor. David Wains reports: "al-Banna's new broad social-welfare program included the provision of alternative institutions to those of the government in the fields of education, public health, and social services, all of which reached both rural and urban populations."[5]

After the war, the Brotherhood turned its attention toward the Egyptian government. The king was immensely unpopular, and those wanting change supported anyone who would give them the change they were seeking. Finally, a small group of junior military officers, led by a junior officer by the name of Gamal Abdel Nasser, overthrew the king. At first the Brotherhood felt that they now could develop their desired society with Sharia as the foundation and other Islamic principles as the building blocks. It was rumored that the MB had even aided in the overthrow of the king. Nasser disappointed them by creating not an Islamic society but rather a secular society, which gave only limited room for the desired Islamic ideas.

A series of events during this period heighted the intrigue. A member of the Brotherhood, Abdel Meguid Ahmed Hassan, assassinated Premier Nokrashy Pasha on December 28, 1948. The Brotherhood was already considered an illegal organization but the conflict between the government and the Brotherhood became even more strained. In 1954, the organization was convicted of attempting to assassinate President Nasser, a charge that was strongly denied.

During this period the Brotherhood was once again a banned organization with some of its members routinely arrested. Several other deaths in this period were linked to conflict between the MB and the government. The Brotherhood's leading intellectual, Sayyid Qutb, was executed by the government in 1966. Nasser's successor, President Anwar Sadat, was subsequently gunned down at a military parade; many believed the MB as responsible.

Unlike many organizations, the Brotherhood flourished under persecution. Since the MB saw itself as an indigenous movement and did not see itself as a political party, the fact that they could not operate as a political party had little or no effect. They simply likened themselves to a community movement that was trying to simply help the poor and needy. One reason they progressed so well during these days of oppression was built into the structure of the organization: "Members were trained and reinforced in their faith. . . . They were carefully selected. . . . They emphasized religious knowledge and moral fitness, and concentrated on moral and social programs."[6]

These actions endeared them in the hearts of the people and reinforced their claims of being a welfare movement rather than a political one. It seems that even within the organization, however, there were debates as to its real purpose. Regardless, there can be little doubt that they felt the best way to achieve their goals was by the creation of an Islamic Republic that would govern under the guise of Sharia law. The bigger question for them is how to achieve this goal.

Although the Brotherhood asserted that they were not a political party but rather an ideological fraternity trying to live after the model of Muhammad, in reality they have been involved in many forms of intrigue, including terrorism and assassinations, in order to accomplish the creation of their ideal Islamic state. There is no doubt that this began as a genuine indigenous movement, and that, from the outset, there was little influence outside of the core of Egyptian believers. The MB did, however, adhere to a more radical form of theology that had been embraced by the Saudi Arabian monocracy. This well-known theology, *Wahabism*, is a very conservative way of thinking that influenced the direction of the movement's ideology, though not its methodology. Some say that both Qutb and *Wahabi* shared in giving the Brotherhood its theology.

Back to politics. The question remained, What would such as Islamic state look like? One author states, "By the turn of the century there were several models that were explored and observed. One was that in Saudi Arabia which seemed to have the purest form of Islam that existed under Wahabi rules."[7] Iran had also developed an Islamic Republic but because it was Shiite it could not really be used as a model. Some have even stated that "the political direction it has been taking lately has tended towards more moderate secular Islamism and so-called Islamic Democracy comparable to Christian

Democrat movements in Europe, the Christian-right in the United States, and the Muslim-oriented democratic parties of Turkey."[8]

Some argue that such a direction was necessary in the development of the ideal state. The Islamic Democracy is not an end goal but rather a means to the end. Also important is that the word "democracy" continues to be foreign in Arabic, thus regulating it to a lower level of acceptance by the masses.

By the 2005 parliamentary elections in Egypt, the Brotherhood's candidates ran as independents since they had been outlawed. They won 88 seats in Parliament or 20 percent of the total, thus making it the largest of the opposition parties. They have used this result to try to prove that they are a moderate influence in the country. During the 2011 revolution that brought down Mubarak's government, the Brotherhood seemed to be at the forefront of the action, and when asked if they would support a real democratic system in Egypt, the answer was always affirmative. Only time will tell if there has been a real moderation within the Brotherhood in Egypt, or if they are waiting in the background to take control and to institute an Islamic Republic with Sharia law as the only law allowed.

EXPANSION INTO THE MIDDLE EAST AND NORTH AFRICA

Soon after the first Brotherhood was founded in 1928, affiliates took root in countries such as Libya and Syria, with many others to follow in time. From its very beginning, the ideology of the MB has found a receptive audience among Muslims, especially those in close proximity to Egypt. As the concept of Islam taking over the world by 2080 became more popularized, many saw the MB as a possible means to achieve this lofty goal. Here is an overview of the creation and growth of these affiliates of the Muslim Brotherhood.

Syria

One of the first offshoots, founded in the 1930s, was in Syria, where the Brotherhood "opposed the French mandate and resented the benefits it conferred on the modernizing sector of the Syrian economy."[9] By 1961, in the parliamentary elections, it had won ten seats, or 5.8 percent of the house. But in 1963, after the Baath party was successful in overthrowing the government, the MB was banned.

From 1963 until 1982, the party existed underground but continued to grow until it began to be a threat to the government. The center of the Brotherhood's activities was located in the northern city of Hama. On February 2, 1982, because of the possibility of a revolt, the Syrian army attacked the town. They did not use rubber bullets or water cannons as is done today but rather used tanks, artillery, and aircraft. After the defeat of the MB, bulldozers completely destroyed the town as a warning to others not to go against the government. It was estimated that between 10,000 and 40,000 were killed. The Brotherhood once again went underground. Today, in many ways, the Palestinian organization Hamas represents the MB in Syria.

Libya

A second country close to Egypt was exposed early to the MB. In the 1940s, when Egyptian MB members were being persecuted, King Idris I of Libya offered the members of the Brotherhood refuge and the right to preach their doctrine. Benghazi, a major city close to the Egyptian border and also the city that hosted the university, became a center of the Brotherhood. Many students with a MB background came to study there and began to win new converts to their belief. It is interesting to note that the center of the uprising against Muammar Gaddafi in the spring of 2011 was in that city, the stronghold of the MB.

Before Gaddafi came to power, the Libyan Brotherhood limited itself to peaceful political, economic, and cultural activities. When Gaddafi came to power, he immediately turned against the Brotherhood and arrested all Egyptian members of the MB that he could identify and sent them back to Egypt. Following this, the MB again went underground but in the first part of the 1980s, the MB renamed itself the "Libyan Islamic Group" and sought to enter mainstream Libyan society. In 1998, Gaddafi's security services launched a crackdown that resulted in more than 200 members imprisoned and hundreds more forced into exile. Again there seemed to be reconciliation when, in 2006, the leaders of the MB were released. One of the leaders, now exiled in Britain, Dr. Abdulmonem Hresha claims that, despite years of repression, "the Brotherhood still has thousands of members scattered across Libya, with chapters in almost every single town, including Sirte, Gadhafi's birthplace on the coast west of Tripoli."[10] The Brotherhood remains a significant force in Libya.

Palestine

When looking at the MB in the Middle East and North Africa, one area always comes to mind: Palestine. The founder of the MB there was the brother of Hassan al-Banna who first established the MB in Egypt. 'Abd al-Rahman al-Banna established the first unit of the Palestinian MB in 1935. The first to lead an armed resistance in the name of Palestine against the British, their actions during the early days were generally against the British as well as moderate local Arab leaders.

During World War II, they became allies with Nazi Germany, both working against common enemies—Britain and Jews. It was reported that in 1945 the group established a branch in Jerusalem, and by 1947 twenty-five more branches had sprung up in towns such as Jaffa, Lod, Haifa, Nablus, and Tulkarm, with a total membership between 12,000 to 20,000.[11]

After the Six Day War, the situation changed radically. Between the years of 1967 and 1987, the year Hamas was founded, the main emphasis of the MB was the building of mosques, tripling them from 200 to 600. This action proved to be successful since now they could use these for political and recruitment purposes (the same tactic now being used by the worldwide Muslim advance). During this period, there was a rise in power for secular Palestinian movements such as Fatah. The MB saw these movements as being too compromising and not ready to combat Israel. This was changed with the coming of the Intifada, and the new conditions led to the creation of a more radical form of the MB, Hamas. Today it is widely recognized as being closely tied into the Brotherhood. Again, at first the major emphasis of Hamas was social help for its people but soon it became militarized and was transformed into one of the strongest Palestinian militant groups. In a major election in Gaza, Hamas had a surprising victory and thus took over the government of the Gaza Strip in 2007. Now a MB group ruled over a significant geographic territory.

Sudan

Until the election of Hamas in Gaza, Sudan was the only geographical area where the MB had been successful in taking political control over a whole country. This happened in 1989 when General Omar Hassan al-Bashir and others overthrew the government. Currently, al-Bashir continues to rule over Sudan.

In Sudan, the Muslim Brotherhood was founded in 1949 and first began organizing in universities in the 1940s. From the very beginning, it had close ties with its Egyptian counterparts, and was very active in the country's intellectual circles. One key figure was a law professor by the name of Hassan al-Turabi, former dean of the college of law at the University of Khartoum.

In the beginning, the MB worked together with Sudan's President Nimeiri, but this cooperation was not always cordial. In fact, during this time, some of the Brotherhood were arrested and put in jail. After the coup in 1989, al-Turabi and others were put into jail but later released. In the early 1970s, al-Turabi was instrumental in the creation of the NIF (National Islamic Front), a strong Brotherhood organization.

From the beginning, the MB attempted to infiltrate political parties, social organizations, banks, and the army. As early as 1955, the MB attempted to infiltrate the Military College. It started in earnest in 1977 during which time they offered a course in "Islamic Ideology and Instruction." Four members that ruled Sudan after the coup of 1989 took the course, including al-Bashir, the president.

Today, Sudan is looked upon as being one of the most repressive countries in the world, and is suspected of having killed one million to two million of their own people in the South of the country. Sudan offers the world the best example of what could happen if other countries are taken over by the MB.

OTHER COUNTRIES IN THE AREA

Other countries with a significant MB presence today include: in Africa—Algeria, Morocco, Somalia, and Tunisia; and in the Middle East—Bahrain, Iran, Israel, Jordan, Kuwait, and Saudi Arabia.

EXPANSION INTO THE WEST

Germany

Western Europe has been a target of Muslim *Da'wah* activity for many years. One country where they have experienced great success is Germany. The Brotherhood seemed to have a head start because of the close relationship of the MB with Nazis during World War II. Another reason for its rapid growth had to do with the political scene during the Cold War. Because of the division of Germany into East and West, West Germany made the decision not to have diplomatic relations with countries that had close ties to the East. During this time, both Egypt and Syria had come under the sphere of influence of Communist countries. Many Islamists were forced to leave their homes in Syria and Egypt because of persecution from their secular governments, which had alienated themselves from West Germany. They were welcomed to come to East Germany as political refugees. Many of those who came were members of the MB; thus, the movement established a solid foundation of well educated radicals in Germany.

The first pioneer in Germany was Sa'id Ramaden, the personal secretary of the MB founder Hassan al-Banna, who came in 1958 and attended law school in Cologne. In Munich, he founded *Islamicsche Gemeinschaft Deutschland* (IGD; Islamic Community of Germany), which today is one of the three largest Muslim organizations in Germany.[12] The IGD is under the full control of the MB and has sixty mosques in Germany alone. Two other MB groups that were international in character but were founded in that country are the Federation of Islamic Organizations in Europe and the World Assembly of Muslim Youth. Both of these organizations have close ties with the Muslim World League, which provides them with finances and political contacts.

Another motivating factor in the creation of these Europe-wide organizations was to give the Brotherhood inroads into the social structures of Europe. Especially in Germany, this was a strong reason for expansion. Because of its persecution of the Jews during World War II there was a mentality expressed by the leadership of Germany to be humanitarian. They wanted to show an openness to peoples who were being persecuted, and the MB seemed to fit into this category. Many favorable decisions were handed down from the government that helped both the MB in particular and the Islamic population in general. Help was given in the construction of mosques as well as social grants to their institutions. Only recently it appears that the overall tone coming out of Berlin from the leaders of Germany is that they have been too generous, especially when it included helping those who were attempting to bring down their country.

In a recent interview Dr. Udo Ulfkote, who has written a book on the Muslim Brotherhood in Germany titled *Der Krieg in unseren Städten* (*The War in Our Cities*), states that "the greatest danger to the German nation today is the Muslim Brotherhood." He goes on to argue that "the Muslims now living in Germany are no longer trying to integrate into the society as were the earlier generations of Muslims but now are being taught to reject the decadent Western culture in the hopes that they can change the country in the future by instilling Islamic values. This now appears to be a grass roots philosophy in Germany that brings about more division."[13]

Great Britain

A second important staging country for the MB is Great Britain. There have been elements of the MB in England since the early 1930s but the actual founding of the MB in Britain was in 1997 with the start of the "Muslim Association of Britain" (MAB) by Arab migrants. It has been said that the creation of the MAB gave new energy to the political process that was already underway to create a shadow government in England. The new organization was decidedly more anti-Western and anti-Israel than other groups. There were several issues that they used to try to influence the Muslim lobby to be more radical. The first was the issue of the book by British author Salman Rushdie, *The Satanic Verses*, which was seen as detrimental to Islam. This issue gained a great amount of publicity but failed to galvanize the Islamic population of Britain as hoped. Another issue was that of Palestine. In the major cities of Great Britain, the MB held street demonstrations against those who would persecute the Palestinians—the Jews and those who propagated the war, namely, the West.

With the election of the Labour Party mayor of London, Ken Livingstone, a close association was created between the Brotherhood and those of the left-leaning spectrum of British politics. This arrangement continues today but because of immense philosophical differences it is doubtful that it will continue. One author states, "MAB [the MB Muslim Association of Britain] influence on Livingstone provides a case book example of political manipulation."[14] The influence of Livingstone was such that the MB gained more credibility than before. The MB also took over the management of the North London Central Mosque, giving them a foothold in the capital of England.

Many articles and books have been written linking the political left in the West (both Europe and the United States) to the MB. They claim that both have a common enemy and that both are active in Western European countries. Among the examples include the Free Gaza Movement, which sent a boat filled with food and medicines that embarked from Turkey and was headed to Gaza. The boat was engaged by Israeli soldiers, and after some violence turned back. The boat had sponsors from both the left and the MB.

There are numerous other organizations that have close ties with the MB in Britain. Sometimes these relationships are easy to understand because of an openness by the Islamic community, but sometimes it is difficult to understand each and every relationship among the various Islamic groups. It is definite that the MB plays a major role in the advancement of Islam in England. One author, in looking at the structure of the MB in England, has stated: "The creation of such a large scale, interdependent financial infrastructure to resource public, educational and media activity spread across the UK and Ireland suggests a long term strategy designed to keep it safe from Arab states' (and American and Israeli) investigations."[15]

Other European Countries

Other countries, such as France, Belgium, the Netherlands, and Denmark, just to name a few, have a very real MB presence. From a practical standpoint, this web of influence is frightening. Far from creating YMCA-type organizations, the Muslim Brotherhood establishes organizations that seek to create Islamic states in all the countries where they are located—by any means necessary, including armed conflict. They are having great success, particularly in Western Europe. This move forward is not just an accident but rather the result of a well-developed strategy generally originating from either Egypt or Saudi Arabia.

The United States

Although its entrance has come rather late, the MB began its activity in the United States during the 1960s. This country has long been on the radar of the Islamists. Ayatollah Khomeini stated that the last bastion of the West to fall to Islam would be the United States. Target groups in the United States include prisoners, African-Americans, military personnel, Hispanics, and other minorities. The MB is very active in educational institutions and in the media. According to a statement by the NEFA Foundation, which cites evidence from the *United States v. Holy Land Foundation* trial, the goal of the Muslim Brotherhood in the United States is the "enablement of Islam in North America, meaning: establishing an effective and stable Islamic Movement led by the Muslim Brotherhood which adopts Muslims' causes domestically and globally, and which works to expand the observant Muslim base, aims at unifying and directing Muslims' efforts, presents Islam as a civilization alternative, and supports the global Islamic state, wherever it is."[16]

The same report from NEFA continues,

> The process of settlement [of Islam in the United States] is a "Civilization-Jihadist Process" with all the word means. The Ikhwan must understand that all their work in America is a kind of grand Jihad in elimination and destroying the Western civilization from within and "sabotaging" its miserable house by their hands and the hands of the believers so that it is eliminated and God's religion is made victorious over all other religions. Without this level of understanding, we are not up to this challenge and have not prepared ourselves for Jihad yet. It is a Muslim's destiny to perform Jihad and work wherever he is and wherever he lands until the final hour comes, and there is no escape from that destiny except for those who choose to slack.[17]

The activities of the MB in the United States are many and varied. Some of the organizations related to the MB and operating in the United States, along with the dates of their inception, are:

Muslim Student Association, 1963
North American Islamic Trust, 1971
Institutional Institute of Islamic Thought, 1980s
The Islamic Society of North America, 1981

The American Muslim Council, 1990
The Muslim Society, 1992[18]

Their activities in the United States range from peaceful intentions that include positive social action to the funding of terror organizations such as Hamas and advocating the fall of the country and replacing it with an Islamic society.

CONCLUSION

It is hard to summarize the Muslim Brotherhood as it is found in many countries on various continents, has many different objectives, and is known under many different names. It is, however, limited in that those who belong have a common goal: the establishment of a global Islamic state, or *ummah*. This Islamic state would be impossible without the conceived laws of human behavior that are described in Islamic Sharia law. This legal system is considered a complete scheme of life that must be adhered to in its totality. For the Muslim, it must replace the depravity of Christian life as it now is practiced.

Once again let us consider the official credo of the MB, which states: "Allah is our objective. The Prophet is our leader. Qur'an is our law. Jihad is our way. Dying in the way of Allah is our highest hope."

Even the opening phase affirms that it is a religious movement and should be seen as such. Neither distinctly political nor distinctly social, it is a combination of these two aspects of the movement, both being subservient to Islamic religious ideas and fervor. It is a mistake to try to look at the Brotherhood as only one way of life or as simply a political party that seeks by due process change in the society. Rather, it is life itself. To describe it any other way is like the blind men trying to describe the elephant. Each feels only a part of the large creature and in attempting to describe it, one person sees that it is similar to a large snake (the trunk), another as a small rope (the tail), a large wall (the side), another as a piece of paper (the ear), another as a tree trunk (the legs). The elephant is all of the things that are named but they are all necessary to make up the whole. The Brotherhood is very similar. It is a large and complex movement.

In looking at it from a modern standpoint, the so-called democratic upheavals that began in North Africa and the Middle East in the winter of 2011 continually named the MB as a part of the so-called process that was necessary in order to overthrow despots and create a new Western-type democracy. It is an oversimplification to say that the MB caused the revolutionary fervor, but it is also simplistic to say they were only bystanders.

In all reports about what is happening in the various countries of the area such as Tunisia, Libya, Syria, Jordan, Saudi Arabia, and Yemen, there is the feeling that the MB is not only an instigator of the uprisings but is also lying in wait so as to move when necessary to take advantage of what is happening. In talking about the uprising in Libya, Dr. Abdulmonem Hresha, who taught physics at Tripoli University but now lives in London and who is a prominent member of the MB, described the situation by saying, "We've been working secretly till this moment."[19]

Teri Schure reports:

> The Muslim Brotherhood is currently playing an active role in the unrest in several Arab countries [for example, at a rally held outside the Egyptian embassy in Amman on Saturday, January 29, 2011, with some one hundred participants]. Hammam Saeed, head of the Muslim Brotherhood in Jordan and a close ally of the Hamas's Damascus-based leader, Khaled Meshaal, recently said, "Egypt's unrest will spread across the Mideast, and Arabs will topple leaders allied with the United States."[20]

The question remains: How much of this unrest is extemporaneous and how much of it has been planned and orchestrated by the Muslim Brotherhood? Several facts remain clear. The theology of the present-day MB movement is dominated by the teachings of Qutb and Wahabi, both of whom were radical in their understanding of the Qur'an, especially Qutb who was very much anti-West. There is no reason to believe that they have or will change their stance concerning the underlying understanding of their faith.

If the MB were to be in the position of completely taking over one of the named countries who are experiencing uprising, what type of government would they establish? Would it be similar to the Islamic Republic of Iran, which has little or no tolerance of other beliefs; or one similar to that of Turkey, which has a secular government but gives a great deal of influence in the society to Islamic leaders; or a more modern-day form of Arab democracy such as is now practiced in Iraq? No one is certain at this time.

Consider the position of Libya, for example. In a statement issued March 22, 2011, the Interim National Council in Benghazi, which is the thirty-one-member opposition leadership group in Libya, stated that it is committed to "the ultimate goal of the revolution; namely to build a constitutional democratic civil state based on the rule of law, respect for human rights and the guarantee of equal rights and opportunities for all its citizens including full political participations by all citizens and equal opportunities between men and women and the promotion of women empowerment."[21] However, speaking about the Libyan situation, Dr. Abdulmonem Hresha has said that "if his organization forms a political party, it would seek to legislate according to Koranic principles, which would include, for example, a continued ban on the sale of alcohol. 'Why shouldn't we be able to press our point of view—we are humans too,' he said."[22]

In conclusion, it can be said that the MB is a transnational religious organization that is actively working in many countries of the Middle East, Africa, and Europe and has as its goal the establishment of a global Islamic state that exists under the Sharia rule of law. Up to now, they have been very successful in their endeavors. Only time will tell if they will ultimately succeed to create a worldwide *ummah*.

If the thesis of this book is correct and Islam plans to change the world in the next several generations, then the MB will play a major part in its march to make the whole world Muslim by the year 2080. It is time for those who live in the Christian West to take the threat of the Muslim Brotherhood seriously and become more aware of their methods, tactics, and goals.

Notes

Chapter 1: Don't Panic

1. John Esposito, *Unholy War: Terror in the Name of Islam* (New York: Oxford University Press, 2002), 117.
2. Patrick J. Buchanan, *The Death of the West: How Dying Populations and Immigrant Invasions Imperil Our Country and Civilization* (New York: St. Martin's, 2002), 118.
3. Ihsan Bagby, Paul M. Perl, and Bryan T. Froehle, "The Mosque in America: A National Portrait" (April 26, 2001). This report is available online at http://www.cair.com/portals/0/pdf/The_mosque_in_America_A_National_Portrait.pdf.
4. This statistic was taken from the work published by the Population Division of the United Nations in *World Population Prospects: The 2000 Revision, Highlights,* released February 28, 2001. The report also shows that by 2050 Germany's 82 million people will have fallen to 59 million and that Europe's population of 728 million today will crash to 600 million.
5. Muslim *imam,* interview by author, Germany, September 14, 1993. For security reasons, his name cannot be published.
6. Hizb-ut-Tahrir website quoted by Steven Emerson, *American Jihad: The Terrorists Living Among Us* (New York: Free Press, 2002), 194.

7. Emerson, *American Jihad*, 194.

8. Ronald de Valderanos, "Terror: The War Against the West," *Imprimis*, November 1988, Hillsdale College, http://www.hillsdale.edu/news/imprimis/archive/issue.asp?year=1988&month=11 (accessed September 8, 2011).

9. Ibid.

10. Dr. James Slack, interview by author, Mill Valley, CA, August 14, 2002.

11. Jerilyn Watson, "Muslims in America," *This Is America*, aired on Voice of America, December 17, 2001, posted online at http://www.manythings.org/voa/usa/72.html (accessed September 8, 2011).

12. Fatema Mernissi, *Islam and Democracy: Fear of the Modern World*, trans. Mary Jo Lakeland (Cambridge, MA: Perseus, 2002), 44.

13. Buchanan, *Death of the West*, 16.

14. Ralph D. Winters, *The Twenty-five Unbelievable Years 1945–1969* (South Pasadena, CA: William Carey Library, 1970). Winters has written an excellent study on the radical changes that took place during these years. It concentrates mostly on the effects of this period on religion and, particularly, on Christian missions.

15. Ibid., 12.

16. Mernissi, *Islam and Democracy*, 190.

17. Larry A. Poston, *The Changing Face of Islam in America* (Camp Hill, PA: Horizon, 2000), chap. 1; quote is from p. 26.

18. Jane I. Smith, *Islam in America* (New York: Columbia University Press, 1999), 179.

19. Ibid.

20. Mernissi, *Islam and Democracy*, 130.

21. "A Brief History of Islam in the United States," found at various sites, including http://www.colostate.edu/orgs/MSA/find_more/iia.html and http://www.islamfortoday.com/historyusa1.htm (accessed December 9, 2011).

22. Fareed Zakaria, "The Politics of Rage: Why Do They Hate Us?" *Newsweek*, October 15, 2001.

23. Buchanan, *Death of the West*, 9.

24. Jim Nelson Black, quoted by Buchanan, *Death of the West*, 187.

25. James Kurth, "The Real Clash," *National Interest* (fall 1994), available at various sites such as findarticles.com or scribd.com.

26. Samuel P. Huntington, *The Clash of Civilizations and the Remaking of World Order* (New York: Simon and Schuster, 1996), 66; emphasis in original.

27. A. J. Bacevich, *Books in Review: The Clash of Civilizations and the Remaking of World Order,* http://www.leaderu.com/ftissues/ft9705 /reviews/bacevich.html. This review was on Huntington's major work, which was a follow-up to his widely read article on the same subject published in *Foreign Affairs* in the summer of 1993.

28. Kabbani quoted in Emerson, *American Jihad,* 162.

29. Dale Hurd, "Hijacking Tolerance: Radical Islam's War with Christianity," CBN News, May 12, 2003, posted online at http://cbn.com /CBNNews/News/030512a.asp.

30. Ibid.

31. The Muslim World League was created in 1962 with one of its purposes as the promotion of Islam worldwide. It has a permanent staff and its headquarters is in Mecca.

32. Kabbani quoted in Emerson, *American Jihad,* 160.

33. Peter Finn, "Saudis Say Iran Cooperating in War on Terror," *Washington Post,* August 11, 2002.

Chapter 2: The Quiet Revolution

1. Jane I. Smith, *Islam in America* (New York: Columbia University Press, 1999), 160.

2. Dr. Ghassan Khalif, interview by author, Spain, July 3, 2002.

3. Ibid.

4. Jamal Badawi, *Islamic Da'wah in the West,* video of lecture delivered at the 24th Annual Conference of the UK Islamic Mission in London, August 1987, produced and directed by Anwar Cara (London: Islamic Foundation, 1988).

5. Lisa Beyer, "Saudi Arabia: Inside the Kingdom," *Time,* September 15, 2003, 50.

6. Badawi, *Islamic Da'wah in the West.*

7. Stuart E. Brown, *Meeting in Faith: Twenty Years of Christian-Muslim Conversation Sponsored by the World Council of Churches* (Geneva: WCC Publications, 1989).

8. Marsha Snulligan Haney, *Islam and Protestant African-American Churches: Responses and Challenges to Religious Pluralism* (San Francisco: International Scholars Publications, 1998), 34.

9. Ibid.

10. Ibid., 122.

11. Mernissi, *Islam and Democracy*, 49.

12. George W. Braswell Jr., *What You Need to Know About Islam and Muslims* (Nashville: Broadman and Holman, 2000), 3.

13. Brian Connor, "Islam Taught in Public Schools," February 8, 2002, http://www.cbn.com/CBNNews/CWN/020802IslamTaught.asp. The article gives a list of statements from the book as well as opinions of California parents concerning the class.

14. Ibid.

15. Ibid.

16. William J. Bennetta, *A Review of Islam: A Simulation of Islamic History and Culture, 610–1100,* http://www.textbookleague.org/filth.htm (accessed online May 7, 2003).

17. Ibid.

18. Wayne Parry, "Hip-hopping on Faith," *San Francisco Chronicle*, January 3, 2003, D10.

19. Smith, *Islam in America,* 165.

20. Jason Ziedenberg and Vincent Schiraldi, "Cellblocks or Classrooms? The Funding of Higher Education and Corrections and Its Impact on African American Men," Washington, DC: Justice Policy Institute, 2002), http://www.justicepolicy.org/images/upload/02-09_REP_Cell blocksClassrooms_BB-AC.pdf (accessed September 20, 2011).

21. From an interview with an area director (name withheld for security reasons) of the Prison Fellowship Ministry on April 14, 2002.

22. Joseph P. Gudel, "Islam's Worldwide Revival," *Forward* magazine, CRI, http://equip.org/articles/islam-s-worldwide-revival (accessed September 20, 2011). Gudel quotes Yvonne Y. Haddad, "The Muslim Experience in the United States," *The Link* (Sept–Oct 1979), 2.

23. John Ogletree, lecture at North American Mission Board meeting in Atlanta, Georgia, July 29, 2002.

24. *The Minaret,* July–August 1993, 38.

25. Dale Neal, "Attacks Continue to Sway Opinions on Islam," *Ashville Citizens Times,* September 11, 2002, 1.

26. Badawi, *Islamic Da'wah in the West.*

27. Ibid.

28. Smith, *Islam in America,* 67.

29. Ibid.

30. Ibid., 68.

31. Ibid.

32. Khurram Murad, *Da'wah Among Non-Muslims in the West* (London: Islamic Foundation, 1986), 9.

33. Ibid., 10.

34. Khurram Murad, *Da'wah Among Non-Muslims in the West,* http://www.masmn.org/books/Khurram_Murad/Dawah_among_Non_Muslims_in _the_West/ (accessed online August 6, 2002).

CHAPTER 3: *Jihad*

1. Azim A. Nanji, ed., *The Muslim Almanac* (Detroit: Gale Research, 1996), 499.

2. Sachiko Murata and William C. Chittick, *The Vision of Islam* (New York: Paragon, 1994), 21.

3. Donna Abu-Nasr, "Bin Ladin's World Revisited," posted online at http://www.lats.com/rights/register.htm (accessed online September 28, 2002). This quote came from an undated press release. The dateline was Damascus. The author quoted from the book *Bin Ladin, Al-Jezeera, and I,* by Jamal Abdul Latif Ismail. The book, which at the time is only in Arabic, includes a fifty-four-page transcript of the complete 1998 interview that was broadcast in abbreviated form on Al-Jezeera, a popular Islamic television program. The book was sold out in the Middle East.

4. Rollin Armour Sr., *Islam, Christianity, and the West: A Troubled History* (Maryknoll, NY: Orbis, 2002), 31.

5. Hammudah Abdulati, *Islam in Focus*, 3rd rev. ed., rev. and ed. by Shaykh Salih al Husayin and Mustapha Abu Sway (Beltsville, MD: Amana, 1998), 146.

6. George W. Braswell Jr., *Islam: Its Prophet, Peoples, Politics and Power* (Nashville: Broadman and Holman, 1996), 74.

7. Christine Schirrmacher, "Islam and Christianity," *Journal of the Institute of Islamic Studies of the Lausanne Movement Germany*, no. 1 (2000): 2.

8. Khaled Abou El Fadl, "Between Functionalism and Morality: The Juristic Debates in the Conduct of War," in *Islamic Ethics of Life: Abortion, War, and Euthanasia*, ed. by Jonathan E. Brockopp (Columbia, SC: University of South Carolina, 2003), 108.

9. Section titled "Newswatch," *Press Democrat*, October 10, 2002, 2.

10. *Imad Shehadeh Self-Published Newsletter* in the hands of the author, October 4, 2001, 2. It should be noted that various authors offer different statistics for the number of mosques in the United States. In this book, we have various quotes suggesting from 1,200 to 3,600 mosques in the United States. The wide variation is due to two reasons: (1) different ways of defining what constitutes a mosque, and (2) the lack of adequate statistics coming out of the Islamic community in the United States.

11. *Imad Shehadeh Self-Published Newsletter*, 3.

12. Malise Ruthven, *Islam in the World*, 3rd ed. (New York: Oxford University Press, 2006), 219.

13. Armour, *Islam, Christianity, and the West*, 177.

14. Ahmed Rashid, *Jihad: The Rise of Militant Islam in Central Asia* (New Haven, CT: Yale University Press, 2002), 1.

15. Ibid., 2.

16. Hussein K. al-Hussein, "Islamic Jihad: Some Misconceptions," *Muslim World League Journal* 16, no. 3 and 4 (1998): 36.

17. Armour, *Islam, Christianity, and the West*, 29.

Chapter 4: If You Build It, They Will Come

1. Bryant L. Meyers, *The New Context of World Missions* (Monrovia, CA: MARC, 1996), 8.

2. Azim A. Nanji, ed., *The Muslim Almanac* (New York: Gale Research, 1996), 465.

3. Ibid.

4. Ibid., 471.

5. John L. Esposito, *Unholy War: Terror in the Name of Islam* (New York: Oxford University Press, 2002), 129.

6. Martin Frishman, "Islam and the Form of the Mosque," in *The Mosque: History, Architectural Development, and Regional Diversity,* ed. Martin Frishman and Hasan-Uddin Khan (New York: Thames and Hudson, 1994), 30.

7. Dogan Kuban, "The Central Arab Lands," in *The Mosque: History, Architectural Development, and Regional Diversity,* ed. Martin Frishman and Hasan-Uddin Khan (New York: Thames and Hudson, 1994), 77.

8. Frishman, "Islam and the Form of the Mosque," 41.

9. Kuban, "Central Arab Lands," 89.

10. Ismail Serageldin, "Introduction: Regionalism," in *The Mosque: History, Architectural Development, and Regional Diversity,* ed. Martin Frishman and Hasan-Uddin Khan (New York: Thames and Hudson, 1994), 72.

11. Frank Charles Thompson, *The Thompson Chain-Reference Bible* (Indianapolis: B. B. Kirkbride, 1978), 1648.

12. J. Christy Wilson, *Afghanistan—The Forbidden Harvest: The Challenging Story of God's Work in a Resistant Land* (Elgin, IL: D.C. Cook, 1981), 59.

13. Nigeria Background Information, "Standard 10: Cultural Mosaics of Nigeria," http://www.uni.edu/gai/nigeria/Background/Standard10.html (accessed October 5, 2011).

14. Marsha S. Haney, *Islam and Protestant African-American Churches: Responses and Challenges to Religious Pluralism* (San Francisco: International Scholars Publications, 1998), 109.

15. Paul Johnson, "What Follows Saddam in Iraq," *Forbes,* August 12, 2002, 41.

16. Lisa Beyer, "Saudi Arabia: Inside the Kingdom," *Time,* September 15, 2003, 50; http://www.time.com/time/magazine/article/0,9171,1005663,00.html.

17. Ibid.

18. Council on American-Islamic Relations (CAIR), "CAIR Report: Number

of American Mosques Grows by 25 Percent" (Washington, DC: CAIR, April 26, 2001); can be viewed at http://www.bangladesh.com/forums /religion/5661-cair-report-no-american-mosques-grow-25-a.html . The study is by Ihsan Bagby, Paul M. Perl, and Bryan T. Froehle, "The Mosque in America: A National Portrait: A Report from the Mosque Study Project" (Washington, DC: Council on American-Islamic Relations, April 26, 2001); http://www.cair.com/portals/0/pdf/The_mosque _in_America_A_National_Portrait.pdf (accessed October 5, 2011).

19. Ibid.
20. Ibid.
21. Nabeel Abraham, "Arab Detroit's 'American Mosque,'" in *Arab Detroit: From Margin to Mainstream*, ed. Nabeel Abraham and Andrew Shryock, Great Lakes Books (Detroit: Wayne State University Press, 2000), 280.
22. Islam Online, "Muslims Harassed for Praying in Cordoba Mosque," March 4, 2002, http://www.islamonline.net/English/News/2002-03 /04/article18.shtml.
23. Zenit: The World Seen from Rome, http://www.zenit.org/english /archive9905/ZE990514.html (accessed online May 14, 1999).
24. This material was taken from the Dar-al-Islam website, which also describes the different ministries of the mosque in vague terms, posted online at http://www.daralislam.org (accessed October 5, 2011).

Chapter 5: Changing Demographics

1. Patrick J. Buchanan, *The Death of the West: How Dying Populations and Immigrant Invasions Imperil Our Country and Civilization* (New York: St. Martin's, 2002), 2.
2. Ibid, 12.
3. Jody K. Biehl, "The Death of a Muslim Woman: 'The Whore Lived Like a German,'" March 2, 2005, Spiegel Online International, http:// www.spiegel.de/international/0,1518,344374,00.html (accessed May 12, 2011).
4. "Islam in Europe," Wikipedia, http://en.wikipedia.org/wiki/Islam_in _Europe (accessed January 4, 2011).

5. Steve Doughty, "Britain Has 85 Sharia Courts: The Astonishing Spread of the Islamic Justice Behind Closed Doors," June 29, 2009, MailOnline, http://www.dailymail.co.uk/news/article-1196165/ (accessed May 12, 2011).

6. Samuel P. Huntington, *The Clash of Civilizations and the Remaking of World Order* (New York: Simon and Schuster, 1996; paperback edition 2003), 198.

7. Ibid., 200.

8. Speech given by Geert Wilders at the Hudson Institute, September 25, 2008. Transcript in the hands of the author.

9. One source that provides specific figures on the distribution of Muslim population by nation-state is Azim A. Nanji., ed., *The Muslim Almanac* (New York: Gale Research, 1996), xxix–xxxv.

10. Daniel L. Pipes and Lars Hedegaaard, quoted by Susan MacAllan in "Salute the Danish Flag: It's a Symbol of Western Freedom," Family Security Matters, July 23, 2007. A copy of this article is in the hands of the author, and can be found at various websites, including http://europenews.dk/en/node/6517 (accessed May 12, 2011).

11. Ibid.

12. MacAllan, "Salute the Danish Flag."

13. See transcripts of the speech given by Geert Wilders on May 12, 2011, at Cornerstone Church, Nashville, TN (available at various sites including http://jihadwatch.org/2011/05/geert-wilders-a-warning-to-america.html.

14. Sam Solomon, "A Proposed Charter of Muslim Understanding," presented to the European parliament on December 13, 2006, by Gerard Batten, available at http://www.islam-watch.org/ExMuslims /Charter-of-Muslim-Understanding.htm (accessed October 13, 2011).

15. Ibid.

CHAPTER 6: IT'S THE LAW

1. Ghulam Sarwar, *Islam: Beliefs and Teachings* (Chicago: Kazi, 1993), 161.

2. A. H. Qasmi, ed., *International Encyclopaedia of Islam* (Delhi: Isha Books, 2006), 20–21.

3. Summarized from Stephen Schwartz, *The Two Faces of Islam: Saudi*

Fundamentalism and Its Role in Terrorism (New York: Doubleday, 2002), 41–42.

4. "Concept of Dhimma," http://www.angelfire.com/az/rescon/DHIM MI.html (accessed December 8, 2011).

5. Quoted by Anthony Flew, "Islam's War Against the West: Can It Abide a Secular State?" *Free Inquiry* 22 (spring 2002): 43.

6. Ian Johnson and David Crawford, "A Saudi Group Spreads Extremism in 'Law' Seminars Taught in Dutch," *Wall Street Journal*, April 15, 2003.

7. Ibid.

8. Ibid.

9. Lisa Beyer, "Saudi Arabia: Inside the Kingdom," *Time*, September 15, 2003, 47.

10. Bernard Lewis, *The Crisis of Islam: Holy War and Unholy Terror* (New York: Random House, 2003), 113.

11. Ibid., 114.

12. Ibid., 114–15.

13. Ibid., 115–16.

14. Ibid., 116.

15. Ibid., 8.

16. Ahmed Rashid, *Jihad: The Rise of Militant Islam in Central Asia* (New Haven, CT: Yale University Press, 2002), 9.

17. David Wallechinsky, "The 10 Worst Living Dictators," *Parade Magazine*, February 16, 2003, 4.

18. Ibid.

19. John L. Esposito and John O. Voll, *Islam and Democracy* (New York: Oxford University Press, 1966), 65.

20. Ibid., 67–68.

21. Christiane Bird, *Neither East nor West: One Woman's Journey Through the Islamic Republic of Iran* (New York: Washington Square Press, 2001), 51–52.

CHAPTER 7: THE WHOLE TRUTH AND NOTHING BUT THE TRUTH

1. Moiz Amjad, "Is 'Truth' Relative or Absolute?" *Understanding Islam* website Q&A, July 3, 2000, http://www.understanding-islam.com

/q-and-a/sources-of-islam/is-truth-relative-or-absolute-4768 (accessed October 21, 2011).

2. "Truth and Relativity," The Way to Truth website, last updated July 24, 2000, http://www.thewaytotruth.org/thinkingstraight/truthandrela tivity.html (accessed October 21, 2011).

3. "Thinking Straight and the Ways to Achieve It," The Way to Truth website blog, http://thewaytotruth.org/blog/2011/10/thinking-straight -and-the-ways-to-achieve-it/ (accessed October 21, 2011).

4. "Truth and Relativity."

5. David Weir, "Honour and Shame," *Islam Watch* website, September 17, 2007 (accessed October 22, 2011).

6. Asghar Ali Engineer, "Islamic Ethic," http://andromeda.rutgers.edu /~rtavakol/engineer/ethics.htm (accessed October 21, 2011).

7. Ibid.

8. "Truth and Relativity."

9. Ibid.

10. Ibid.

11. Caesar E. Farah, *Islam*, 7th ed. (Hauppauge, NY: Barron's, 2003), 82.

12. See, e.g., "5 Pillars of Islam," Islamic-World.Net website, http://islamic -world.net/children/muslim_facts/5pillars.htm; or "Six Kalimas," *Lover of Islam* website, http://loverofislam.webs.com/sixkalimas.htm (both accessed October 21, 2011).

13. *Comparative Index to Islam: Lying,* http://islamacevap.net/Index/L /lying.html (accessed October 21, 2011).

14. Sami Zaatari, "Examining the Issue of the Prophet Muhammad Al- lowing Muslims to Lie," http://www.answering-christianity.com/sami _zaatri/are_we_allowed_to_lie.htm (accessed December 6, 2011), em- phasis in original.

15. *Comparative Index to Islam: Lying.*

16. Fatema Mernissi, *Islam and Democracy: Fear of the Modern World*, trans. Mary Jo Lakeland (Cambridge, MA: Perseus, 2002). A thorough study of the book will explain what the author meant by the different types of fear.

17. Sura al-Hujurtt 49:1.

18. Munkar and Nakeer are two of Allah's angels who appear to a person after death. They are blue-black in color. After death they come and ask the person what he said or proclaimed in his life before; if he states that he followed Allah and recites the confession of what he believed, the angels will say that they knew he was going to say that which he did. His grave is then enlarged to seventy cubits by seventy cubits. The grave is also illuminated, whereafter the person is told to sleep like a bridegroom who will only be wakened by his beloved. He will remain that way until Allah raises him up. If the angels ask a hypocrite the same question, it is stated that he will answer that he only recited that which he heard other people saying. Upon hearing these words, the angels will tell him that they knew he was going to say that and command the earth to crush him until his ribs are interlocked, in which position he will remain until Allah raises him up ("Al-malaa'ikah [Angels]," *Allaahuakbar .net*, http://www.allaahuakbar.net/barelwiyat/angels.htm [accessed October 24, 2002]).

19. Imaam al-Ghazali, Imaam Ibn ul-Qayyim, and Ibn Rajab al-Hanbali, "The Signs of Fear of Allah: Its Reasons, Its Fruits and Some Poems" (London: Al-Firdous Ltd., 1995), http://www.sunnahonline.com/ilm /purification/0072.htm (accessed October 24, 2011).

20. Ibn ul Qayyim's Madaarij us-Saalikeen, "Remembering the Destination of Mankind in the Hereafter—A Cure for Weak," http://www.mis sionislam.com/knowledge/Hereafter.htm (accessed October 24, 2011).

21. See "Pillars of Belief: Belief in the Hereafter," *Explore Islaam*, http:// www.exploreislaam.com (accessed December 1, 2011).

22. K. M. Islam, "'The Infidel Hell,' from *The Spectacle of Death*" in *Extreme Islam: Anti-American Propaganda of Muslim Fundamentalism*, ed. Adam Parfrey (Los Angeles: Feral House, 2001), 310.

23. "When Does a Muslim Become an Apostate?" *Light of Life*, http:// www.light-of-life.com/eng/ilaw/ (accessed October 24, 2011), 11.

24. "Bahá'i Executed in Iran," *The Baha'i Faith Index*, July 22, 1988, http://www.bahaindex.com/it/news/human-rights/271-mrruhollah -rowhani-executed-in-iran-21-july-1988 (accessed October 24, 2011).

25. Human Rights Watch World Report 1997: Events of 1996 (New York:

Human Rights Watch, 1996), 279; "Egypt Secular Thinker Nasr Hamed Abu Zeid Dies" AFP, July 5, 2010.

26. Mernissi, *Islam and Democracy*, 13.

27. Ibid., 51.

CHAPTER 8: POWER SHORTAGE

1. Charles H. Kraft, *Anthropology for Christian Witness* (Maryknoll, NY: Orbis, 1998), 453. Kraft is one of America's outstanding authorities on power encounter on a global scale.

2. R. James Woolsey, "World War IV" (lecture, University of California at Los Angeles, November 16, 2002), http://www.globalsecurity.org/mili tary/library/report/2002/021116-ww4.htm (accessed October 25, 2011).

3. Ibid.

4. This was at www.islamicbookstores.com as of August 6, 2002, but appears not to be available there any longer.

5. Steve Hawthorne and Graham Kendrick, *Prayer Walking: Praying on Site with Insight* (Lake Mary, FL: Charisma House, 1993), 85–87.

6. Quoted in "Terror in America (22): Egypt's Al-Azhar Clerics: We Declare War on America," The Middle East Media Research Institute special dispatch no. 296 (Washington, DC: MEMRI, November 6, 2001), memri.org/report/en/print542.htm (accessed October 25, 2011).

7. Ibid.

8. Ibid.

9. *Webster's New English Dictionary* (New York: Simon and Schuster, 1994), s.v. "intimidation."

10. Daniel Pipes, "How Dare You Defame Islam," November 1999, http://www.danielpipes.org/321/how-dare-you-defame-islam (accessed October 25, 2011).

11. "Iraq's Tiny Christian Communities Brace for Heightened Persecution," by Baptist Press staff reporter, March 19, 2003, http://www .bpnews.net/bpnews.asp?id=15483 (accessed October 25, 2011).

12. Erica Goode and Suadad Al-Salhy, "Christians Fleeing Mosul After Targeted Killings," *New York Times*, October 10, 2008, http://www

.nytimes.com/2008/10/10/world/africa/10iht-iraq.4.16857852.html (accessed January 17, 2012).

13. "Nigerian Government Rejects 'Fatwa,'" BBCNews World Edition, November 26, 2002, http://news.bbc.co.uk/2/hi/africa/2514821.stm (accessed October 25, 2011).

14. "Bomb Kills Christian Convert," *Pakistan Christian Post*, May 8, 2003, http://www.pakistanchristianpost.com/headlinenewsd.php?hnewsid =147 (accessed October 25, 2011).

15. David B. Barrett, George T. Kurian, and Todd M. Johnson, *World Christian Encyclopedia* (New York: Oxford University Press, 2003), 1:11.

16. David B. Barrett, Todd M. Johnson, and Peter F. Crossing, "Statistical Overview of the World's 2.2 Billion Christians and Their Activities" *International Bulletin of Missionary Research* 33, no. 1 (January 2009): 32.

17. Name and location withheld; private interview by author, 1990.

Chapter 9: Muhammad, the Message, and the Mass Media

1. Daniel Pipes, "How Dare You Defame Islam," November 1999, http://www.danielpipes.org/321/how-dare-you-defame-islam (accessed October 25, 2011).

2. Ibid.

3. Gwynne Dyer, "Media and Terrorism: How to Cover Terrorism: The New Media Rules," October 27, 2002, http://gwynnedyer.com/2002/media-and-terrorism/ (accessed October 26, 2011).

4. Islamic Net Article 200.08.2002-09-06 6. This was opened in the Middle East and was in Arabic. This was the only information available in identifying the source.

5. "Islamic Cooperation," *Middle East Newspaper,* Religion, March 3, 2003.

6. Pipes, "How Dare You Defame Islam."

7. Charles Krauthammer, "The Truth About Daniel Pipes," editorial *Washington Post*, August 15, 2003.

8. Pipes, "How Dare You Defame Islam."

9. Bassam Za'za', "Insight: Projecting True Picture of Islam," *Gulf News,*

November 1, 2002, http://gulfnews.com/news/gulf/uae/general/insight
-projecting-true-picture-of-islam-1.402261 (accessed October 26, 2011).

10. Caryle Murphy, "Muslim U.S. Workers Hope to Break Image," *Washington Post,* November 6, 2002.

11. Martha Graybow, "US Filmmakers Tread Carefully in Mohammed Biography," Worldwide Religious News, http://tv.yahoo.com/news/va/20021212/103972897200.html, 2.

12. Daniel Pipes, "PBS, Recruiting for Islam," *New York Post,* December 17, 2002, http://www.danielpipes.org/982/pbs-recruiting-for-islam (accessed October 26, 2011).

13. Asma Gull Hasan, *American Muslims: The New Generation* (New York: Continuum, 2000), 100.

14. Posted online at http://www.islamicmedia.net/mission1.htm (accessed August 2003). No longer available there. At the time of publication of the updated edition, this was available at http://www.kuficgraphics.com/dev/imfflash/ (accessed October 26, 2011).

15. Ursula Owre Masterson, "American Muslims Launch PR-style Campaigns to Defend Islam," *Muslim News* (Harrow, Middlesex, UK), November 6, 2002.

16. "Muslim Ramadan Begins, So Does Acceptance," WBAY TV (Green Bay, Wis.), November 8, 2002.

17. Donna Gehrke-White, "Moving Beyond the Mosque: Muslims Seek to Enter Mainstream," *Muslim News,* November 4, 2002, http://www.muslimnews.co.uk/ramadan (accessed 15 January 2003; not available there as of December 2011).

18. Jane Lampman, "A Muslim Scholar Builds Bridges to the West," *Christian Science Monitor,* November 7, 2002.

19. Murphy, "Muslim U.S. Workers Hope to Break Image."

20. Masterson, "American Muslims Launch PR-style Campaigns to Defend Islam."

21. John Rivera, "As Ramadan Begins, Cleric Urges Tolerance," *The Baltimore Sun,* http://articles.baltimoresun.com/2002-11-06/news/0211060343_1_muslim-arafat-islam (accessed October 26, 2011).

22. "Da'wah Is Our Mission," Islamic Media Foundation home page, http://www.imf-ibn.net/ (accessed January 17, 2012).

23. "About Us . . . Did You Know?" *The Muslim News*, October 26, 2011 http://www.muslimnews.co.uk/index/section.php?page=about_us (accessed October 26, 2011).

24. Kari Lynn Dean, "Muslim TV Network in the Making," *Wired News*, May 10, 2003, http://www.wired.com/culture/lifestyle/news/2003 /05/58773 (accessed October 26, 2011). Bridges TV did indeed premier in November 2004. Since then, one of its founders has been sentenced to prison for beheading his wife, who was beginning divorce proceedings.

25. Ibid.

26. Michael Isikoff, "It's All a Matter of Bias," *Newsweek*, December 30, 2002–January 6, 2003, 14.

27. Ibid.

28. Noelle Knox and Theresa Howard, "Anti-war Protesters Take Aim at American Brands," *USA Today*, April 4, 2003.

29. Ibid.

30. "Dr. Al-Turki Meeting with the European parliament," *Middle East Newspaper*, Religion, May 24, 2002.

31. *Muslim Holland*, http://www.islamway.net.

32. *Middle East Newspaper*, Religion, June 23, 2002.

CHAPTER 10: WHAT IN THE WORLD IS ALLAH DOING?

1. Patrick Johnstone and Jason Mandryk, *Operation World: Twenty-first Century*, 6th ed. (London: Bethany, 2001), 2. Updated statistics can be found in Jason Mandryk, *Operation World*, 7th ed. (Colorado Springs: Biblica, 2010), 2.

2. Ibid., 3.

3. Danielle Haas, "Iraqi Crowds Welcome Ayatollah Home," *San Francisco Chronicle*, May 11, 2003.

4. Ibid.

5. Pierre Francis, *The Civil War in Lebanon (1975–1992) and the Christian Evangelical Message: Toward Survival, Extinction or Expansion* (Th.D. dissertation, Evangelical Theological Faculty, Louvin, Belgium, September 1993), 3. The dissertation looks at the causes of the war and

its effects on the traditional Christian community. Francis sees the war as a continued attempt by Islamic forces to drive all remnants of Christianity out of the Middle East. Beirut had been the center for evangelical Christian missions to the Middle East, but the war drove them out. Many mission agencies then placed their headquarters in either Cyprus or Western Europe.

6. Johnstone and Mandryk, *Operation World,* 21. Updated statistics can be found in Mandryk, *Operation World* (2010), 32.

7. Quoted in the preliminary draft of a paper titled *Spreading the Word of God Among Muslims in South Africa,* 3. This draft was produced by the United Bible Societies. The date of the draft was September 26, 2002. The paper is in the hands of the author.

8. Christian missionary to Nigeria, interview by author, February 3, 2001. For the sake of security, the name of the missionary cannot be revealed.

9. Christian missionary to Rwanda, lecture given in Introduction to Missions at Golden Gate Baptist Theological Seminary, November 3, 2002. For the sake of security, the name of the missionary cannot be revealed.

10. "Religious Freedom in the Majority Islamic Countries, 1998 Report," *Cristianità,* http://www.agonet.it/cristianita/acs/acs_english/report _98/malawi.htm. As of December 2011, this web address is no longer available.

11. Dr. Martinus Pretoria, interview by author, Leuven, Belgium, September 14, 2002.

12. Johnstone and Mandryk, *Operation World,* 41.

13. Justin D. Long, "Asia 1900–2025: The Rise and Fall of World Religions," http://www.gem-werc.org/mmrc/mmrc9723.htm (accessed November 28, 2002).

14. John L. Esposito, "An Introduction," in John L. Esposito, ed., *Islam in Asia: Religion, Politics, and Society* (New York: Oxford University Press, 1987), 15.

15. Satu Limaye, "Islam in Asia: Asia-Pacific Center for Security Studies," April 16, 1999, http://www.apcss.org/Publications/Report_Islam_in_ Asia_99.html (accessed November 21, 2011).

16. Ibid.

17. Indian Christian Fellowship, *Conversion of Millions in India*, http://www.webedelil.com/church/delhi411.htm. As of December 2011, this web address is no longer available.

18. Ibid.

19. Ibid.

20. Syed Shahabuddin and Theodore P. Wright Jr., "India: Muslim Minority Politics and Society," in *Islam in Asia: Religion, Politics and Society*, ed. John Esposito (New York: Oxford University Press, 1987), 152.

21. Johnstone and Mandryk, *Operation World*, 339.

22. Limaye, "Islam in Asia."

23. These were statements taken from prayer letters sent to me between January 1, 2002, and March 30, 2003. The names of the missionaries cannot be given due to security reasons.

24. Ibid.

25. Caesar E. Farah, *Islam*, 7th ed. (Hauppauge, NY: Barrons, 2000), 262–63.

26. Ibid., 284.

27. Limaye, "Islam in Asia."

28. Farah, *Islam*, 277.

29. Ibid.

30. Ahmed Rashid, *Jihad: The Rise of Militant Islam in Central Asia* (New Haven, CT: Yale University Press, 2002), 115.

31. Ibid., 116.

32. Chris Moss, "Latin America's First Mega-Mosque Opens Eyes to Islam," from *Islam Online*, http://www.hispanicmuslims.com/articles/other/openseyes.html.

33. Johnstone and Mandryk, *Operation World*, 33.

CHAPTER 11: MEASURING SUCCESS ONE COUNTRY AT A TIME

1. Samuel P. Huntington, *The Clash of Civilizations and the Remaking of World Order* (New York: Simon and Schuster, 1996), 312.

2. David Dolan Newsletter, (*Israel Update) Pieces on the Ground*, February 3, 2003.

3. Huntington, *Clash of Civilizations,* 304.
4. Ibid.

CHAPTER 12: WHAT CAN WE DO ABOUT IT?

1. Todd M. Johnson, David B. Barrett, and Peter F. Crossing, "Christianity 2010: A View from the New *Atlas of Global Christianity,*" *International Bulletin of Missionary Research* 34, no. 1 (January 2010): 36.
2. Donald McGavran, *The Bridges of God* (New York: Friendship Press, 1955), 55.
3. Gregg R. Allison, "Resurgence: An Evaluation of Emerging Churches on the Basis of the Contextualization Spectrum (C1–C6)," paper delivered at the annual meeting of the Evangelical Theological Society, Washington, D.C., November 17, 2006. The original article by John Travis was published in *Evangelical Missions Quarterly* 34, no. 4 (1988): 407–8.
4. Paul G. Hiebert, "The Flaw of the Excluded Middle," *Missiology* 10, no. 1 (January 1982): 35–47.
5. *The Holy Qur'an,* trans. Abdullah Yusuf Ali (Beltsville, MD: Amana Publications, 1997), 535.
6. Dennis Grill, "Love and Affection," *Encyclopedia of the Qur'an,* vol. 3, ed. Jane Dammen McAuliffe (Boston: Brill, 2002), 132.
7. Gerhard Bowering, "God and His Attributes," *Encyclopedia of the Qur'an,* vol. 2, ed. Jane Dammen McAuliffe (Boston: Brill, 2002), 322.
8. J. Windrow Sweetman, *Islam and Christian Theology: A Study of Interpretation of Theological Ideas in the Two Religions,* vol. 2 (London: Lutterworth Press, 1947), 60.
9. R. E. O. White, "Love," *Baker Encyclopedia of the Bible,* vol. 2, ed. Walter A. Elwell (Grand Rapids: Baker, 1988), 324.
10. Peggy Starkey, "Agape: A Christian Criterion for Truth in the Other World Religions," *International Review of Missions* (October 1985), 445.
11. David J. Hesselgrave, *Paradigms in Conflict* (Grand Rapids: Kregel, 2005), 197.
12. Quoted in ibid., emphasis in original.

APPENDIX A: QUOTES FROM MIDDLE EASTERN SOURCES (2002)

1. *Middle East Newspaper,* Religion, May 3, 2002, interview with Sheik Aqil Alaqil.
2. *Middle East Newspaper,* Religion, May 3, 2002, interview with Jussif Haji.
3. *Middle East Newspaper,* Religion, January 31, 2002, Abdulaziz bin Baz Charity Foundation.
4. *Middle East Newspaper,* Religion, March 11, 2002, meetings in Jeddah.
5. Islamic Net Article, 8E20.02-09-06 6.
6. *Middle East Newspaper,* Religion, May 25, 2002, Islamic cooperation.
7. *Middle East Newspaper,* Religion, April 5, 2002, interview with Dr. Fahad al Tajash.
8. *Middle East Newspaper,* Religion, March 3, 2002, Islamic cooperation.
9. 'Abdallah 'Abd al-Fadi, *Is the Qur'an Infallible?* (Villach, Austria: Light of Life, first English edition, 1995), 143–46.
10. *Middle East Newspaper,* Opinions, February 26, 2002, what we can learn from the war in Afghanistan.
11. *Middle East Newspaper,* Religion, n.d., interview with Dr. Al-Turki.
12. *Middle East Newspaper,* Opinions, January 23, 2002, Sheik Ibin Taimeja.
13. *Middle East Newspaper,* Religion, May 3, 2002, Islamic delegation to Europe.
14. *Middle East Newspaper,* Religion, May 18, 2002, meetings concerning dialogues with the West.
15. *Middle East Newspaper,* High Education Research, March 29, 2001, the American Company (amidst).
16. *Middle East Newspaper,* front page, May 10, 2002, new studies to understand Qur'an.
17. *Middle East Newspaper,* front page, March 11, 2002, Islamic delegation visiting the U.K.
18. *Middle East Newspaper,* Religion, June 17, 2002, Islamic delegation in Germany.
19. *Middle East Newspaper,* front page, March 11, 2002, Islamic delegation visiting the U.K.

20. *Middle East Newspaper,* Religion, February 19, 2002, interview with Dr. Al-Turki.
21. *Middle East Newspaper,* Religion, May 25, 2002, humanity studies from an Islamic point of view.
22. *Middle East Newspaper,* Religion, August 16, 2002, Islamic organizations in the Earth Summit.
23. *Middle East Newspaper,* Religion, March 29, 2002, the Da'l Yussif Islam new exhibition.
24. Al Jazeera, http://www.aljazeera.com, n.d., interview with Dr. Yussif Qaradawe.
25. *Middle East Newspaper,* Religion, March 20, 2002, meetings between Islamic organizations in Saudi Arabia.
26. *Middle East Newspaper,* Religion, April 13, 2002, interview with the president of the Islamic American University.
27. *Middle East Newspaper,* Religion, April 8, 2002, King Fahd interview.
28. *Middle East Newspaper,* Religion, June 21, 2002, meeting with Dr. Al-Turki about the relationship between Islam and the West.
29. *Middle East Newspaper,* Religion, February 2, 2002, meeting with executive director of the Council on American-Islamic Relations, Nihad Awad.
30. Al Jazeera, August 2, 2002, Paul rejected the Islamic wrong ideas about Islam.
31. http://english.islamway.com (accessed August 2, 2002).
32. "Dr. Al-Turki Meeting with the European parliament," *Middle East Newspaper,* Religion, May 24, 2002.
33. *Muslim Holland,* http://www.islamway.net.
34. *Middle East Newspaper,* Religion, May 16, 2002, new branches for Al-Azhar University.
35. *Middle East Newspaper,* Religion, November 9, 2001, interview with Dr. Taricha.
36. *Middle East Newspaper,* Religion, February 2, 2002, the mosque of King Fahd.
37. *Middle East Newspaper,* Religion, February 8, 2002, conference for the World Islamic Universities.

38. Al Jazeerah channel, program (a Sharee'ah wal Haiat), December 7, 2000. As of the updated edition of this book, Islamic schools can be seen popping up all over the country.

39. *Middle East Newspaper*, Religion, August 10, 2001, interview with Dr. Ali Qara Daghi.

40. "Europe's Muslims," *The Economist*, August 10, 2002, http://www.economist.com/node/1270621 (accessed November 21, 2011).

41. Islamic Net, July 3, 2002, interview with a businessman.

42. Islamic Net, July 13, 2002, Islamic media under the ecumenical.

43. *Middle East Newspaper*, Religion, May 3, 2002, interview with Tantawee.

44. *Middle East Newspaper*, Religion, September 20, 2002, conference for the leaders of an Islamic organization in South America.

45. Islamic Net, July 16, 2002, Islamic satellite.

46. Islamic Net, August 12, 2002, Islamic satellite.

47. *Middle East Newspaper*, TV, Radio, August 7, 2002, Arabic channel in Germany.

48. Larry Allan Poston, "The Institutionalization of *Da'wah* in the West, Islamic *Da'wah* in North America," Ph.D. dissertation, Northwestern University, 1988.

49. Larry Poston, *Islamic* Da'wah *in the West: Muslim Missionary Activity and the Dynamic of Coversion to Islam* (New York: Oxford University Press, 1992), 94.

50. Ibid., 97–98.

51. Ibid., 98.

52. Poston, "Institutionalization of *Da'wah* in the West."

53. Ibid.

54. Ibid.

55. Ibid.

Appendix C: A Brotherhood of Conquest

1. "Muslim Brotherhood," Wikipedia, http://en.wikipedia.org/wiki/Muslim_Brotherhood (accessed March 6, 2011).

2. These are available, with slight variation, from various sources, in-

cluding the Global Muslim Brotherhood Daily Report, June 2, 2007, http://globalmbreport.org/?p=5.

3. Bernard Lewis, *The Crisis of Islam: Holy War and Unholy Terror* (New York, Random House, 2003), 81.

4. "Muslim Brotherhood" (accessed May 11, 2011).

5. David Waines, *An Introduction to Islam*, 2nd ed. (Cambridge: Cambridge University Press, 2004), 242.

6. John L. Esposito, *Islam: The Straight Path*, 3rd ed. (New York: Oxford University Press, 2005), 150.

7. Malise Ruthven, "Islam in the Modern World," *The Muslim Almanac*, ed. Azim A. Nanji (Detroit: Gale Research, 1995), 436.

8. Ibid.

9. Bruce B. Lawrence, *Shattering the Myth: Islam Beyond Violence* (Princeton, NJ: Princeton University Press, 1998), 70.

10. Paul Cruickshank and Tom Lister, "Energized Muslim Brotherhood in Libya Eyes a Prize," CNN World, March 25, 2011, https://www.cnn.com/2011/WORLD/africa/03/25/libya.islamists/ (accessed March 25, 2011).

11. "Muslim Brotherhood" (accessed July 25, 2011).

12. Lorenzo Vidino, "The Muslim Brotherhood's Conquest of Europe," *Middle East Quarterly*, March 6, 2011, http://www.meforum.org/687/the-muslim-brotherhoods-conquest-of-europe?gclid=CleAqY.

13. Udo Ulfkotte, private interview by author, Bonn, Germany, January 11, 2011.

14. Michael Whine, "The Advance of the Muslim Brotherhood in the UK," *Current Trends in Islamist Ideology*, vol. 2, Hudson Institute, September 12, 2005, http://www.currenttrends.org/research/detail/the-advance-of-the-muslim-brotherhood-in-the-uk (accessed May 11, 2011).

15. Ibid.

16. Douglas Farah and Ron Sandee, "The Ikhwan in North America: A Short History," The NEFA Foundation, p. 9, http://www.nefafoundation.org/newsite/file/hefahlf0807.pdf; which quotes "An Explanatory Memorandum on the General Strategic Goal for the Brotherhood in North America" by Mohamed Akram, May 19, 1991, Government Exhibit 003-0085; 3:04-CR-240-G; *U.S. v. HLF, et al.*, p. 18.

17. Farah and Sandee, "The Ikhwan in North America," p. 9; which quotes "An Explanatory Memorandum" by Akram, Government Exhibit 003-0085, p. 21.

18. "Muslim Brotherhood" (accessed March 6, 2011).

19. Cruickshank and Lister, "Energized Muslim Brotherhood."

20. Teri Schure, "Muslim Brotherhood: Who Are They?" Worldpress.org, February 4, 2011, http://www.worldpress.org/Mideast/3694.cfm (accessed May 11, 2011).

21. "The Interim Transitional National Council Statement," March 22, 2011, The Libya Interim National Council official website, http://ntclibya.org/English/the-statement/ (accessed May 11, 2011).

22. Cruickshank and Lister, "Energized Muslim Brotherhood."

Glossary

al-houdh. The pool of water in hell.

al-jisr. The bridge over hell.

Allah. The name for God in Islam.

Allahu Akbar. "God is greatest"; phrase used by Muslims in the form of a battle cry, in the call to prayer, and often used in general conversation.

ayatollah. "Sign of God"; title used since the twentieth century for a high-ranking *Shiite* leader.

burka. Heavy, dark clothing worn by Muslim women that covers most of the body.

caliph. Successor to Muhammad's temporal, but not spiritual, authority over the Muslim community.

daa'i. A missionary in Islam.

dar-al-bughd. The community of non-Muslims who are hated by Muslims.

dar-al-harb. "The house of war"; Islamic doctrine and language divides the world into two parts (the other is *dar-al-Islam*). This one is for the non-Muslim world and means the "unpeaced" abode.

dar-al-Islam. "The house of Islam"; the Islamic world.

dar-al-kuffer. Community of non-Muslims or unbelievers.

Da'wah. "Call" or "invitation" summoning others to heed the call of God to Islam; propagation of the faith.

dhimmi. A conquered Jew or Christian who lives under Islamic rule.

fatwa. An official pronouncement from a leader in Islam; also a nonbinding legal opinion.

fiqh. The legal system of Islam as practiced in the courts.

gharaba. "Strangeness"; used in reference to the West, it is a derivative of *ghareeb* ("strange").

gharb. "The West" or "darkness."

Hadith. The Islamic writings describing the life and sayings of Muhammad.

hajj. Pilgrimage to Mecca.

halal. Clean by Islamic standards.

imam. The spiritual leader in a Muslim community.

injil. The gospels describing Jesus that are accepted by Islam.

irsalyaat. Negative word used to describe Christian missions.

jihad. "Struggle"; it need not be physical but could be. Also used to mean holy war.

jizya. Poll tax for *dhimmis* living under Islamic rule, exempting them from military duty.

Ka'aba. The most sacred shrine in Islam, believed to have been erected by Abraham and located in the courtyard of the Grand Mosque in Mecca.

kaffir. Infidel or pagan.

madrassa. Muslim religious school. Many of the Taliban were educated in Saudi-funded madrassas in Pakistan that teach a particularly austere form of Islam.

Mahdi. The awaited one, the *imam* who will return and unite all Muslims into one *ummah,* according to Shiite Muslims.

minaret. The tower of a mosque, from which the call to prayer is issued five times daily.

mosque. From the Arabic *masjid;* a place of Muslim worship.

Muslim. Literally, "one who submits himself to the will of God"; a follower of the religion of Islam.

Qur'an. The holy book of Islam; God's word as revealed to Muhammad.

Ramadan. Ninth month of the Muslim lunar year and the month of fasting during daylight hours.

shahada. The profession of faith; a statement of fundamental belief in

Islam. "There is no god but Allah and Muhammad is the messenger of Allah."

Sharia. The compiled code of laws and rules governing the life and behavior of Muslims.

Shiite. A follower of Islam in the *Shia* branch of Islam. Shiites differs from the Sunnis in that they accept the spiritual authority of Ali, the fourth caliph who was the cousin and son-in-law of Muhammad.

Sufism. Islamic mysticism; brotherhoods of Sufis, or mystics, exist throughout the Muslim world.

Sunnite. A Muslim of the majority *Sunni* group who follow the *Sunna* or practices of Muhammad, comprising about 85 percent of all Muslims.

Surah. One of the 114 chapters or sections of the Qur'an.

ta'a. Obedience.

tabshir. A negative word used to refer to Christian evangelism.

takffir. The practice of declaring that an individual or a group previously considered Muslim are, in fact, nonbelievers.

Tawrah. The first five books of Moses as accepted by Islam.

ummah. The community of all those who affirm Islam.

Zabur. The book of Psalms.

zakat. The "alms-tax," a mandatory donation to charity, and one of the essential duties of all Muslims.

zulm. Structures of oppression.

Selected Bibliography

Abdulati, Hammudah. *Islam in Focus*. 3rd rev. ed. Rev. and ed. by Shaykh Salih al Husayin and Mustapha Abu Sway. Beltsville, MD: Amana, 1998.

Abdullah Yusuf Ali, trans. *The Meaning of the Holy Qur'an*. Seattle, WA: Pacific Publishing Studio, 2010.

Abraham, Nabeel, and Andrew Shryock, eds. *Arab Detroit: From Margin to Mainstream*. Detroit: Wayne State University Press, 2000.

Armour, Rollin Sr.. *Islam, Christianity, and the West: A Troubled History*. Maryknoll, NY: Orbis, 2002.

Bagby, Ihsan, Paul M. Perl, and Bryan T. Froehle. "The Mosque in America: A National Portrait." April 26, 2001. Available online at http://www.cair -net.org/mosquereport/.

Bird, Christiane. *Neither East nor West: One Woman's Journey Through the Islamic Republic of Iran*. New York: Washington Square Press, 2001.

Braswell, George W., Jr. *Islam: Its Prophets, Peoples, and Power*. Nashville: Broadman and Holman, 1996.

———. *What You Need to Know About Islam and Muslims*. Nashville: Broadman and Holman, 2000.

Buchanan, Patrick J. *The Death of the West: How Dying Populations and Immigrant Invasions Imperil Our Country and Civilization*. New York: St. Martin's, 2002.

Emerson, Steven. *American Jihad: The Terrorists Living Among Us.* New York: Free Press, 2002.

Esposito, John L. *Islam: The Straight Path.* 3rd ed. New York: Oxford University Press, 2005.

————, ed. *Islam in Asia: Religion, Politics and Society.* New York: Oxford University Press, 1987.

————. *Unholy War: Terror in the Name of Islam.* New York: Oxford University Press, 2002.

————, and John O. Voll. *Islam and Democracy.* New York: Oxford University Press, 1966.

Farah, Caesar E. *Islam.* 7th ed. Hauppauge, NY: Barron's, 2000.

Flew, Antony. "Islam's War Against the West: Can It Abide a Secular State?" *Free Inquiry* 22 (spring 2002).

Frishman, Martin, and Hasan-Uddin Khan, eds. *The Mosque: History, Architectural Development, and Regional Diversity.* New York: Thames and Hudson, 1994.

Haddad, Yvonne Yazbeck, and Jane Idleman Smith, eds. *Muslim Communities in North America.* Albany: State University of New York Press, 1994.

Haney, Marsha Snulligan. *Islam and Protestant African-American Churches: Responses and Challenges to Religious Pluralism.* San Francisco: International Scholars Publications, 1998.

Hasan, Asma Gull. *American Muslims: The New Generation.* New York: Continuum, 2000.

Hesselgrave, David J. *Paradigms in Conflict.* Grand Rapids: Kregel, 2005.

Huntington, Samuel P. *The Clash of Civilizations and the Remaking of World Order.* New York: Simon and Schuster, 1996.

Kraft, Charles H. *Anthropology for Christian Witness.* Maryknoll, NY: Orbis Books, 1998.

Lewis, Bernard. *The Crisis of Islam: Holy War and Unholy Terror.* New York: Random House, 2003.

Mandryk, Jason. *Operation World: The Definitive Prayer Guide to Every Nation.* 7th edition. Colorado Springs: Biblica, 2010.

McAuliffe, Jane Damen, et al. *Encyclopedia of the Qur'an.* 5 volumes plus index. Leiden: Brill, 2001–2006.

McGavran, Donald. *The Bridges of God*. New York: Friendship Press, 1955.

Mernissi, Fatema. *Islam and Democracy: Fear of the Modern World*. Trans. Mary Jo Lakeland. Cambridge, MA: Perseus Publishing, 2002.

Meyers, Bryant L. *The New Context of World Missions*. Monrovia, CA: MARC, 1996.

Murad, Khurram. *Da'wah Among Non-Muslims in the West*. London: Islamic Foundation, 1986.

Murata, Sachiko, and William C. Chittick. *The Vision of Islam*. New York: Paragon, 1994.

Nanji, Azim A., ed. *The Muslim Almanac*. New York: Gale Research, 1996.

Parfrey, Adam, ed. *Extreme Islam: Anti-American Propaganda of Muslim Fundamentalism*. Los Angeles: Feral House, 2001.

Poston, Larry A. *The Changing Face of Islam in America*. Camp Hill, PA: Horizon Books, 2000.

Rashid, Ahmed. *Jihad: The Rise of Militant Islam in Central Asia*. New Haven, CT: Yale University Press, 2002.

Ruthven, Malise. *Islam in the World*. 3rd ed. New York: Oxford University Press, 2006.

Smith, Jane I. *Islam in America*. New York: Columbia University Press, 1999.

Sweetman, James Windrow. *Islam and Christian Theology: A Study of Interpretation of Theological Ideas in the Two Religions*. 2 vols. London: Lutterworth Press, 1947.

Waines, David. *An Introduction to Islam*. 2nd ed. Cambridge: Cambridge University Press, 2004.

Wilson, J. Christy. *Afghanistan—The Forbidden Harvest: The Challenging Story of God's Work in a Resistant Land*. Elgin, IL: D. C. Cook, 1981.

Winters, Ralph D. *The Twenty-Five Unbelievable Years, 1945–1969*. South Pasadena, CA: William Carey Library, 1970.